DISARMING THE PAST

This volume is the fourth in the *Advancing Transitional Justice Series*, a joint project of the International Center for Transitional Justice and the Social Science Research Council. Other volumes include:

Alexander Mayer-Rieckh and Pablo de Greiff, eds., *Justice as Prevention: Vetting Public Employees in Transitional Societies*

Ruth Rubio-Marín, ed., *What Happened to the Women? Gender and Reparations for Human Rights Violations*

Pablo de Greiff and Roger Duthie, eds., *Transitional Justice and Development: Making Connections*

ADVANCING TRANSITIONAL JUSTICE SERIES

# DISARMING THE PAST
## Transitional Justice and Ex-combatants

EDITED BY ANA CUTTER PATEL, PABLO DE GREIFF & LARS WALDORF,
INTERNATIONAL CENTER FOR TRANSITIONAL JUSTICE

SOCIAL SCIENCE RESEARCH COUNCIL • NEW YORK • 2009

INTERNATIONAL CENTER FOR TRANSITIONAL JUSTICE

The International Center for Transitional Justice (ICTJ) assists countries pursuing account-ability for past mass atrocity or human rights abuse. The Center works in societies emerging from repressive rule or armed conflict, as well as in established democracies where historical injustices or systemic abuse remain unresolved.

In order to promote justice, peace, and reconciliation, government officials and nongov-ernmental advocates are likely to consider a variety of transitional justice approaches includ-ing both judicial and nonjudicial responses to human rights crimes. The ICTJ assists in the development of integrated, comprehensive, and localized approaches to transitional justice comprising five key elements: prosecuting perpetrators, documenting and acknowledging violations through nonjudicial means such as truth commissions, reforming abusive institu-tions, providing reparations to victims, and facilitating reconciliation processes.

The field of transitional justice is varied and covers a range of disciplines, including law, public policy, forensics, economics, history, psychology, and the arts. The ICTJ works to develop a rich understanding of the field as a whole, and to identify issues that merit more in-depth research and analysis. Collaborating with colleagues in transitional societies and often commissioning outside studies, the Center targets its research to address the complex issues confronting policymakers and activists. Identifying and addressing the most important gaps in scholarship, it provides the benefit of comparative analysis to its staff and to practitioners worldwide.

## SOCIAL SCIENCE RESEARCH COUNCIL

The Social Science Research Council (SSRC) leads innovation, builds interdisciplinary and international networks, and focuses research on important public issues. Independent and not-for-profit, the SSRC is guided by the belief that justice, prosperity, and democracy all require better understanding of complex social, cultural, economic, and political processes. The SSRC works with practitioners, policymakers, and academic researchers in all the social sciences, related professions, and the humanities and natural sciences. With partners around the world, the Council mobilizes existing knowledge for new problems, links research to practice and policy, strengthens individual and institutional capacities for learning, and enhances public access to information. The SSRC brings necessary knowledge to public action. A new publications initiative, represented here in this co-publication with the ICTJ, complements and enhances the SSRC's mission to disseminate necessary knowledge in innovative ways.

Published by the Social Science Research Council
Printed in the United States of America

Editorial production by the International Center
for Transitional Justice

Cover illustration by Orlando José Plata Martinéz

Typesetting by Julie Fry with Donald Fox


Library of Congress Cataloging-in-Publication Data

Disarming the past : transitional justice and ex-
    combatants / edited by Ana Cutter Patel, Pablo
    de Greiff, and Lars Waldorf.
    p.  cm.
ISBN 978-0-9841257-0-8
1. Disarmament. 2. Transitional justice. 3. Postwar
    reconstruction. 4. Peace-building. I. Patel, Ana
    Cutter. II. De Greiff, Pablo. III. Waldorf, Lars.

JZ5588.D58 2009
341.6'6–dc22

2009027235

# Contents

# Contributors

*Pablo de Greiff* is the Director of Research at the International Center for Transitional Justice (ICTJ) in New York. Born in Colombia, he graduated from Yale University (B.A.) and from Northwestern University (Ph.D.). Before joining the ICTJ he was Associate Professor (with tenure) in the Philosophy Department at the State University of New York at Buffalo, where he taught ethics and political theory. He was Laurance S. Rockefeller Fellow at the Center for Human Values, Princeton University, and held a concurrent fellowship from the National Endowment for the Humanities. De Greiff has published extensively on transitions to democracy, democratic theory, and the relationship between morality, politics, and law. He is the editor of nine books, including Jürgen Habermas's *The Inclusion of the Other* (MIT Press, 1998), and in areas related to transitional justice, *Global Justice and Transnational Politics* (MIT Press, 2002) and *The Handbook of Reparations* (Oxford, 2006), among others. He authored the Office of the High Commissioner for Human Rights' "Rule-of-Law Tools for Post-Conflict States: Reparations Programmes."

*Roger Duthie* is a Senior Associate in the Research Unit at the International Center for Transitional Justice in New York, where he recently managed a research project on transitional justice and development. His publications include *Transitional Justice and Development: Making Connections* (SSRC, 2009) (co-edited with Pablo de Greiff), and "Toward a Development-Sensitive Approach to Transitional Justice," *International Journal of Transitional Justice* (2008). He previously worked at KPMG, the Carnegie Council on Ethics and International Affairs, and Oxford University Press. He has an M.A. from Yale University and a B.A. from Cornell University.

*Mark Freeman* is the Director of External Relations with the International Crisis Group. Previously, he worked in a variety of capacities with the International Center for Transitional Justice in both New York and Brussels. He has an extensive publication record that includes books on international human rights law and truth commissions. He is currently completing a book entitled *Amnesty and Accountability* (Cambridge University Press, 2009). As a specialist in the field of transitional justice, he has led missions and worked closely with victims of gross human rights violations in more than a dozen countries.

*Luisa Maria Dietrich Ortega* is a doctoral candidate in political science at the University of Vienna, Austria. She has worked as the gender and disarmament, demobilization, and reintegration (DDR) consultant for the United Nations Development Programme, and as the Reparation and Reconciliation Specialist as well as Gender Focal Point of the DDR programme, both at the International Organization for Migration's mission in Colombia. Recent publications include a coedited piece on demobilization of female ex-combatants in Colombia published by *Forced Migration Review* (University of Oxford). She holds an M.Sc. in comparative politics in Latin America from the London School of Economics and a B.A. in international relations.

*Ana Cutter Patel* is the Deputy Director for the International Policymakers Unit at the International Center for Transitional Justice, and the project manager for the Center's research initiative on Transitional Justice and Disarmament, Demobilization, and Reintegration. Her publications include "DDR and Transitional Justice," a module in the United Nations integrated DDR standards, and "Transitional Justice and DDR," in Robert Muggah (ed.), *Security and Post-Conflict Reconstruction: Dealing with Fighters in the Aftermath of War* (Routledge Global Security Studies, 2008), among others. She has been a Lecturer at Columbia University since 2001. Prior to her work with ICTJ, she was a consultant with the United Nations Development Programme. From 1993 to 2002, she held positions at the Carnegie Council for Ethics and International Affairs, the Carnegie Commission on the Prevention of Deadly Conflict, the Newmarket Company, the *Journal of International Affairs*, and the Corporación Andina de Fomento in Caracas, Venezuela. She served as a United States Peace Corps Volunteer and has a master's in international affairs from Columbia University.

*Irma Specht* is an anthropologist with broad experience in the transition from war to peace. She is currently the director of the consultancy firm Transitions International, providing advisory services to many international organizations and governments. She has an international reputation in the field of reintegration of ex-combatants, including children associated with armed groups. Seven years of field and headquarter experience in the International Labour Organization's (ILO) Programme on Crisis Response and Reconstruction has provided her with a specific focus on employment issues and the inclusion of vulnerable/special groups in the transition processes. She has, over the past fifteen years, been involved in most of the DDR processes around the world. Additionally, she is involved in the design and delivery of several training modules and courses on reintegration, youth, gender, and conflict transformation and is a well-known resource person in international conferences and networks. She is an active writer, and is the coauthor of the book *Young Soldiers, Why They Choose to Fight* (Lynne Rienner Publishers, 2004), and the author of *Red Shoes: Experiences of Girl Combatants in Liberia* (ILO, 2006) and several chapters in edited volumes on children associated with armed forces and reintegration. In addition, she coauthored modules on youth and socio-economic reintegration in the United Nations integrated DDR standards.

*Lars Waldorf* is Senior Lecturer in International Human Rights Law at the Centre for Applied Human Rights and York Law School, University of York. He ran Human Rights Watch's field office in Rwanda from 2002 to 2004 and reported on genocide trials at the International Criminal Tribunal for Rwanda in 2001. He was a Visiting Fellow at Harvard Law School's Human Rights Program in 2004. He has authored numerous publications on Rwanda, including "Mass Justice for Mass Atrocity: Rethinking Local Justice as Transitional Justice," *Temple Law Review* 79, no. 1 (August 2006). He is currently writing a book on Rwanda's community genocide trials (with a grant from the United States Institute of Peace) and co-editing a book entitled *Reconstructing Rwanda: State Building and Human Rights after Mass Violence*. He also co-edited *Localizing Transitional Justice* (Stanford University Press, forthcoming 2010). He is principal organizer of a Mellon Foundation Sawyer Seminar Series on "Fratricide and *Fraternité*: Understanding and Repairing Neighborly Atrocity."

*Eric A. Witte* is an independent consultant in the fields of human rights and transitional justice and a Senior Associate at the Democratization Policy Council (DPC). In addition to occasional op-eds for DPC, his recent writings include an assessment of war crimes prosecutions at the Bosnian State Court for the Open Society Justice Initiative, the Europe and Middle East chapters of the *Minority Rights Group's State of the World's Minorities 2007*, and the Africa and Middle East chapters of the same report for 2006. Until June 2005, he spent nearly two years as political advisor and special assistant to the chief prosecutor at the Special Court for Sierra Leone, where he focused on efforts to bring the former Liberian president Charles Taylor to justice. Before that he worked on Balkan, African, and transitional justice issues in Washington at the Coalition for International Justice, International Crisis Group, and Balkan Institute. He has a Magister Artium in political science from the University of Regensburg, Germany.

# Acknowledgments

The editors are extremely grateful to acknowledge the Federal Public Service of Foreign Affairs of the Government of the Kingdom of Belgium, the Ministry of Foreign Affairs of the Republic of Finland, the Ministry of Foreign Affairs of the Kingdom of the Netherlands, and the Ministry for Foreign Affairs of the Kingdom of Sweden, for grants that supported the research, website, and this publication. The United Nations Department of Peacekeeping Operations deserves special thanks for encouraging and engaging with this project from an early stage and for publishing a module on DDR and Transitional Justice as part of the Integrated DDR Standards that marks one of the important policy contributions resulting from this work.

Individuals, as well as institutions, deserve recognition and gratitude for advancing this research: Nat Colletta, Lotta Hagman, Lena Sundh, Kelvin Ong, Lucie Viersma, Irma Specht, Kees Steenken, Kees Kingma, Desmond Malloy and Mauricio Romero, provided valuable insight and guidance at various moments during this process. We are deeply in debt to Roger Duthie, Paige Arthur and Debbie Sharnak of the ICTJ's Research Unit for their constant support and help, as well as many other current and former staff members and interns at the ICTJ including: Lizzie Goodfriend, Briony MacPhee, Allegra Panetto, Chloe Poynton, Joanna Rice, Nadia Siddiqui, Meg Tierney and Zoe So.

We are also grateful to the authors of the papers in this volume and the authors of the country case studies including: Patricia Gossman (Afghanistan), Mohamed Suma and Gibril Sesay (Sierra Leone), Sergio Jaramillo, Yanet Githa and Paula Torres (Colombia), Massimo Morrati and Amra Sabic-El-Rayess (Bosnia and Herzegovina), Hugo van de Merwe and Guy Lamb (South Africa), Alex Segovia (El Salvador), Peter Bartu and Neil Wilford (Cambodia), Lars Waldorf (Rwanda) and Thomas Jaye (Liberia). The case studies are available on the ICTJ website at http://www.ictj.org/en/research/projects/ddr/index.html. We also thank the experts who joined us at the initial expert meeting and two meetings of authors and commentators convened in New York in 2006 and 2007.

*Ana Cutter Patel, New York; Pablo de Greiff, New York; Lars Waldorf, London*

# Linking DDR and Transitional Justice

*Lars Waldorf*

"[W]hen designing [DDR] reintegration programmes, UN practitioners should coordinate and, where possible, jointly plan programmes with actors working on the reintegration of other war-affected groups, reconciliation, justice, governance, political reform, human rights, gender equality, poverty reduction and development."
— UN *Integrated Disarmament, Demobilization and Reintegration Standards (IDDRS)* (2006)[1]

"There are so many complications with either [DDR or transitional justice] that you don't simplify by putting them together."
— Gromo Alex, Senior Demobilization and Reintegration Specialist, World Bank (2006)[2]

## INTRODUCTION

Since the fall of the Berlin Wall in 1989, there have been at least 111 civil wars around the world. In its efforts to quell some of these conflicts, the international community has dispatched United Nations (UN) blue helmets, ordered humanitarian interventions, conducted peace negotiations, and occasionally issued international arrest warrants. Once the fighting is over (or nearly over), the international community often rushes into these now postconflict states with humanitarian assistance, aid packages, and recovery programs.[3] The postconflict landscape has altered dramatically over the past twenty years as international donors have set up large-scale disarmament, demobilization, and reintegration (DDR) programs to transform combatants into former combatants—and to ensure they remain that way. More than a million ex-combatants (and their dependents) participated in DDR programs in twenty countries in 2005 (at a cost of $1.9 billion).[4]

During this same period, there has been a proliferation of transitional justice mechanisms to help render truth, justice and reparations in the aftermath of state violence and civil war. These mechanisms range from international criminal tribunals to national truth commissions to local justice processes. These mechanisms are much less generously supported than DDR programs. To give just one stark figure: in 2005, none of those twenty countries with DDR programs had implemented a reparations program for victims. This clearly reflects the international community's priorities: former combatants over current victims, peace over justice. That makes some sense, of course. After all, ex-combatants are potential "spoilers" of a peace process in the short term in a way that civilian victims rarely are. Yet, this discrepancy is still deeply troubling: perpetrators of violence are rewarded while war-affected civilians get little or nothing, perhaps creating a moral hazard for the future.

DDR programs coexist or overlap with transitional justice mechanisms in several postconflict states. They are usually run by the same national governments, funded by the same donors, and work with the same civil society and community-based organizations. Consequently, ex-combatants sometimes perceive DDR programs and transitional justice mechanisms as being "[a]ll the same thing."[5] But there is little, if any, coordination between the two. This is largely explicable because of their different beneficiaries and aims: ex-combatants and security, on the one hand, and victims and justice, on the other.

The divide between DDR and transitional justice is slowly starting to narrow. In 2004, Kofi Annan, then UN secretary-general, committed the UN to promote transitional justice and the rule of law in its postconflict recovery programming. Subsequently, the UN adopted an "integrated" approach to DDR in 2006. Now, DDR is supposed to be linked to other recovery processes, rather than existing as a "stand-alone intervention."[6] As the UN *Integrated Disarmament, Demobilization and Reintegration Standards* (*IDDRS*) quoted above makes clear, DDR practitioners (at least those working for the UN) should now "coordinate and, where possible, jointly plan programmes" with other actors, such as transitional justice practitioners.

It will not be easy, however, to change the attitudes of DDR practitioners. Gromo Alex, then the World Bank's DDR expert in the Great Lakes, stated that "you don't simplify by putting [DDR and transitional justice] together." He was not alone in that view. One of Rwanda's top DDR officials told me, "If you want to make DDR that makes all these things fairly and effectively, you would never have a DDR. It's best to isolate DDR and leave others to do their work."[7] Similarly, a donor official who finances DDR stated, "if you want to design something that's manageable, don't be too holistic."[8]

In some ways, this book is an initial response to such doubts. It is an effort to convince both DDR and transitional justice practitioners that they have something to learn from each other and that they can benefit from greater coordination when it comes to designing and implementing their respective programs. Remarkably, there has been very little written on the relationship between DDR and transitional justice up until now.[9] This book is the culmination of a three-year project by the International Center for Transitional Justice (ICTJ) to research and reflect on that relationship, as well as to provide lessons learned and future guidance (there are, as yet, no best practices) for policymakers, practitioners, and scholars. This collection of thematic essays builds on eight in-depth case studies that ICTJ commissioned, and that are being published simultaneously on its Web site. This has been more than a scholarly exercise, for ICTJ researchers have also helped shaped DDR policy-making at the international level, first with the Stockholm Initiative on Disarmament Demobilisation Reintegration (SIDDR) and more recently with the drafting of a transitional justice module for the *IDDRS*.[10]

Several themes or arguments run through the chapters of this book. First, DDR and transitional justice do not clash as often or as much as commonly supposed—even when it comes to amnesties and prosecutions. Second, the very real tensions that do sometimes exist in the early stages of DDR can usually be mitigated, for example, through sequencing—something that often happens naturally, as DDR programs usually start more quickly than transitional justice mechanisms. Third, there is greater congruence between DDR and transitional justice in the reintegration phase of DDR. Indeed, most of the book's chapters argue that transitional justice mechanisms can help some ex-combatants reintegrate into local communities. This assistance can be direct, as when ex-combatants are given a forum to express remorse to those they harmed, or it can be less direct, as when victims are given reparations and thereby are possibly less aggrieved when ex-combatants receive DDR benefits. In the opposite direction, DDR programs can assist transitional justice efforts: not just in the obvious way of creating the requisite security and stability, but also, for example, through sharing information about the causes and patterns of an armed conflict. Overall, this book argues that DDR programs and transitional justice mechanisms can both benefit from greater coordination and linkages.

In this introduction, I focus more on DDR than on transitional justice, because the chapters that follow set out detailed descriptions of various transitional justice mechanisms, including amnesties, prosecutions, truth commissions, local justice processes, reparations, and security sector reforms. I begin by presenting an overview of DDR before turning to reintegration, which is the more neglected dimension of DDR but also the more promising arena for cooperation with transitional justice. Next, I briefly sketch what is meant by transitional justice. I then discuss the rationales for and benefits of linking DDR and transitional justice. Finally, I conclude by suggesting several ways to take the agenda forward.

## DISARMAMENT, DEMOBILIZATION, AND REINTEGRATION (DDR)

### DDR OVERVIEW

DDR programs are peacekeeping, peacebuilding, and conflict-prevention measures meant to shore up fragile security situations. DDR programs also enable states to shift from a war economy to economic development by reducing military expenditures and reallocating resources to reconstruction. DDR programs are a relatively new tool in negotiated peace agreements, peacekeeping missions, and even non-peacekeeping contexts, having been used first in 1989 with the UN Observer Group in Central America.[11] Since then, DDR programs have become a familiar feature of postwar reconstruction: approximately thirty-four DDR programs were created between 1994 and 2005.[12]

Most donors and practitioners have treated DDR largely as a short-term technical process typified by counting weapons, establishing demobilization camps, and handing out reinsertion and reintegration packages—the "guns, camps and cash" approach.[13] The results have been disappointing. As the United Nations Development Programme acknowledged, "[m]any DDR interventions have in the past failed because of their narrow focus and short-term approach."[14] Consequently, the UN secretary-general stressed the "vital" need to "integrate" DDR "with the wider peace, recovery, and development frameworks."[15] In 2006, the UN launched the *IDDRS*, which set forth lessons learned and best practices for DDR programming.[16]

While DDR's shift to an integrated approach is a welcome move, there is now the opposite danger that DDR is becoming too ambitious in its goals and too unfocused in its methods. The *IDDRS*, for example, suggests tying DDR into national-level and community-level development. As Pablo de Greiff rightly warns, "Assigning DDR programs the responsibility to, say, make a significant contribution to economic development and then criticizing the program for failing to achieve this goal is an example of how conceptual profligacy with the goals of DDR programs may discredit them in general."[17] There is a real need to scale back the expectations of what DDR can accomplish—both for donors and beneficiaries. If the expectations of ex-combatants are not carefully managed, this can trigger new rounds of violence.

Before going further, it is helpful to define DDR and its constituent parts more precisely. Currently, the UN defines DDR as

> [a] process that contributes to security and stability in a post-conflict recovery context by removing weapons from the hands of combatants, taking the combatants out of military structures and helping them to integrate socially and economically into society by finding civilian livelihoods.[18]

Disarmament involves the collection, registration, storage, and often destruction of small arms and light weapons.[19] Demobilization is "the formal and controlled discharge of active combatants."[20] Reintegration is the long-term process whereby "ex-combatants acquire civilian status and gain sustainable employment and income."[21] Disarmament, demobilization, and reintegration need not occur in this sequential order.[22]

During disarmament and demobilization, combatants are screened to make sure they are eligible for DDR and for program assistance. While the eligibility criteria are usually laid out in peace accords or national legislation, DDR programs encounter difficulties ascertaining just exactly who are bona fide combatants, especially in the context of civil wars, where many combatants are irregular, part-time, or coerced.[23] Women and children pose particular challenges for DDR screening. Early programs often restricted eligibility to those with ownership of or expertise in weapons—a requirement that excluded many women and children, who often play crucial support roles for armed combatants (as porters, cooks, messengers, "war wives," and so on).[24]

### PAYING GREATER ATTENTION TO REINTEGRATION

Many DDR programs have given short shrift to the reintegration phase, focusing instead on the more easily deliverable and measurable goals of disarmament and demobilization.[25] Now, with the advent of the UN's integrated DDR standards, this is starting to change.[26] The UN defines reintegration as follows:

> Reintegration is the process by which ex-combatants ... gain sustainable employment and income. Reintegration is essentially a social and economic process with an open time-frame, primarily taking place in communities at the local level. It is part of the general development of a country ... and often necessitates long-term external assistance.[27]

It is now generally recognized that "reintegration" is a somewhat misleading term, as many ex-combatants do not return to their home communities.[28] In addition, in countries like Liberia, "re-marginalisation and not reintegration is the natural outcome awaiting most ex-combatants."[29]

Reintegration has economic, social, and political aspects. First, it aims to create sustainable livelihoods for ex-combatants.[30] Second, reintegration seeks to rebuild social capital and social cohesion.[31] Finally, it offers ex-combatants an opportunity to resolve political grievances through legitimate channels rather than through force of arms.[32] In this introduction and this volume, the focus is mostly on social reintegration.[33]

There are several rationales for providing ex-combatants with reintegration assistance. From a security perspective, ex-combatants need to be given an economic stake in a stable social order so they do not become "spoilers" or do not turn to organized crime or banditry. From a humanitarian or needs-based approach, ex-combatants are a vulnerable group that lacks education, marketable skills, and social links.[34] From a developmental approach, ex-combatants constitute a large pool of potential human capital.[35]

The main debate about reintegration assistance is whether it should narrowly target ex-combatants (and their dependents) or broadly help war-affected groups and communities. The IDDRS carves out a middle position by arguing for targeted ex-combatant assistance in the short run and community-based reintegration in the long run. The IDDRS justifies preferential treatment for ex-combatants early on:[36]

> Returning ex-combatants are potential "spoilers" of peace. This is why, while other war-affected groups, such as refugees and internally displaced persons (IDPs), may far outnumber them, ex-combatants will usually need focused, sustainable support if they are to succeed in making the transition from military to civilian life.[37]

Yet, as the IDDRS is quick to observe, this risks "turning [ex-combatants] into a privileged group within the community"—something clearly not conducive to their reintegration.[38] The IDDRS proposes a twofold solution to this thorny problem. First, reintegration assistance "must be harmonized with the assistance given to other returnees to minimize competition and resentment."[39] Second, direct assistance to ex-combatants should be phased out over time and replaced with community-based reintegration (what it equates with "sustainable reintegration"): "Ultimately it is communities who will, or will not, reintegrate ex-combatants and it is communities who will, or will not, benefit from a successful DDR programme."[40] While this is a useful start, it remains to be seen how this will play out in practice. In one of her fieldwork sites in Sierra Leone, Rosalind Shaw found that community-level reintegration may have actually improved when assistance to ex-combatants ran out: "Now that ex-combatants' DDR stipends were gone, several civilians attributed their improved relationship with ex-combatants to the fact that they shared everyday problems of survival.... Both the struggle for a sustainable livelihood and the sense of having been forgotten were common among ex-combatants and civilians alike, and sometimes formed the basis of bonds among them."[41]

We still know quite little about reintegration. To date, few empirical studies of reintegration have been conducted.[42] This is not altogether unexpected given the difficulties in defining and measuring reintegration, as well as the greater attention paid to disarmament and demobilization. So, what do we know so far? There seems to be surprisingly little correlation between DDR programs and successful reintegration. Based on surveys with more than 1,000 ex-combatants in Sierra Leone, Humphreys and Weinstein found little evidence that participation in DDR programs helped individuals find employment, break ties with their factions, gain acceptance from families and communities, or develop democratic attitudes.[43] They are quick to point out that a lack of correlation does not mean DDR had no positive impact at the individual level (let alone the macro level). Still, "the nonfindings should be seen as a wakeup call to advocates of these programs"—both to moderate their claims and to devise better methodologies for measuring DDR's impact.[44]

There are two intriguing findings from Humphreys and Weinstein's Sierra Leone study. Reintegration is largely premised on the need to break down former command structures and dissolve combatant identities. Yet, they discovered that reintegration does not appear to depend on reducing connections between ex-combatants and their former comrades and commanders.[45] This is good news given the difficulty of loosening those bonds, especially in states and societies characterized by high levels of patronage and clientelism, and where many remain prepared for the resumption of conflict.[46] Second, their data suggest that an ex-combatant's wartime role has the greatest impact on reintegration. Most critically, "[p]ast participation in an abusive military faction is the strongest predictor of difficulty in achieving social reintegration."[47] This latter finding, if borne out by further empirical research elsewhere, has important implications for linking DDR and transitional justice.

## TRANSITIONAL JUSTICE

Having now reviewed DDR (and particularly the issues surrounding ex-combatant reintegration), I want to look briefly at transitional justice before going on to examine how they might be linked. Transitional justice consists of all the mechanisms that states, societies, and communities use to provide accountability and redress for genocide, crimes against humanity, and war crimes (collectively referred to here as international crimes). Transitional justice is simultaneously backward- and forward-looking: addressing past abuses with the aim of preventing future ones. As such, it often involves difficult choices between punishment and forgiveness, accountability and reconciliation, remembrance and forgetting. The term "transitional justice" is something of a misnomer as it frequently concerns more than justice, occurs in the absence of transitions, and unfolds over a lengthy period.[48] But that term reflects transitional justice's emergence as a field at the time of the post–Cold War transitions from authoritarian to democratic regimes.[49]

Over the years, transitional justice has become a globalized paradigm as international donors, nongovernmental organizations (NGOs), and legal elites export, import, apply, and adapt a growing assortment of "tools" to diverse settings.[50] While the transitional justice "tool kit" was initially best known for truth commissions, it now commonly contains international and internationalized criminal tribunals, local justice processes, reparations, lustration (vetting), and memorials, among other tools. States have increasingly used a mix of tools: for example, East Timor had a hybrid international-national tribunal, a truth commission, and local reconciliation ceremonies running concurrently. There is often a division of labor, with internationalized mechanisms prosecuting those most responsible for international crimes and local mechanisms emphasizing restitution and reconciliation. What unites all transitional justice mechanisms—in theory, if not always in practice—is that they are victim-centered.[51] At bottom, the legitimacy of transitional justice mechanisms depends on how much they serve victims' needs and aspirations.[52]

## LINKING DDR WITH TRANSITIONAL JUSTICE

There are clearly significant, perhaps inherent, tensions between DDR and transitional justice in the short term, with DDR emphasizing security and transitional justice aiming for accountability. In other words, DDR and transitional justice occupy different sides of the "peace versus justice" debate in

postconflict states.[53] As such, they are initially addressed to separate beneficiary groups with seemingly divergent interests: whereas many ex-combatants
(some of whom may have perpetrated international crimes) want impunity,
many victims want some form of accountability.[54]

An argument can be made that the long-term goals of DDR and transitional
justice are "broadly analogous" in that they both seek to rebuild social trust
and social capital.[55] In the *IDDRS*'s formulation, DDR is about creating "social
cohesion" between ex-combatants and other members of their communities.[56]
Similarly, transitional justice mechanisms are designed to foster reconciliation
among perpetrators, victims, bystanders, and rescuers.[57] As Ana Patel writes,
"Trust-building, the prevention of renewed violence and reconciliation therefore emerge as essential objectives for both types of processes."[58] From this
perspective, short-term tensions between DDR and transitional justice can be
fixed with more institutional linkages and coordination.[59] Most of the chapters
in this book adopt this approach.

Over the past few years, there have been moves to have DDR programs
pay more heed to victims' interests and transitional justice. For example, the
Stockholm Initiative stated that DDR programs "should not only seek to minimize potential tensions with transitional justice measures (by e.g. avoiding
blanket amnesties), but should capitalize on the potential complementarities
with transitional justice measures to reconstitute civic trust and smooth the
process of reintegration."[60] The secretary-general's 2006 report on integrated
DDR standards makes three important points in this regard. First, DDR should
be planned in close coordination with rule of law reforms and transitional
justice. Second, it should respect international humanitarian law and human
rights — in other words, there should be accountability for perpetrators of
international crimes and reparations for their victims. Finally, DDR should balance security with equity by providing benefits not just to ex-combatants, but
also to receiving communities. Consequently, the integrated DDR standards
recognize that postconflict reconstruction requires *both* peace and justice.
Still, it realistically acknowledges a need for sequencing: "the security situation
often dictates that, in the short term at least, a specific focus on ex-combatants
is required."[61]

In the remainder of this section, I want to touch on two rationales for linking DDR and transitional justice. The first, and most obvious, reason is that
DDR programs must conform to international human rights norms, international humanitarian law, and international criminal law.[62] Broadly speaking,
these international norms and laws provide victims with three rights: (1) the

right to justice;[63] (2) the right to truth;[64] and (3) the right to reparations.[65] These correspond to the main transitional justice mechanisms: prosecutions, truth commissions, and reparations. The UN High Commissioner for Human Rights has made clear that "the legal framework governing the disarmament, demobilization and reintegration process of illegal armed groups should guarantee the rights to truth, justice and reparations."[66] To do this, DDR programs need to make sure that, at a minimum, they are not hindering transitional justice mechanisms.

Second, as the chapters in this book argue, more coordination and cooperation can benefit *both* DDR and transitional justice. From DDR's perspective, transitional justice mechanisms may assist the reintegration of former combatants.[67] In other words, those mechanisms can relieve demands on DDR programs to provide assistance and, most important, redress to other war-affected groups—something that is beyond their mandate and their expertise. From transitional justice's perspective, DDR can provide the secure and stable environment necessary for establishing transitional justice mechanisms. In addition, DDR can produce information about the workings of armed groups (such as the use of forcible recruitment) that could further truth-seeking and reparations.

The following chapters show how transitional justice mechanisms may promote DDR's goal of reintegration. Ex-combatants may reintegrate more easily if they are given public spaces, such as those provided by truth commissions and local justice processes, where they can tell the truth, apologize to victims and communities, and explain their actions (including possible forced participation).[68] Such actions may help reduce the fears that ex-combatants and receiving communities often have of one another. As one former combatant in Liberia told the anthropologist Mats Utas, "They all believe that we (ex-combatants) have gunpowder in our heads."[69] Transitional justice mechanisms, particularly reparations, may help blunt the resentment and envy that victims and communities sometimes feel toward returning ex-combatants who receive reintegration assistance.[70] They also may assure victims and receiving communities that perpetrators of international crimes will pay some price for their actions, whether through being punished or publicly shamed or forced to make reparation. Finally, transitional justice mechanisms may help individualize responsibility, so that victims and communities do not perceive all ex-combatants as having committed international crimes.[71] Overall, then, these mechanisms may help reduce reprisal, stigmatization, or discrimination against ex-combatants—something that will obviously benefit DDR.[72]

## CONCLUSION

The chapters in this volume set forth how DDR can benefit from transitional justice and how, in turn, transitional justice can benefit from DDR. The chapters do this by examining specific transitional justice mechanisms—namely, amnesties, prosecutions, truth commissions, local justice, reparations, and security sector reform—and by exploring cross-cutting issues—namely, gender and children. In the end, this volume may present more questions than solutions. That is partly because DDR and transitional justice are still "adolescent" disciplines and there has been little empirical testing of their assumptions and impacts. It also reflects how new it is to consider DDR and transitional justice together. This volume is intended to advance this new conversation about how best to minimize tensions and exploit opportunities between DDR and transitional justice.

Finally, I want to suggest a few helpful ways to move forward. First, policy-makers should consider the implications for transitional justice when designing and implementing DDR programs—and vice versa. As DDR programs normally come first, there is perhaps less of a problem with sequencing. Nevertheless, it is important that policy-makers, peace negotiators, and DDR practitioners not foreclose transitional justice options.[73] Second, there needs to be more creative thinking about how to link DDR and transitional justice. In ongoing cases, such as Colombia, efforts are being made for the first time to link demobilization benefits to justice measures.[74] Third, there needs to be more micro- and macro-level empirical research into the impact of both DDR and transitional justice that is connected to the recent growth in empirical research on conflict and violence.[75] Finally, we need to be careful not to freight DDR and transitional justice with too many unrealizable expectations. Neither can produce peace and justice, but, acting in tandem, they may just bring those goals a bit closer.

## NOTES

1   United Nations Department of Peacekeeping Operations (DPKO), *Integrated Disarmament, Demobilization and Reintegration Standards (IDDRS)* (New York: DPKO, 2006), sec. 4.30, 20.

2   Interview by the author, Kigali, Rwanda, May 17, 2006.

3   The term "postconflict" will be used as shorthand for the period following a (formal or informal) peace accord. In fact, many postconflict states exist in a limbo of what the anthropologist Paul Richards terms "no peace, no war." Paul Richards, "New War: An Ethnographic Approach," in *No Peace, No War: An Anthropology of Contemporary Armed Conflicts*, ed. Paul Richards (Oxford: James Currey, 2005), 13–14. Similarly, Robert Muggah points out that violence often increases after peace agreements. Robert Muggah, "No Magic Bullet: A Critical Perspective on Disarmament, Demobilization and Reintegration (DDR) and Weapons Reduction in Post-Conflict Contexts," *Round Table* 94, no. 379 (April 2005): 239–52, esp. 240–42. The eastern Democratic Republic of Congo is perhaps the worst example of this.

4   Albert Carames, Vicenc Fisas, and Daniel Luz, *Analysis of Disarmament, Demobilization and Reintegration (DDR) Programmes Existing in the World During 2005* (Barcelona: Escola de cultura de pau, 2006), 9.

5   Rosalind Shaw, "Linking Justice with Reintegration? Ex-Combatants and the Sierra Leone Experiment" in Rosalind Shaw and Lars Waldorf, *Localizing Transitional Justice* (Palo Alto: Stanford University Press, forthcoming) (quoting ex-combatant), 3. Chris Coulter found the same perception among female ex-combatants she interviewed in Sierra Leone. Chris Coulter, "Reconciliation or Revenge: Narratives of Fear and Shame among Female Ex-combatants in Sierra Leone" (Uppsala: Department of Cultural Anthropology and Ethnology, 2006).

6   Nicole Ball and Luc van de Goor, "Disarmament, Demobilization and Reintegration: Mapping Issues, Dilemmas and Guiding Principles" (The Hague: Netherlands Institute of International Relations, August 2006), 7.

7   John Zigira, Commissioner, Rwanda Demobilization and Reintegration Commission, interview by the author, Kigali, May 22, 2006.

8   Diplomat, interview by the author, Kigali, May 23, 2006.

9   See Kimberly Theidon, "Transitional Subjects: The Disarmament, Demobilization and Reintegration of Former Combatants in Colombia," *The International Journal of Transitional Justice* 1, no. 1 (March 2007), 66-90; Pablo de Greiff, "Contributing to Peace and Justice: Finding a Balance Between DDR and Reparations" (Nuremberg: Working Group on Development and Peace [FriEnt], 2007); Roger Duthie, "Transitional Justice and Social Reintegration," in Stockholm Initiative on Disarmament Demobilisation Reintegration, *Background Studies* (Stockholm: Ministry for Foreign Affairs, 2005); and Ana Cutter Patel,

"Transitional Justice and DDR," in *Security and Post-Conflict Reconstruction: Dealing with Fighters in the Aftermath of War*, ed. Robert Muggah (London: Routledge, 2009). The latter three authors are based at the International Center for Transitional Justice (ICTJ) and have been deeply involved in ICTJ's research project on DDR and transitional justice.

10  United Nations, "IDDRS Module: Transitional Justice and DDR" (unpublished draft, 2009).

11  For brief historical overviews of DDR, see Muggah, "No Magic Bullet," 243–44; and Macartan Humphreys and Jeremy M. Weinstein, "Demobilization and Reintegration," *Journal of Conflict Resolution* 51, no. 4 (August 2007): 531–67.

12  Stockholm Initiative on Disarmament Demobilisation Reintegration (SIDDR), "Final Report" (Stockholm: Ministry for Foreign Affairs, 2006), 9.

13  Mark Knight and Alpaslan Özerdem, "Guns, Camps and Cash: Disarmament, Demobilization and Reinsertion of Former Combatants in Transitions from War to Peace," *Journal of Peace Research* 41, no. 4 (July 2004): 499–516.

14  United Nations Development Programme (UNDP), *Practice Note: Disarmament, Demobilization and Reintegration of Ex-Combatants* (New York: UNDP, 2005), 18.

15  United Nations, "Disarmament, Demobilization and Reintegration: Report of the Secretary-General," A/60/705 (March 2, 2006), 3.

16  DPKO, *IDDRS*.

17  Pablo de Greiff, "Establishing Links Between DDR and Reparations," in this volume. Several authors have voiced similar concerns. Kathleen Jennings argues that DDR has become "so broad in scope and aims as to undermine chances of effective implementation." Kathleen Jennings, "Unclear Ends, Unclear Means: Reintegration in Postwar Societies— The Case of Liberia," *Global Governance* 14 (2008): 341. Nicole Ball and Luc van de Goor write that "DDR processes have the capacity to influence only a fairly narrow range of political and security objectives… [they] cannot produce development…." Ball and van de Goor, "Disarmament, Demobilization and Reintegration: Mapping Issues," 1. The SIDDR attributes DDR's expanding aims to the fact that it is one of the few, immediate sources of funding in postconflict environments. SIDDR, "Final Report," 9.

18  DPKO, *IDDRS*, sec. 1.20, 6.

19  The term "disarmament" with its connotation of defeat proved problematic in Sudan. Richard Barltrop, *The Negotiation of Security Issues in Sudan's Comprehensive Peace Agreement* (Geneva: Centre for Humanitarian Dialogue, 2008).

20  DPKO, *IDDRS*, sec. 1.20, 6. Demobilization consists of two stages: (1) processing combatants in cantonment sites or temporary centers; and (2) providing a support package, commonly called reinsertion, which can last for up to a year. Ibid.

21  Ibid., 19. Sami Faltas rightly criticizes the first part of this definition:

It is not in reintegration, but during demobilization (either formal or informal) that combatants acquire civilian status. In reintegration, they do not so much change their status, but rather their behaviour, roles, identity and social environment. If demobilization is about becoming an ex-combatant, then reintegration is about becoming a civilian in every sense of the word.

Sami Faltas, "DDR without Camps" (2004), 7.

22  DPKO, *IDDRS*, sec. 4.30, 20. Anders Nilsson rightly notes that retroactive DDR may be needed for individuals or groups that self-demobilized. Anders Nilsson, "Reintegrating Ex-Combatants in Post-Conflict Societies" (Stockholm: Swedish International Development Cooperation Agency, 2005), 17.

23  The *IDDRS* defines combatant more broadly than the Third Geneva Convention as a person who

is a member of a national army or an irregular military organization; or
is actively participating in military activities and hostilities; or
is involved in recruiting or training military personnel; or
holds a command or decision-making position within a national army or an armed organization; …

DPKO, *IDDRS*, sec. 1.20, 4. The International Committee on the Red Cross has clarified the distinction between combatants and civilians:

All members of the armed forces are combatants, and only members of the armed forces are combatants. This should therefore dispense with the concept of quasi-combatants, which has sometimes been used on the basis of activities related more or less directly with the war effort. Similarly, any concept of a part-time status, a semi-civilian, semi-military status, soldier by night and peaceful citizen by day, also disappears. A civilian who is incorporated in an armed organization such as that mentioned in paragraph 1, becomes a member of the military and a combatant throughout the duration of the hostilities (or in any case, until he is permanently demobilized by the responsible command referred to in paragraph 1), whether or not he is in combat, or for the time being armed.

*Prosecutor v Blaskic*, ICTY Case No. Case No. IT-95-14, Appeals Chamber Judgment, July 29, 2004, para. 114 (quoting ICRC Commentary). See Megan Hirst, *An Unfinished Truth: An Analysis of the Commission of Truth and Friendship's Final Report on the 1999 Atrocities in East Timor* (New York: International Center for Transitional Justice, Mar. 2009), 22–23.

24  In some cases, male commanders took weapons from female and child combatants and gave them to male civilians "for personal financial or political gain." DPKO, *IDDRS*, sec. 4.10, 11. See, e.g., Susan McKay and Dyan Mazurana, *Where are the Girls? Girls in Fighting Forces in Northern Uganda, Sierra Leone, and Mozambique: Their Lives During and After War* (Montreal: International Centre for Human Rights and Democratic Development, 2004); Coulter, "Reconciliation or Revenge."

25  See, e.g., Muggah, "No Magic Bullet," 246; Jennings, "Unclear Ends, Unclear Means," 333–34; Theidon, "Transitional Subjects," 67.

26   See, e.g., Sarah Michael, *Reintegration Assistance for Ex-Combatants: Good Practices and Lessons for the MDRP* (Washington, DC: The World Bank Multi-Country Demobilization and Reintegration Program, 2006).

27   DPKO, *IDDRS*, sec. 4.30, 2.

28   This can be for any number of reasons: (1) some never left in the first place; (2) some search for economic betterment in urban areas; (3) some fear returning to communities they or their armed groups have harmed; or (4) some no longer have communities left to return to. More fundamentally, Caspar Fithen and Paul Richards observe, "If the roots of conflict are to be found in pre-war society, sending ex-combatants home risks rekindling hostility." Caspar Fithen and Paul Richards, "Making War, Crafting Peace: Militia Solidarities & Demobilisation in Sierra Leone," in *No Peace*, 117. They therefore adopt a perspective that is "less concerned with reintegration than with societal transformations embracing ex-combatants and civilians alike." Ibid.

29   Mats Utas, " Building a Future? The Reintegration and Remarginalisation of Youth in Liberia" in *No Peace*, 150.

30   For, as Paul Collier and Anke Hoeffler have shown, the larger the pool of unemployed young men, the greater the risk of conflict. Paul Collier and Anke Hoeffler, "Military Expenditure in Post-Conflict Societies" (Centre for the Study of African Economies, Oxford University, April 8, 2004).

31   Nat J. Colletta, Markus Kostner, and Ingo Wiederhofer, "Disarmament, Demobilization, and Reintegration: Lessons and Liabilities in Reconstruction," in *When States Fail: Causes and Consequences*, ed. Robert I. Rotberg (Princeton: Princeton University Press, 2004). Another set of authors contend that DDR should be seen as creating a new social contract between ex-combatants and both the state and society. Knight and Özerdem, "Guns, Camps and Cash," 506, 513.

32   See DPKO, *IDDRS*, sec. 2.10, 6.

33   To date, most of the literature on reintegration focuses on the economic dimension. Of course, further empirical studies may reveal that economic reintegration is more important than social or political reintegration.

34   Still, they are usually less vulnerable than war-affected civilians. The *IDDRS* recognizes that "the civilian population often go through far worse war experiences than combatants." DPKO, *IDDRS*, sec. 4.20, 6. See Jennings, "Unclear Ends, Unclear Means," 337.

35   Muggah, "No Magic Bullet," 248.

36   This sits uneasily with the UN's core principles of nondiscrimination and equal treatment, as the *IDDRS* acknowledges. See DPKO, *IDDRS*, sec. 4.30, 6.

37   Ibid., 3.

38   Ibid., 3, 6–7.

39   Ibid., sec. 2.20, 8. The Stockholm Initiative proposed creating a multi-donor trust fund that would support both the needs of ex-combatants and their receiving communities.

SIDDR, "Final Report," 35–36.

40    DPKO, *IDDRS*, sec. 4.30, 12–13.

41    Shaw, "Linking Justice with Reintegration?" 43–44.

42    The *IDDRS* recognizes that DDR programs have focused on short-term, quantitative outcomes rather than longer-term, qualitative impacts. DPKO, *IDDRS*, sec. 4.30, 14–15. Anders Nilsson goes further: he bluntly criticizes reintegration as "a theoryless field" of untested assumptions, descriptive case studies, and lessons learned. Nilsson, "Reintegrating Ex-Combatants," 35. In similar fashion, Kathleen Jennings states that "DDR's effectiveness…owes more to assumption than to evidence." Jennings, "Unclear Ends, Unclear Means," 327. For her recommendations on how to evaluate reintegration, see ibid., 338. There is now more empirical research being conducted. See, e.g., Humphreys and Weinstein, "Demobilization and Reintegration"; and Ana M. Arjona and Stathis Kalyvas, "Preliminary Results of a Survey of Demobilized Combatants in Colombia" (May 11, 2006) (draft).

43    Humphreys and Weinstein, "Demobilization and Reintegration," 549. They helpfully disaggregate the economic, social, and political components of reintegration. Other scholars argue on the basis of limited case studies that DDR programs can have unintended negative consequences for the reintegration of ex-combatants. According to Jennings, these include "cementing divisions between ex-combatants and non-combatants; hardening group identity; buttressing harmful prewar authority structures…; and contributing to participation in criminalized economies." Jennings, "Unclear Ends, Unclear Means," 338.

44    Humphreys and Weinstein, "Demobilization and Reintegration," 560.

45    Ibid., 533.

46    Utas, "Building the Future?" in *No Peace*, 138–139. Anders Nilsson has argued that it is difficult, if not impossible, to remove ex-combatants' identity and their command structure. Nilsson, "Reintegrating Ex-Combatants," 90. In fact, those identities and command structures can help ex-combatants create successful businesses, cooperatives, and development enterprises. See, e.g., Fithen and Richards, "Making War, Crafting Peace" in *No Peace*, 134–35; Utas, "Building the Future?" in *No Peace*, 149–150; Theidon, "Transitional Subjects," 87. In addition, veterans' associations can enhance political reintegration, at least in the short term. See Nilsson, "Reintegrating Ex-Combatants," 8. In El Salvador, the FMLN's (Farabundo Martí National Liberation Front) continuing command structures helped it maintain its unity as it made the transition from a guerrilla movement to a political party. Alexander Segovia, *Disarmament, Demobilization and Reintegration (DDR) and Transitional Justice: The Case of El Salvador* (New York, International Center for Transitional Justice, 2009), 31.

47    Humphreys and Weinstein, "Demobilization and Reintegration," 533.

48    See Naomi Roht-Arriaza, "The New Landscape of Transitional Justice," in *Transitional*

*Justice in the Twenty-First Century: Beyond Truth Versus Justice*, ed. Naomi Roht-Arriaza and Javier Mariezcurrena (Cambridge: Cambridge University Press, 2006), 1–2.

49   Thus, it is debatable whether the mechanisms that developed in that specific context are really applicable to the very different transitions from war to peace.

50   Ruti Teitel, "Transitional Justice Genealogy," *Harvard Human Rights Journal* 16 (2003): 69–94. There are four main critiques of the transitional justice paradigm: (1) it rests largely on untested assumptions; (2) it pays insufficient attention to local needs and the ways that local actors reshape transitional justice mechanisms; (3) it too often simplistically categorizes individuals as either perpetrators or victims; and (4) it often reinforces state power even though the state played a large (and sometimes predominant) role in the perpetration of gross human rights abuses. See, e.g., Kieran McEvoy and Lorna McGregor, *Transitional Justice from Below: Grassroots Activism and the Struggle for Change* (Oxford: Hart Publishing, 2008); Rosalind Shaw and Lars Waldorf, *Localizing Transitional Justice.*

51   Some mechanisms are more victim-centered than others. Criminal trials almost invariably wind up focusing on the perpetrators in the dock. By contrast, "at least in terms of potential direct impact on victims, reparations do occupy a special place among transitional measures." Pablo de Greiff, "Repairing the Past: Compensation for Victims of Human Rights Violations," in *The Handbook of Reparations*, ed. Pablo de Greiff (Oxford: Oxford University Press, 2006), 2. Some scholars have faulted the workings of transitional justice for not paying sufficient attention to victims. For example, Ruth Rubio-Marin stated, "The transitional justice debate has been overwhelmingly more about what to do against perpetrators than about what to do for victims...." Ruth Rubio-Marin, "The Gender of Reparations: Setting the Agenda," in *What Happened to the Women? Gender and Reparations for Human Rights Violations*, ed. Ruth Rubio-Marin (New York: Social Sciences Research Council, 2006), 22.

52   See United Nations, "The Rule of Law and Transitional Justice in Conflict and Post-Conflict Societies: Report of the Secretary-General," S/2004/616 (August 23, 2004), paras. 16, 18; Shaw and Waldorf, *Localizing Transitional Justice.*

53   In his 2004 report on transitional justice, the UN secretary-general stated:

Justice and peace are not contradictory forces. Rather, properly pursued, they promote and sustain one another. The question, then, can never be whether to pursue justice and accountability, but rather when and how. (UN, "The Rule of Law," para. 21)

That still leaves open the difficult questions of deciding when and how, as northern Uganda makes clear. For further reframing of the peace versus justice debate, see Priscilla Hayner, *Negotiating Justice: Guidance for Mediators* (Geneva: The Centre for Humanitarian Dialogue, 2009); Mark Freeman, "Amnesties and DDR," and Eric Witte, "Beyond 'Peace vs. Justice': Understanding the Relationship Between DDR Programs and the

Prosecution of International Crimes," in this volume.

54 Of course, this is often not so clear-cut on the ground. Child soldiers, who are both perpetrators and victims, may want impunity for their own crimes, but accountability for the commanders who recruited them.

55 Patel, "Transitional Justice and DDR," 248; see Duthie, "Transitional Justice and Social Reintegration," 59; and de Greiff, "Establishing Links Between DDR and Reparations," in this volume.

56 DPKO, *IDDRS*, sec. 4.30, 33.

57 The term "reconciliation" is vague and problematic, but it will be used here for lack of better alternatives. David Crocker helpfully distinguished three conceptions of reconciliation, ranging from "thinner" to "thicker": (1) simple coexistence where former enemies live together non-violently; (2) mutual respect as fellow citizens; and (3) mutual forgiveness." David A. Crocker, "Truth Commissions, Transitional Justice, and Civil Society" in *Truth v. Justice: The Morality of Truth Commissions*, ed. Robert I. Rotberg and Dennis Thompson (Princeton: Princeton University Press, 2000), 108.

58 Patel, "Transitional Justice and DDR," 251; see Duthie, "Transitional Justice and Social Reintegration," 81.

59 Patel, "Transitional Justice and DDR," 251.

60 SIDDR, "Final Report," 32. Rosalind Shaw rightly worries that: "If, as these SIDDR statements imply, the 'guns, camps, and cash' approach to DDR is replaced by axiomatic transitional justice assumptions, this simply exchanges one standard toolkit for another." Shaw, "Linking Justice with Reintegration?" in *Localizing Transitional Justice*, 6.

61 DPKO, *IDDRS*, sec. 4.30, 6.

62 Ibid., sec. 2.10, 9–10; see ibid., Annex B, 17–19.

63 International and regional human rights treaties obligate states to make the rights provided by those treaties judicially enforceable. As of mid-April 2009, 108 states had ratified the Rome Statute, which established the International Criminal Court to prosecute perpetrators of genocide, crimes against humanity, and war crimes. Universal jurisdiction and alien tort claims have expanded the reach of criminal prosecutions and civil actions against perpetrators of international crimes. See, e.g., William A. Schabas, *An Introduction to the International Criminal Court*, 3rd ed. (Cambridge: Cambridge University Press, 2007); and Stephen Macedo, ed., *Universal Jurisdiction: National Courts and the Prosecution of Serious Crimes Under International Law* (Philadelphia: University of Pennsylvania Press, 2006).

64 Over the past twenty years, a growing body of international and regional human rights law has recognized a freestanding and non-derogable right to truth about gross human rights violations. In 2006, the UN High Commissioner for Human Rights affirmed a broad right to truth. See, e.g., UN Commission on Human Rights (UNCHR), "Study on the Right to the Truth, Report of the Office of the United Nations High Commissioner

for Human Rights, 8 February 2006," E/CN.4/2006/91; Mark Freeman, *Truth Commissions and Procedural Fairness* (Cambridge: Cambridge University Press, 2006), 6–9; and Yasmin Naqvi, "The Right to the Truth in International Law: Fact or Fiction?" *International Review of the Red Cross* 88, no. 862 (June 2006), pp. 245–73.

65 Victims of human rights violations have a right to remedy under numerous human rights instruments. See, e.g., United Nations, *Basic Principles and Guidelines on the Right to a Remedy and Reparations for Victims of Gross Violations of International Human Rights Law and Serious Violations of Humanitarian Law*, G.A. Res. 60/147, U.N. Doc. A/Res/60/147/ Annex (March 21, 2006), para. 8. This was reinforced by the Rome Statute, which authorized the International Criminal Court to award reparations to victims of genocide, crimes against humanity, and war crimes out of a Victim's Trust Fund. Rome Statute of the International Criminal Court (1998), arts. 75, 79. See, e.g., de Greiff, *Handbook of Reparations*; Rubio-Marin, *What Happened to the Women?*; and C. Ferstman, M. Goetz, and A. Stephens, eds., *Reparations for Victims of Genocide, Crimes Against Humanity and War Crimes* (Leiden: Martinus Nijhoff Publishers, 2009).

66 UNCHR, "Right to the Truth," para. 16 and n. 28.

67 Theidon makes this argument as well. Theidon, "Transitional Subjects," 67.

68 This is much less the case for female-ex-combatants who often quietly self-demobilize to avoid shaming themselves and their families: for example, one talked about her "fear of people's mouths." Coulter, "Reconciliation or Revenge" (quoting a female ex-combatant).

69 Utas, "Building a Future?" in *No Peace*, 138. Other researchers have documented similar fears. See, e.g., Theidon, "Transitional Subjects," 83.

70 Peter Uvin found that "the jealousy problem is much less severe than is often thought" in a small-scale, ethnographic study in Burundi. Peter Uvin, *Ex-combatants in Burundi: Why They Joined, Why They Left, How They Fared* (Washington, DC: The World Bank Multi-Country Demobilization and Reintegration Program, 2007), 21.

71 See DPKO, *IDDRS*, sec. 2.10, 9. See also Duthie, "Transitional Justice and Social Reintegration," 63.

72 Several studies have raised questions about whether trials do, in fact, individuate guilt. See Eric Stover and Harvey M. Weinstein, eds., *My Neighbor, My Enemy: Justice and Community in the Aftermath of Mass Atrocity* (Cambridge: Cambridge University Press, 2004).

73 As one author notes, "Transitional justice norms change the legal and political climate in which peace negotiations occur; the issues of truth, justice and redress may no longer be ignored nor indefinitely postponed." Theidon, "Transitional Subjects," 89. See Louise Mallinder, *Amnesty, Human Rights and Political Transitions: Bridging the Peace and Justice Divide* (Oxford: Hart Publishing, 2008); Leslie Vinjamuri and Aaron P. Boesenecker, *Accountability and Peace Agreements: Mapping Trends from 1980 to 2006* (Geneva: Centre for Humanitarian Dialogue, 2007).

74　On Colombia, see, e.g., Theidon, "Transitional Subjects," 70-73; Catalina Diaz, "Challenging Impunity from Below: The Contested Ownership of Transitional Justice in Colombia," in *Transitional Justice from Below*, 189-215; Catalina Diaz, "Colombia's Bid for Justice and Peace" (Nuremberg: Working Group on Development and Peace [FriEnt], 2007); Sergio Jaramillo, Yanet Giha, and Paula Torres, *Disarmament , Demobilization and Reinsertion Amidst the Conflict: The Case of Colombia* (New York: International Center for Transitional Justice, 2009).

75　See, e.g., Stathis Kalyvas, *The Logic of Violence in Civil War* (New York: Cambridge University Press, 2006); Scott Straus, *The Order of Genocide: Race, Power, and War in Rwanda* (Ithaca: Cornell University Press, 2006); and Jeremy Weinstein, *Inside Rebellion: The Politics of Insurgent Violence* (New York: Cambridge University Press, 2007). The UN and World Bank have put increasing emphasis on understanding the causes and dynamics of conflict. See, e.g., Paul Collier and Nicholas Sambanis, *Understanding Civil War: Evidence and Analysis* (2 vols.) (Washington, DC: World Bank, 2005). Similarly, the *IDDRS* recommends that DDR practitioners conduct a "conflict and security analysis" in which they look at the root causes of conflict. DPKO, *IDDRS*, sec. 4.30, 7–8.

# CHAPTER 1

# Amnesties and DDR Programs[1]

*Mark Freeman*[2]

## INTRODUCTION

Transitional justice experts and disarmament, demobilization, and reintegration (DDR) experts have traditionally worked in separate professional and academic silos, with contact between them being the exception, not the rule. This appears to have led to wide gaps in perception and practice on one of the crucial issues of concern to both fields: the place of amnesties in conflict resolution and peacebuilding. This chapter endeavors to offer analysis and recommendations to begin to overcome the gap in a manner that better serves the concurrent and sometimes competing interests of DDR, on the one hand, and transitional justice, on the other.

I begin with an observation that is symptomatic of this gap. Speaking from within my own discipline, I would say that most transitional justice practitioners treat the subject of amnesty as highly controversial. Amnesties are typically, though not always fairly, viewed as sources of impunity that significantly threaten the underlying values and operational prospects of transitional justice because they appear to remove the possibility of criminal accountability. By contrast, when discussing amnesties with DDR practitioners, the subject tends to be treated as *un*controversial. Amnesties are usually seen as one of the key incentives or preconditions for a successful DDR program. These divergent practitioner perceptions are mirrored in academic scholarship. The transitional justice literature on amnesties is vast and the analyses are, especially in the last decade, overwhelmingly antagonistic to amnesties. By comparison, DDR literature on amnesties is scant, and where one finds a reference to the topic at all, it is usually positive in the sense of treating amnesties as conducive, rather than antagonistic, to the aims of DDR.

This gap in perception also reflects profound differences about the paramount priority of each field in the context of a peace process: security, if one is in the DDR field; or accountability, if one is in the transitional justice field. This chapter will examine to what degree, in doctrine and in practice, such differences can be overcome through a restructured relation between DDR programs and amnesties. The chapter will suggest, ultimately, that both fields reconsider their current positions so that amnesties can find their proper place as tools, and not necessarily obstacles, of peacebuilding. A subsidiary goal of this chapter is to familiarize practitioners in both fields, but especially in DDR, with the diversity of amnesty models and options in order to foster new thinking on amnesty's role in peacebuilding generally.

In ideal conditions, this chapter would offer a strong empirical case for assertions about the proper relation between DDR programs and amnesties. In that regard, there is some scholarship on the relation between amnesties and peace outcomes in general, which, while not specifically addressing the DDR-amnesty relation, is relevant to the underlying issues. Unfortunately, much of it involves assertions based on unprovable counterfactuals,[3] broad conclusions generated from narrow data sets,[4] and questionable attributions of cause and effect that remain largely untested through peer evaluation.[5] While this is unsurprising given the novelty of the DDR and transitional justice fields, it is perhaps best to treat today's findings with a significant degree of caution. As more reliable data becomes available in the future, it will be easier to empirically measure the nature and depth of the impact of amnesties on DDR programs.

In light of the foregoing, this chapter's principal aim is to provide a cogent analytical framework—rather than a "how-to" guide or "lessons learned" manual—on the range of possible or ideal relationships between DDR programs and amnesties. In doing so I will employ two general, but arguably defensible, premises to underpin what follows. First, I will treat as an accepted fact that DDR programs are generally beneficial for the durability of peace in the short term.[6] Second, I will assume that transitional justice tends to enable sustainable peace. Putting these claims together, I can thus describe the broad aim of this chapter as follows:

> To assess whether and how amnesties can serve to maximize the effectiveness of a DDR program, *which is generally assumed to be beneficial for disarming and demobilizing ex-combatants and hence beneficial for the durability of peace in the short term,* while doing the least harm possible to the transitional justice values of truth, justice, reparation, and reform, *which arguably contribute to the effective reintegration of ex-combatants and hence to the durability of peace in the long term.*[7]

So much for the goals, now what of the challenges? As the reader may already appreciate, the main dilemma in this matter is that the "DD" phases tend to rely for their successful operation on a lack of overt judicial threat to combatants. In some contexts, this may naturally imply a need for some form of amnesty right from the outset. Yet depending on the content and scope of any such amnesty, there is a consequent risk of undermining the "R" phase *by virtue of* the impunity conferred through the amnesty that was necessary to reach the "R" phase in the first instance.[8] In one sense, therefore, the central challenge appears to be one of sequencing. This chapter will explore various options in the area of amnesty design that can help to mitigate the acuteness of this dilemma.

The chapter encompasses four main sections. The first section defines the term "amnesty." The second section examines international law and policy issues that are directly pertinent to amnesties. The third section sets out the different types of amnesty that are applicable in DDR contexts. The fourth and longest section examines a broad range of amnesty design choices that are relevant to consider in the context of DDR program implementation.

## I  DEFINING AMNESTY

For the purposes of this chapter, I use the following definition of amnesty:

> Amnesty is a legal measure, adopted in exceptional circumstances, whose primary function is to remove, conditionally or unconditionally, the prospect and sometimes the consequences of a legal proceeding against designated individuals or classes of persons in respect of designated types of offenses.

In my view, this definition is sufficiently broad to cover the diverse types of amnesties that are observable in state practice. For example, it encompasses amnesties established in peace accords and later implemented in national legislation;[9] amnesties adopted in mid-conflict, postconflict, as well as nonconflict situations; and amnesties that extinguish liability for a wide variety of offenses, and not merely those of a political character.

The definition is also sufficiently narrow to avoid confusion with analogous, yet different, types of legal measures. For example, it excludes pardons, which eliminate only the consequences but not the prospect of adverse legal proceedings; it excludes statutes of limitations and various types of immunities (for example, parliamentary, executive, diplomatic), all of which are forms of standing rather than extraordinary legislation; it excludes reduced sentence regimes, which lower but do not eliminate legal responsibility; and it excludes asylum and sanctuary arrangements, which are political measures but not legal ones.

In practice, the term "amnesty" is used rather loosely. For example, one can often find references to "de facto" amnesties,[10] a misleading expression since one of the definitional elements of an amnesty is that it is a legal (that is, de jure) measure. Thus, while it is perfectly appropriate to discuss the phenomenon of impunity, it makes no sense, properly speaking, to use the term "de facto amnesty." Similarly, one can find references to such terms as "pseudo" amnesties, meaning legal measures that have the same effect as amnesties but are drafted in a disguised form, and "blanket" amnesties, meaning amnesties that are unlimited or unconditional or both. Since both of these terms are used inconsistently to mean different things in the literature on amnesties, this chapter does not use either of them.

## II  INTERNATIONAL LAW AND POLICY ON AMNESTIES

Before analyzing the main types of amnesties, as well as their interrelationships with DDR programs, it is important to note some of the relevant international treaty and non-treaty standards on amnesties. Amnesty is not defined in international treaty law. Amnesties are neither explicitly prohibited nor explicitly required by international treaty law. In fact, there is only one explicit reference found in international treaty law and it takes the form of a limited encouragement in the context of internal armed conflicts. Article 6(5) of "Additional Protocol II to the Geneva Conventions" (APII) provides as follows:

> At the end of hostilities, the authorities in power shall endeavor to grant the broadest possible amnesty to persons who have participated in the armed conflict, or those deprived of their liberty for reasons related to the armed conflict, whether they are interned or detained. [11]

The relevant International Committee of the Red Cross (ICRC) commentary on Article 6(5) declares, "The object of this sub-paragraph is to encourage gestures of reconciliation which can contribute to re-establishing normal relations in the life of a nation which has been divided."[12] However, it does not provide any guidance on the types of amnesties that would be legally admissible or inadmissible in response to internal armed conflicts. Not surprisingly, therefore, Article 6(5) has been interpreted on several occasions to justify the granting of amnesties for a wide range of different offenses, including serious war crimes.[13] Yet the ICRC and leading international humanitarian law (IHL) experts now commonly observe that the article was not intended to encourage all types of amnesty. Instead, they argue, Article 6(5) aims to encourage amnesty only for wartime crimes of hostility that are consistent with international humanitarian law obligations (for example, rebellion, sedition, treason) and not for wartime crimes that would violate them.[14] The ICRC interpretation is arguably not reflected in state practice.[15] Nor is it clear whether this legal interpretation of Article 6(5) has reached the attention of DDR practitioners.[16]

Of equal or greater relevance for DDR policy and practice is the evolving UN secretariat's position on amnesties since 1998. The new position was initially expressed in the form of a handwritten reservation placed by the former Special Representative of the Secretary-General of the UN, Francis Okelo, on a single copy of the 1999 Lomé Peace Accord for Sierra Leone. The reservation stated, "the UN holds the understanding that the amnesty provisions of the Agreement shall not apply to international crimes of genocide, crimes against humanity, war crimes and other serious violations of international humanitarian law."[17] The substance of the reservation has since become the foundation of the new UN position.[18]

This position was formally affirmed in the "Report of the Secretary-General on the Rule of Law and Transitional Justice in Conflict and Post-Conflict Societies."[19] Paragraph 64(c) of the report urges that peace agreements and Security Council resolutions and mandates

> reject any endorsement of amnesty for genocide, war crimes, or crimes against humanity, including those relating to ethnic, gender and sexually based international crimes, and ensure that no such amnesty previously granted is a bar to prosecution before any United Nations-created or assisted court....

Over time, the secretariat's position expanded to include gross human rights violations. In one of the most prominent applications of the new position, the UN boycotted the Commission on Truth and Friendship set up jointly by Indonesia and Timor-Leste because it authorized the Commission to recommend amnesty for crimes against humanity and other gross violations of human rights. The UN secretary-general's spokesperson stated that UN policy "is that the Organization cannot endorse or condone amnesties for genocide, crimes against humanity, war crimes or gross violations of human rights, nor should it do anything that might foster them."[20]

The UN secretariat's position stands in stark relief with its own previous practice[21] and with long-standing opinions about the issue in general.[22] In brief, we have gone from treating amnesties as a political issue, fully within the exclusive and sovereign domain of states, to treating them above all as a legal issue that extends beyond the prerogative of any one state.[23] The new reality of amnesty negotiations today for states is that they need to factor in not only a new jurisdictional reality—namely, the risk of sealed and public arrest warrants and prosecutions by international or hybrid tribunals, or by foreign courts with competence to try extraterritorial violations—but also the risk of potentially offending the UN position. The latter in particular could engender donor disengagement from DDR programs and the withdrawal of related technical and financial support.

Defenders of the UN position assert it will force UN mediators, and encourage non-UN mediators, to think about justice and international law questions more seriously and deeply than in the past.[24] Yet skeptics contend that the position could instead result in such mediators losing a place at the negotiation table, thus leaving mediation to parties with less commitment to accountability.[25] In addition, amnesties for international crimes are those most likely to be challenged by international, hybrid, and foreign courts. The effect of the UN position is to force mediators to negotiate hardest on the elements of an amnesty that are more likely to be overturned by the courts, and thus will present the least impediments to justice in practice. Rigid application of the UN position could also, of course, lead to the entrenchment of tyrants or rebel groups, with all of the terrible human consequences that would entail.[26] A more moderate and compelling view expressed by some backers of the UN position focuses on the need to be flexible in the case-by-case application. But even that view evades the issue of the position's "costs," because the mere existence of the position shifts how parties negotiate in the first place, including on issues of DDR. In other words, the UN does not openly indicate it is flexible in application, and therefore parties do not expect such flexibility in practice.

Another argument advanced by defenders of the new UN position is that it will strengthen the ability of accountability-amenable states or governments to resist "amnesty blackmail" by those with the capacity to perpetuate renewed or ongoing violence. The idea is that, in difficult negotiations, such states will be able to rely on the UN position to say to their blackmailers, "We are internationally prohibited from giving the amnesty you want, and therefore let's focus on what is negotiable."[27] Skeptics can, however, respond that one may accept the general premise of the counterweight argument without endorsing the specific content of the new UN position (that is, a slightly different norm or "red line" could also serve as a counterweight).[28] DDR practitioners may also consider that the UN position ends up removing a key bargaining chip needed to achieve a peace agreement in the first place, thus contradicting any counterweight benefit.[29] In addition, there is a risk that the UN position could prompt a negotiator to offer leniency and concessions in potentially riskier areas (for example, allowing violators to retain powerful positions in the country's security apparatus) to "compensate" for the inability to offer a broad amnesty. In short, there is much room and much need for debate on the UN's current position.[30]

The UN does at least recognize that certain limited amnesties may be necessary for DDR purposes. Paragraph 32 of the "Report of the Secretary-General on the Rule of Law and Transitional Justice in Conflict and Post-Conflict Societies" provides:

> Carefully crafted amnesties can help in the return and reintegration of both [displaced civilians and former fighters] and should be encouraged, although, as noted above, these can never be permitted to excuse genocide, war crimes, crimes against humanity or gross violations of human rights.[31]

While this passage is of limited guidance on how to overcome the dilemmas mentioned above, it does affirm the important and often overlooked point that amnesties can potentially be a *tool* for meeting the dual needs of peace and justice.

A possibly bigger factor than the UN position on amnesty negotiations is the existence of the ICC — *a permanent* court with an *international* criminal mandate and the power to issue sealed or public arrest warrants, which is not necessarily bound by any national amnesty.[32] As a 2005 International Center for Transitional Justice (ICTJ) report asserts:

> ICC obligations now make the prospect of amnesties for war crimes, crimes against humanity, and genocide unlikely even where the UN is not leading the mediation. The ICC itself will not be bound by them and they may contravene the legal obligations of State Parties to investigate or prosecute under the Statute. While this is unlikely to stop parties to negotiations from seeking assurances of immunity from prosecution, it at least allows all negotiators to make clear that the matter is essentially out of their control and to concentrate less on the issue of amnesty and more on the question of what other measures that address past abuses may be appropriate.[33]

From a DDR perspective, however, a major dilemma of the ICC system is that it largely precludes the sequencing of peace and justice. Other than the possibility of a Security Council–imposed, renewable, one-year suspension in proceedings under Article 16 of the Rome Statute, the system, at least in theory, does not allow for any transition-sensitive time horizon in the planning of trials. They must happen immediately at the national level or, failing that, at the international level — in either case creating a likelihood of major blockages in peacemaking.

## III  TYPES OF AMNESTY

Just as there are no two identical DDR programs, there are no two identical amnesties. Some amnesties are given in postconflict contexts (for example, Croatia, 1996)[34] and others in nonconflict contexts (for example, Spain, 1977)[35]; some are given to correct past injustices (for example, Morocco, 1994),[36] and others to entrench impunity (for example, Chile, 1978)[37]; some cover acts of violence (for example, Algeria, 2005),[38] while others do not (for example, U.S. immigration and tax amnesties); some appear in constitutions (for example, Ghana, 1992),[39] others in legislation (for example, Guatemala, 1996),[40] and still others in executive decrees (for example, Greece, 1974)[41]; some apply only to state agents (for example, Turkey, 1982),[42] others only to opponents of the state (for example, Colombia, 2003),[43] and others to both (for example, Sierra Leone, 1999)[44]; some are sweeping in nature (for example, Angola, 1996),[45] and others are more circumscribed (for example, Ivory Coast. 2002).[46] This is only a small list of the many fundamental differences between different amnesty types and amnesty contexts.[47]

In thinking about the types of amnesties most relevant to the operation of DDR programs, at least two observations are in order. First, the existence of DDR implies, as a matter of contextual fact, the existence of some form of armed conflict, irrespective of whether the conflict is new, long-standing, or recently ended. Second, within the subset of amnesties linked to armed conflicts, there are at least four broad types of amnesty that could apply in situations in which a DDR program is in place or under consideration:

1.  Amnesties that are designed as part of a DDR process or mechanism but that grant a very *broad scope* of impunity to former combatants, thus tending to facilitate disarmament and demobilization. For example, the Ugandan Amnesty Act (2000), as amended, created a DDR program that offers amnesty for any conflict-related acts by nonstate combatants involved in the armed conflicts there, with the exception of a handful of leaders against whom the ICC has issued arrest warrants.

2. Amnesties that are designed as part of a DDR process or mechanism but that grant a more *narrow scope* of impunity to former combatants, thus potentially complicating disarmament and demobilization. For example, most DDR programs include "weapons amnesties," which are grants of amnesty issued upon a combatant's disarmament and that cover only the crime of illegal possession of arms (and not any other wartime crime).[48]

3. Amnesties that are *not* designed as part of a DDR process or mechanism but that grant a very *broad scope* of impunity to former combatants, thus tending to facilitate disarmament and demobilization. For example, the amnesty adopted in Mozambique in the 1992 peace accord was not a formal part of the DDR program, but granted a sweeping scope of impunity to the actors in the civil war there.[49]

4. Amnesties that are *not* designed as part of a DDR process or mechanism but that grant a more *narrow scope* of impunity to former combatants, thus potentially complicating disarmament and demobilization. For example, a 2005 amnesty law adopted in the DRC was not a formal part of any DDR program, and granted a limited scope of impunity because it excluded from its ambit, inter alia, the crimes covered in the Rome Statute.[50]

There is admittedly a high degree of artificiality to this typology. For example, the variance within each type can be extremely broad (for example, the South Africa 1995 and Macedonia 2001 amnesties are radically different on a number of levels, but both would fit under category 4 above). In addition, there may be more than one of these amnesty types in force in a state at a given moment (for example, a weapons amnesty and a separate and broader type of amnesty outside the DDR framework). At the same time, these categories help set the framework of policy design choices that bear on the relationship of amnesties and DDR programs, with a view to balancing the nominal DDR "interest" in broad amnesties (whether structurally internal or external to a DDR program) with the nominal transitional justice "interest" in limited amnesties (whether structurally internal or external to a DDR program).

## IV   DESIGNING AMNESTIES TO SUPPORT
## BOTH TRANSITIONAL JUSTICE AND DDR

As previously noted, the UN secretary-general's 2004 report on transitional justice promotes the goal of "carefully crafted amnesties" that can assist in the reintegration of ex-combatants. This important, albeit general, goal will be the focus of this section. In taking up the issue, however, there will be no discussion of "weapons amnesties." These are often integral elements of DDR programs, but they are uncontroversial from a transitional justice perspective.[51] For the same reason, there will be no discussion of so-called corrective amnesties, which provide relief from punishment for acts that (1) were not wrong in the past (such as breaking an illegitimate law), or (2) acts that violated a legitimate law but are no longer considered wrong.[52] Instead, this section will examine only amnesties that have the primary function of removing, conditionally or unconditionally, the prospect or consequence of legal proceedings in respect of more serious offenses. I have divided the analysis into three parts: first, an assessment of amnesty's procedural dimension in relation to DDR programs; second, an analysis of its substantive or "content" aspects; and third, an assessment of its implementation dimension.

## IV.I  PROCESS ISSUES

### AMNESTIES AS LAST RESORT

The use of amnesties tends to encounter little opposition in the DDR community. After all, combatants will be more likely to disarm and demobilize when they do not risk prosecution for their prior acts of violence. However, on the continuum of leniency measures considered necessary to facilitate a DDR process, an amnesty sits at the extreme end. Amnesties that cover grave acts of violence are often viewed as a direct affront to states' remedial obligations, and correspondingly to victims' rights, under international law.[53] In addition, by preventing the punishment of heinous criminal acts, such amnesties may run the risk of damaging public confidence in the rule of law, which may be crucial at a time when society is seeking to transition out of armed conflict.[54] Amnesties of a broad nature also eliminate the possibility of removing war criminals from society (via trial and imprisonment), and can possibly have the effect of emboldening the amnestied class to commit further crimes, thus undermining the specific deterrence goal of criminal law. On occasion they may even provoke victims into committing violent acts against perpetrators, thus undermining the goal of general deterrence.[55] It is for all of these reasons that amnesties should not be considered except as a last resort.

In some cases the concession of an amnesty may not be necessary for a DDR program to operate, whether because of the absence of a functioning justice system or because of a favorable balance of political and military power. In Liberia, where an extensive DDR process occurred, the 2003 Comprehensive

Peace Agreement "left the question of amnesty to be decided in the future, indicating only that there may be consideration of an amnesty by the two-year transitional government."[56] In the case of Afghanistan, which also had a DDR program, many of the parties to the 2001 Bonn Agreement invoked the need for amnesty during negotiations, but the final text did not include one. As noted by Patricia Gossman: "During the closed sessions at Bonn, a heated discussion took place over the idea [of an amnesty]. The original draft of the agreement—written by the U.N.—stated that the interim administration could not decree an amnesty for war crimes or crimes against humanity. This paragraph nearly caused the talks to break down … but in the end, the paragraph was removed…."[57] This left open the possibility of justice, which in the context of the Afghan justice system was more theoretical than real. The point is that the agreement preserved justice options—that is, until the national parliament adopted a broad and general amnesty six years later.[58]

In other DDR contexts, it may be possible to consider other concrete options, short of amnesty. A first and less radical option might be the adoption of a reduced sentence regime. The case par excellence for this is Colombia, where a 2005 "Law on Peace and Justice" offers the possibility of a conditional and reduced sentence, but not amnesty, to persons who have committed certain international crimes and who comply with the various procedural requirements of the legislation.[59] Admittedly, the law is accompanied by a parallel amnesty process for persons responsible for having committed less serious offenses.[60] However, the fact that there is not an across-the-board amnesty is commendable in and of itself.

Another less radical option in lieu of amnesty is asylum in a third country. Sometimes all that may stand between war and peace, and perhaps between the possibility and impossibility of DDR, is a single notorious leader. Assuming it is not feasible to get such a person "out of the way" by military means, asylum is, all else being equal, a better option than amnesty because it avoids the *legal* entrenchment of impunity. Asylum may produce de facto impunity—indeed, that is its intended function—but it is still less debilitating to the rule of law than amnesty. Asylum deals, however, are much less likely to entice tyrants and war criminals as a result of the recent overturning of the asylum deal for the former Liberian president Charles Taylor.[61]

It is true that those who run DDR programs do not usually negotiate peace deals, but instead "inherit" the particular leniency measures conceded or adopted in the course of peace talks or in legislation. This means that managers of DDR programs will tend to have a limited ability to control the impact of the prior, and external, conferral of leniency on the effective implementation of their programs. DDR actors, especially those involved in the design of DDR systems, should nevertheless be aware of this "amnesty as last resort" threshold so that peace through DDR is pursued using leniency measures that violate to the least extent possible a state's ethical and international legal obligations.[62]

## PUBLIC CONSULTATION AND DEBATE

The second procedural point when it comes to amnesty's relation to DDR concerns the issue of public consultation and debate. Although difficult to operationalize in DDR settings, the idea of consultation has recently become a popular cause in human rights, conflict resolution, and many other fields.[63] Patrick Vinck and Eric Stover explain that "survivors of mass violence are rarely given a 'voice' in the development of policies that will affect both their individual and collective lives for years to come."[64] They stress that, "to the extent possible, all sectors of a war-ravaged society—the individual, community, society, and state—should become *engaged participants in*—and not merely *auxiliaries to*—the process of transitional justice and social reconstruction."[65] On few issues is this truer than amnesty, which tends to be negotiated and decided at the elite level.[66]

A consultation process, and any accompanying public and democratic debate, can help reinforce national and international awareness and legitimacy for any amnesty (and to the extent they are connected, for any simultaneous or subsequent DDR program). As importantly, soliciting the views of the most relevant constituencies for amnesty and DDR processes—including victims, combatants, civilian returnees, and conflict-affected communities—can help ensure any eventual legislation or policy maximally reflects the realities on the ground and maximally balances the competing needs, preferences, and expectations of relevant stakeholders.[67] However, because amnesties concern fundamental human rights, this author does not believe they should be adopted through a public referendum (unless, for example, they are adopted as part of a broader constitutional reform or peace agreement package that follows a full and transparent national debate involving a free and independent press).[68]

Nonetheless, consultation may reveal ambivalent public attitudes, rather than a clear majority in favor of a particular approach. One must also be aware that those responsible for the bulk of past violence may remain sufficiently powerful to block or threaten those seeking public input or a more accountability-oriented amnesty-DDR mix. Participation by the international community can, therefore, be a crucial element in ensuring that meaningful consultation and public debate occur. International participation can also be important when the parties to a negotiation have a mutual interest in an unprincipled amnesty, as when serious crimes were committed on a large scale by all sides.

### STATE MOTIVATION

A final procedural threshold when it comes to amnesty's relation to DDR concerns the issue of state motivation. "Good faith" is a core principle of international law.[69] Where it is present, in the sense of a good faith effort to come to terms with a past conflict, the legitimacy of any amnesty or DDR program necessarily increases. Conversely, where it is absent, the prospect of legitimacy necessarily decreases. This may sound self-evident, yet the UN's current position on amnesties ignores this factor in the evaluation of whether a specific amnesty is acceptable. Instead, the UN position effectively lumps together well-intentioned leaders who reluctantly accept broad amnesties as the price for peace, with ill-intentioned leaders seeking to immunize their own systematic misconduct. This author believes that the motivations behind a state decision to grant amnesty—motivations that, admittedly, may be difficult to discern[70]—ought to be a central consideration by those in decision-making or other influential positions in an amnesty negotiation. As other authors suggest, "In a world of failed states and weak institutions—a world where politics in fact often trumps law—prosecutors should show deference to responsible political leaders who have the skills and the mandate to make choices based on prudence and political consequences."[71]

An important indicator of state motivation concerns who is "giving" amnesties and who is "receiving" them. At one end of the spectrum are so-called self-amnesties, amnesties given by a state to itself and its allies. Such amnesties should be cause for immediate suspicion. At the other end of the spectrum are what might be called "non-self-amnesties," amnesties given by a state to benefit only its opponents, whether political dissidents or armed rebel movements, either as an incentive to leave the field of battle or as a means to correct a past injustice. Such amnesties may be political ploys, but the motivation of a state in adopting such amnesties may generally be presumed to be bona fide absent clear evidence to the contrary.

Between the extremes of self-amnesty and non-self-amnesty are so-called reciprocal amnesties,[72] which encompass anything from an amnesty negotiated by state and nonstate actors in which both sides benefit, to an amnesty adopted unilaterally by a state but which benefits both itself and its opponents.

Reciprocal amnesties require careful scrutiny, especially in the latter case, because they may be tantamount to disguised self-amnesties, as when the overwhelming majority of offenses are attributable to the state.[73] Where reciprocal amnesties result from negotiation, however, the motivations are less suspicious. Yet even then it is important to carefully scrutinize the facts because the amnesty could be tantamount to a collective self-amnesty, as when both sides have committed a comparable and significant number of grave crimes. Reciprocal amnesties adopted by democratically elected governments and bolstered by public debate and consultation, as occurred most famously in South Africa with the 1995 Promotion of National Unity and Reconciliation Act, are the least suspect.[74]

## IV.II  CONTENT ISSUES

In contexts of armed conflict, amnesties cannot always be avoided. Military victory may be impossible. Other peacemaking tools, such as sanctions, may be ineffective or inappropriate. In addition, prosecutions (or the threat of prosecutions) may push back rather than facilitate the prospects of peace, and the procedural options outlined above, such as reduced sentence regimes, may be insufficient "carrots" to convince combatants to disarm and demobilize. In short, sometimes amnesty truly is a last option, without which there would be no serious prospect for DDR or the end of conflict.[75] Although well-informed tyrants and warlords may realize that amnesties can be disregarded by foreign and international tribunals, or scaled back by national courts or future national governments, such awareness would rarely make them seek anything less than the broadest amnesty possible.[76] For these reasons, and in order to achieve the most effective reintegration of ex-combatants possible, the question of an amnesty's content is crucially important.

In terms of an overall litmus test for the proper content of an amnesty, this chapter argues against using a simple and rigid rule. Instead it argues that the content of an amnesty should be evaluated on the basis of the degree to which it promises to: (1) *fulfill* a state's core justice obligations in regard to human rights crimes (that is, investigation, redress, suppression, and prevention); and (2) *impair* each of those obligations as little as possible. Such a test lends itself to detailed case-by-case evaluation — precisely as it should. It also corresponds to the reality that, in most cases of a negotiated amnesty, the final content will include both elements of accountability and elements of leniency. It is all a question of careful balancing and attention to the specifics of the context.

In examining the issue of an amnesty's content, while bearing in mind the possible relevance to DDR programs, four clusters of questions will be explored: the first cluster focuses on how to limit the scope and legal consequences of the amnesty; the second examines ways to add elements of accountability to the process; the third centers on the need to impose the most demanding conditions possible for an individual to retain the legal and other benefits an amnesty offers; and the fourth concerns relevant aspects of the juridical character of an amnesty.

### VI.II.A  LIMITING THE SCOPE AND LEGAL CONSEQUENCES OF AN AMNESTY

The first cluster of questions centers on the notion that the scope of an amnesty should be as narrow as possible. This is examined with reference to three common elements of an amnesty: the categories of *crimes* covered, the categories of *persons* covered, and the *legal consequences* for any potential beneficiary.[77]

#### I  THE CATEGORIES OF CRIMES

Unless it is blanket in scope, an amnesty will generally set out specific types of crimes as being expressly eligible for amnesty. In many cases, an amnesty will also establish certain crimes as being expressly ineligible. Such specifications in an amnesty have a direct impact on the operation of a DDR program. Usually the main eligible forms of crime are those deemed "political" or those associated with a particular conflict. The main ineligible forms of crime tend to be one or more of the following: international crimes, economic crimes, or "context-specific" crimes (meaning crimes considered especially repugnant in the particular context that do not fit under the other mentioned categories).

*Political/conflict-related versus ordinary offenses*  In the context of an ongoing or recently ended armed conflict, it is important to avoid granting amnesty for offenses that lack a clear nexus with the conflict. In other words, an amnesty established because of a conflict should not serve as a pretext for extinguishing the prospect or consequence of criminal accountability for those guilty of ordinary offenses (that is, nonpolitical and non–conflict-related offenses). In this regard, an amnesty should ideally specify that it applies only to acts related to the armed conflict and for which there was some kind of underlying "political" (that is, conflict-related) motivation.[78] It may, however, be difficult in some cases to distinguish political crimes from common crimes (for example, theft to raise funds for the purchase of weaponry, rather than for self-enrichment).[79]

*International crimes*  As previously noted, the UN has adopted the position that amnesties "can never be permitted to excuse genocide, war crimes, crimes against humanity or gross violations of human rights."[80] Beyond this list there are several other types of international crimes, such as international terrorist acts, that should be excluded on the same basis (that is, because of a treaty- or custom-based obligation to prosecute).[81] Indeed, *all* relevant international crimes ideally should be excluded from an amnesty. This has both a symbolic impact, in implicitly denouncing such crimes, and a practical impact, in preserving justice options in respect of them at the national level.

*Economic crimes* Beyond the exclusion of international crimes from an amnesty, it may be important to also explicitly exclude crimes committed "for personal gain," whether or not they were linked in some way to the conflict.[82] This, too, has both symbolic and practical implications. A typical example of such a crime would be drug trafficking by rebel groups or paramilitaries.[83] Interestingly, crimes of this sort may be easier to exclude from an amnesty than human rights violations.[84]

*Selected context-specific crimes* Beyond the acts mentioned above, it may be possible for an amnesty to also exclude other categories of crime that were especially prevalent in prior armed conflict and that engendered significant social opprobrium—whether from the local population, the international community, or both. The types of offenses falling into this category include, for example, violent crimes against children[85] and assassination of religious leaders.[86] Such crimes may be easier to exclude from an amnesty because the conflict's chief actors may want to avoid the impression of seeking impunity for them (which would imply responsibility for their commission in the first instance).

## II   THE CATEGORIES OF PERSONS

Negotiating whom to include or exclude from an amnesty is often central to the prospects of DDR and peace. Unless there has been a complete military vanquishing of one side by the other, one is invariably negotiating with parties that have the capacity to continue or renew serious violations, and who are themselves the most vulnerable to prosecution. Is it realistic to expect such individuals to agree to disarm and demobilize if immediately after signing a peace accord they and their allies face certain punishment? As two leading authors on amnesty have noted, "Where human rights violators are too weak to derail the strengthening of the rule of law, they can be put on trial. But where they have the ability to lash out in renewed violations to try to reinforce their power, the international community faces a hard choice: either commit the resources to contain the backlash or offer the potential spoilers a deal that will leave them weak but secure."[87] Often that deal has included compromises in the form of policies of inclusion and power sharing, including the conversion of militarized movements into political parties.[88] For example, "At every critical juncture, those steering the state-building process in Afghanistan have undervalued and deemphasized transitional justice.... [I]n the immediate aftermath of the Taliban's defeat, preventing a return to civil war necessitated a policy of inclusion, according to which faction leaders, 'war lords' and other commanders were awarded positions in the interim and transitional administrations regardless of their past records...."[89] But a negotiated deal in such circumstances could just as likely include an amnesty. In that context, it is important for an amnesty to clearly demarcate the categories of persons who are expressly eligible or ineligible according to such metrics as affiliation, rank, and the nature of one's participation in particular crimes.

*Affiliation* An amnesty can cover persons with a very wide range of possible affiliations, whether at the state level (for example, army, police, intelligence agency), the para-statal level (for example, militia, self-defense groups, paramilitaries), or the nonstate level (for example, rebel groups, private companies, religious institutions). There is also a wide range of possible sub-affiliations that may be pertinent, as when one or more special units of a security sector institution are responsible for the acts covered in an amnesty. In this regard, the text of an amnesty should be as precise as possible about the affiliation requirements necessary to benefit from the amnesty, especially when it concerns serious crimes. Language that is too general or ambiguous may risk extending the scope of the amnesty to unintended beneficiaries, thus unduly undermining future transitional justice options.

*Rank* In addition to specifying affiliation, it may be important to specify rank. This issue is crucial for the effectiveness of DDR programs, especially ones issued mid-conflict that seek to entice lower-level combatants away from the field of battle in order to reduce the strength of the nonstate armed group in question. Here we return to the issue of the current UN position on amnesties, which omits any rank specification. In particular, the position does not specifically limit its application to "those bearing greatest responsibility"[90] or some similar formulation. Such a specification would seem to be in keeping both with the practice of international and hybrid criminal tribunals and with the reality that no justice system will be in a position to try more than a small percentage of the total number of perpetrators of international crimes in a context of mass abuse. As one author observes (albeit without proposing a different UN position), it would be "unwise to dissuade people from DDR participation based on a threat of prosecution that cannot realistically be fulfilled."[91]

However, as previously noted, in a negotiation the exclusion of leaders from an amnesty's scope is difficult to achieve because the leaders (or their proxies) are the ones with whom one is negotiating and whose endorsement of a DDR program is necessary for it to operate most effectively. Such leaders may be able to compromise in some areas and accept certain unfavorable conditions of a peace agreement, but they are unlikely to sign an agreement that exposes them to immediate and full prosecution.

*Forms of participation* In addition to limitations based on affiliation and rank, amnesty eligibility can also be limited based on the nature of a person's participation in the crimes in question. Although some amnesties cover persons irrespective of how they participated in an eligible crime, many others expand or narrow eligibility based on the nature of one's participation. Consistent with the ideal of excluding those in command positions from eligibility for amnesty, it is desirable to exclude persons who gave orders to commit crimes.[92]

*Specific groups* There may be specific categories of persons that ought to be explicitly excluded from the benefit of an amnesty, such as "recidivists,"[93] beneficiaries of prior amnesties,[94] and foreign mercenaries.[95] There also may be specific categories of persons that could or should be explicitly *included* in the benefit of an amnesty, such as children, who even in ordinary times are often completely immune from criminal responsibility.[96]

## III THE LEGAL CONSEQUENCES FOR ANY POTENTIAL BENEFICIARY

There are many possible legal consequences of a grant of amnesty for the beneficiary. For example, beneficiaries may receive immunity from prosecution only, or they may additionally receive immunity from civil liability. In addition, the legal consequences can be varied within the terms of an amnesty according to the gravity of the offense or other similar criteria. There can also be prospective prohibitions placed on amnesty beneficiaries.

*Immunities from legal process* Ideally an amnesty will be expressly limited to immunity from prosecution, which tends to be what combatants fear most, in any case.[97] By limiting an amnesty in this way, the possibility of civil suits and nonjudicial disciplinary proceedings remains open, thus achieving a better overall balance between the values of transitional justice and the needs of a DDR program. In legal systems in which civil redress is structurally dependent on the availability of criminal redress, however, the "gain" in limiting the amnesty to immunity from prosecution may be largely illusory.[98]

*Variation in consequences* Consistent with standard criminal sentencing practice and with the principle of proportionality,[99] it may be appropriate to avoid a uniform set of consequences for all eligible amnesty beneficiaries in respect of all eligible crimes. Instead, within an amnesty—and provided the administrative time and costs would be reasonably manageable—the legal consequences may be structured in a manner that achieves greater individuation and specificity by, for example, varying the consequences according to the type and number of crimes committed by the individual in question and the form of participation in each.[100] In addition, and analogous to the truth commission model adopted in Timor-Leste, the legal consequences could be made contingent on the gradual fulfillment of various amnesty conditions, such as participation in a DDR process, the revelation of one's crimes, or community repentance measures. In other words, the degree of immunity for the beneficiary could increase in a sequential manner tied to the individual's step-by-step fulfillment of such conditions. (The issue of amnesty conditions is discussed in more detail below.)

*Prospective prohibitions* In addition to any favorable legal consequences for someone covered by an amnesty law, various *un*favorable legal consequences could also be incorporated. For example, one possible consequence of receiving amnesty might be the placement of prospective prohibitions on the individual beneficiary. Depending on a wide range of possible factors—such as the gravity of the crime committed, the level of remorse expressed, and the likelihood of recidivism—prohibitions might be placed on the beneficiary's ability, for example, to secure certain forms of public employment in the security sector or to purchase or carry arms during a prescribed period. Such prohibitions would clearly support the general aims of DDR.

### IV.II.B CONDITIONS FOR OBTAINING AN AMNESTY

The second cluster of amnesty content questions centers around the notion that an amnesty should impose the most demanding conditions possible for an individual to *obtain* the legal and other benefits it confers. Unlike the prior cluster of questions, which was primarily concerned with how to limit the scope and legal consequences of the amnesty, this second cluster of questions concerns ways to add elements of accountability to the process.[101] It is important, however, to reiterate that the degree to which elements of accountability can be added will be inversely related, in most cases, to the power of the party seeking a grant of amnesty. The more powerful the party, the fewer and the weaker the elements of accountability will be. Conversely, the less powerful the party, the more and the stronger the elements of accountability will be. That said, the range of possible conditions is almost limitless and can be combined in different ways. While such conditions will generally make the amnesty more acceptable in transitional justice terms, they will generally make it less conducive to DDR.

*Disarmament and demobilization*  Amnesties issued in contexts of armed conflict often make voluntary surrender, or disarmament and demobilization, an explicit condition of a beneficiary's eligibility.[102] For such a condition to be effective, it is naturally important that the government, as well as the body designated to oversee disarmament and demobilization, enjoys at least a minimum degree of credibility. Failing that, the carrot of amnesty will likely not work.[103] Cash inducements may also be required to make such an amnesty effective. As Louise Mallinder has noted: "In many amnesty processes, insurgents do not simply have to turn themselves in, but are also encouraged or required to surrender their weapons, ammunitions and explosives. Sometimes, cash incentives, known as 'buy back' programmes, are introduced. These offer payments usually on a varying scale depending on the type of weaponry that is surrendered."[104] Yet another approach is to tie the individual benefits of amnesty to a broader organizational commitment to disarm.[105] Whatever choice is made, one must appreciate that disarmament and demobilization may not be sufficient in and of itself to reduce the power of an armed faction.[106] Therefore, it may be advisable in the future to condition the legal benefits of an amnesty on effective participation in the reintegration phase of a DDR program. For example, DDR and amnesty conditions could be linked in such a way that at every turn when an ex-combatant has to perform some amnesty-related act of accountability (for example, an act of restitution in a community of reception), there is an acknowledgment and a benefit (for example, an increase in the economic support package).

*Requirement of renunciation of violence*  There are a number of amnesties that are made conditional on an express renunciation of violence or the maintenance of a cease-fire or both.[107] Provided the renunciation is voluntary, a condition of this sort would seem to be unobjectionable from a normative and legal standpoint, as well as actionable and verifiable in practice. A complementary approach, not found in any amnesties discovered in this research, might be to condition amnesty not only on the applicant's renunciation of violence and pledge to obey the law, but also on a related legal and financial pledge by parents, guardians, or community leaders, akin to the procedures for posting bail in a criminal court.

*Release of hostages and prisoners of war*  There is a long-standing practice as part of cease-fire and final peace agreements to include conditions for the exchange and release of prisoners and missing persons in accordance with the require- ments of international law.[108] Consistent with that practice, and taking into account the widespread abduction of children and women in modern warfare, amnesties should ideally be conditioned on the release and return of hostages and other prisoners of war.[109]

*Temporary supervised relocation*  Along with other preconditions of eligibility, the conferral of amnesty could be conditioned on temporary relocation to a part of the country where the risk of violence is significantly lower and where the activities of the amnesty applicant can be effectively monitored prior to long-term reintegration efforts. This could be akin to a release-on-bail scheme, and could include regular supervision as well as reporting appearances by the applicant.[110] This would also be a means of serving criminal law's objective of incapacitation and DDR's objective of enhanced public security.[111] How- ever, such a precondition could only be applied if it was clearly presented and understood by the applicant as a condition of amnesty eligibility, considering that it affects his right to freedom of movement.[112] As a condition of eligibil- ity for amnesty, it could not be a permanent supervised relocation but would instead need to be for a limited and fixed duration—whether predetermined by the amnesty law or decided by the body responsible for administering the amnesty. No precedent for such an amnesty condition was discovered in the course of this research, but it would seem an idea worthy of future consider- ation, especially in contexts in which an immediate reintegration effort would be destabilizing.

*Cooperation with law enforcement authorities*  Some amnesties require as a condi- tion of eligibility the cooperation of the applicant with national, or possibly international, law enforcement authorities. This could include the requirement to fully disclose relevant information about command structures, arms suppli- ers, illicit trade routes, and assisting in locating bodies of missing persons.[113] The insertion of such a condition would generally advance the underlying pub- lic security goals common to DDR and transitional justice.

*Submission of a formal application within a specified time*  Most amnesties do not provide for the administration of individual grants of amnesty. Eligibility is presumed (that is, automatic) and individuals as such need not affirmatively apply. There are, however, an increasing number of examples of amnesties that require persons to apply for eligibility, whether formally (for example, by submitting a written application or request) or informally (for example, by simply presenting themselves to the competent authority).[114] The chief advantage of requiring an application is the addition of a level of individual decision-making and accountability to the process.[115] However, for application-based amnesties to work there needs to be a short yet reasonable application deadline and, ideally, the threat of increased military pressure after the deadline against those who fail to come forward.[116] With a fixed deadline in place, the incentive for combatants to return to civilian life is increased, since there is no future guarantee of amnesty, whether through renewal of the original amnesty or enactment of a new one.

*Full disclosure of past crimes*  Some application-based amnesties, including the one devised for the TRC in South Africa, obligate applicants to provide a full description of the crimes they committed and for which they claim entitlement to amnesty.[117] Amnesties may also require applicants to disclose knowledge or evidence about the crimes of others.[118] In both cases, an amnesty applicant should if possible be required to provide a full description of such crimes, including a list of documentary and physical evidence within his possession or control. This should occur ideally via a public hearing.[119] However, expectations around the implementation of such disclosure and hearing procedures should be kept in check. There are many reasons why perpetrators may prefer to remain silent and forgo the possibility of amnesty, including the risk of family and community humiliation, fear of revenge attacks, and concern about breaking rank with former comrades. While such abstention from an amnesty process will have the negative effect of reducing the amount of truth that is revealed out of court, it will have the positive effect of preserving the option of truth and justice in court against those who fail to come forward.[120] Prior to adopting disclosure and hearing procedures of this sort, a serious evaluation should also be done of the domestic capacity to implement such an operationally complex and demanding scheme.

*Acknowledgment of wrongdoing*  It may be important to condition grants of amnesty on unqualified public apologies, particularly in contexts where apologies are broadly considered as beneficial or necessary to the successful reintegration of ex-combatants.[121] Apology or acknowledgment could alternatively be a precondition of amnesty at the organizational rather than individual level such that a rebel, militia, or paramilitary group could be required to acknowledge its systemic wrongdoing as a first step in a broad amnesty process (though I am not aware of any example of this).[122] The idea of explicit acknowledgment of wrongdoing may, however, be inappropriate in various circumstances. If it is a condition of obtaining amnesty, there may be no way for it to seem voluntary and sincere, thus eviscerating its symbolic value. It may also be difficult to condition amnesty on an apology when the crimes in question were committed with a strong ideological motivation.

*Acts of restitution and community service* In addition to or in lieu of any formal apology, and with the aim of contributing to a successful ex-combatant reintegration process, perpetrator restitution or community service could also be made a condition of amnesty eligibility.[123] Such acts of restitution and service are habitually taken into account in criminal sentencing procedures. They are also sometimes part and parcel of "tradition-based justice mechanisms," which can play a potentially important role in the success of DDR programs in their own right.[124] The return of illicit economic gains acquired through wartime activity can also be made an express condition of amnesty eligibility in order to reinforce further the link between past crime and the obligation of restitution.[125]

### IV.II.C  CONDITIONS FOR RETAINING AN AMNESTY

The third cluster of amnesty content questions centers around the need to impose the most demanding conditions possible for an individual to *retain*, as opposed to obtain, the legal and other benefits an amnesty offers. First, amnesty benefits should be explicitly revocable when an individual fails to comply with one or more of its central conditions, such as the failure to fulfill the requirements of a DDR program.[126] Concerning revocability based on a material misrepresentation by the amnesty applicant, the person should ideally be prosecuted both for the crime of perjury or fraud and for the original crimes (subject to the right against self-incrimination).[127] Second, amnesty benefits should normally be subject to revocation when any new human rights crime of comparable gravity is committed.[128] Indeed, all else being equal, the general population is probably more likely to accept amnesty for past crimes if *both* of the mentioned conditions of retention are included in the text.

### IV.II.D  THE JURIDICAL FORM OF AN AMNESTY

The fourth cluster of content questions concerns an amnesty's legal nature, and in particular, whether it is enacted as a permanent or temporary legal measure. Ron Slye notes that amnesties "are not meant to be temporary."[129]

However, where possible they ought to be made expressly temporary rather than permanent (for example, by limiting the period of application to five years).[130] There are some examples of this, including the Burundian Loi No. 1/004 du 8 mai 2003, which grants provisional immunity from prosecution for perpetrators of international crimes until an international judicial commission of inquiry (foreseen in an earlier peace accord) shall have issued findings on the occurrence of such crimes.[131]

At the conclusion of the period of prescribed immunity provided for under any temporary amnesty, the immunity benefit should either come to an end (thus raising the possibility of prosecutions) or be reenacted and extended (thus prolonging the suspension of prosecutions) in accordance with pre-defined criteria and following a formal review by the president, parliament, or the courts.[132] Until now the situation has seldom arisen because those seeking amnesty have naturally tended to insist on a permanent amnesty, even if they are aware that in some countries the guarantees of permanence have diminished with the passage of time.[133] In terms of the impact on DDR, one would also have to assess the risk—within the specific context—that a temporary amnesty would increase the risk of the resumption of hostilities, thus undermining the peace as well as the DDR program.

### IV.III   IMPLEMENTATION QUESTIONS

In addition to questions of procedure and content vis-à-vis amnesties, there is the crucial question of implementation. Amnesties are merely legal instruments, and thus no more or less likely to be honored in the breach than any other laws. In this respect, it is quite possible for principled amnesties to coexist with de facto impunity. Examples of principled amnesties that are belied by de facto impunity include, perhaps most starkly, the 1996 amnesty in Guatemala,[134] but also the much-heralded South African amnesty process.[135] Such impunity may be due in part to the very nature of amnesties, which tend to encompass only the "negative obligation" to refrain from prosecuting certain classes of persons. Stated otherwise, the fact that an amnesty excludes certain categories of crime from eligibility does not guarantee that those responsible for such crimes will in fact be investigated or prosecuted by the state.

Concerning DDR programs, there are some general rules of thumb to consider in order for amnesties to directly contribute to their effectiveness. First, just as war crimes prosecutions need to include information and outreach programs, amnesties also need to be publicized and explained in the plainest language possible—both to combatants who may stand to benefit from the amnesty and any related DDR program, and to the communities that may be expected to receive and reintegrate them upon demobilization. An example of such outreach occurred in Sierra Leone, where early efforts with combatants helped clarify the fact that only a handful of them risked prosecution by the Special Court.[136] Since few combatants are legally trained or familiar with how trials operate, such education and outreach efforts tend to be essential in order to explain whether the threat of prosecution they perceive for themselves is exaggerated or underrated, as the case may be.[137] Outreach efforts are also important in order to allay any fears of violence they might face upon demobilization.[138] Indeed, combatants may see amnesty as a guarantee not just against prosecutions but also against future harassment or violence by state authorities or future neighbors. No longer bearing weapons, ex-combatants may not only feel more vulnerable, but may actually be more vulnerable.

In addition to the foregoing it is important to note that amnesties, especially ones intended to catalyze and assist DDR programs, tend to be most effective where there is both a credible external threat (for example, a threat of increase in military strength and activity by the state or a threat to issue an international arrest warrant)[139] and a credible external incentive (for example, the offer of job training, small loans, or family reunification).[140] Such a "carrot and stick" approach has been important in the operation of several amnesties, including in South Africa, where many perpetrators of gross human rights violations submitted amnesty applications due to the "carrot" of potential amnesty and the "stick" of potential prosecution due to any failure to apply. However, a key variable in South Africa, as elsewhere, is the *credibility* of both the threat and the incentive. If credibility is absent, the amnesty and any related DDR program will likely under-deliver and potentially foster resentment rather than reintegration.[141]

In addition to the above considerations, many other more general contextual factors will naturally affect the prospects of successful implementation. These include the following:

- *The nature of the conflict* If the conflict is or was of an interstate or cross-border character, that factor will tend to complicate the effectiveness of amnesties and DDR programs.[142] The form of its suspension or termination (for example, stalemate versus clear military victor) will also of course be a major factor in the amnesty's implementation.
- *The overall security situation* If the conflict persists or if broad security fears remain even after the end of conflict, this too will tend to make it difficult for either amnesty or DDR to succeed.

- *The overall economic situation* Widespread poverty and unemployment, combined with scarce state resources, will obviously tend to have a detrimental effect on amnesties and DDR programs. In the context of armed actors, the question of who controls the informal or illicit economy will also of course be relevant to amnesty and DDR outcomes.
- *The absorption capacity of receiving communities* If communities are not prepared and equipped for the eventual reception of ex-combatants into their midst, this will normally undermine amnesty and DDR prospects.[143]
- *The administrative scheme* The bodies responsible for overseeing amnesty and DDR schemes are also critical factors in their outcomes. Ensuring the bodies are adequately resourced is important, but so too may be the direct participation by international agencies in order to increase operational capacity and the perception of impartiality.
- *The overall state of the domestic judicial system* If the domestic legal system is shattered and there is a generalized and ongoing context of impunity for war criminals, there would be little penal risk for perpetrators to engage in fresh acts of violence. This would tend to subvert the benefits of well-intentioned amnesties and DDR programs.
- *Uncontrollable threats of prosecution* International and foreign prosecutors decide their prosecution strategies with broad independence and they are not bound by national amnesties. This, too, can affect the prospects of successful implementation of amnesties and DDR programs, especially in situations where the domestic legal system is weak and where impunity is thus of greater concern to international and foreign prosecutors.[144]

As a final point it is worth recalling that in contexts of armed conflict the question of amnesty is usually only *one* issue within a much larger negotiation process that involves other important bargains on peace, justice, and power.[145] One should avoid passing judgment on any amnesty in isolation from these other bargains. Instead, the concessions and gains agreed to in respect of the content of any particular amnesty should be weighed against possible external concessions and gains, which could include, on the positive side, the restoration of democracy and civil and political rights, the provision of reparation to individual victims or their next of kin, the allocation of special development funds for victim communities, the creation of repatriation and reintegration programs for refugees and internally displaced persons, the establishment of a truth commission or similar investigative body, and the implementation of various reforms to the national security system. Such measures can partially mitigate the negative impact of an amnesty, and hence improve the prospects of success for any parallel DDR program.[146]

## CONCLUSIONS

The broad aim of this chapter was to assess whether and how amnesties can serve to maximize the effectiveness of a DDR program, while doing the least harm possible to the transitional justice values of truth, justice, reparation, and reform. This involved, among other things, an analysis of various international law and policy issues, and an examination of the possible interrelation of amnesties and DDR programs.

In terms of final reflections, it is difficult to offer any definitive conclusions. The subject of this chapter falls into an inescapably gray zone, in terms of both theory and practice, given the absence of any literature on the relation between DDR programs and amnesties covering human rights crimes. There are, however, at least three very general concluding remarks that might be offered.

First, just as DDR programs are not an unqualified good, amnesties are not an unqualified bad. Amnesties can be a *positive* tool of peacebuilding. In this respect, it is high time for the debate on amnesty to be fundamentally reframed. The debate is not between peace and justice, or even between impunity and justice. It is between competing conceptions of justice. It is a debate between those who privilege the human dignity and interests of victims of past abuse (that is, the "justice camp" that is opposed to amnesties for serious crimes) and those who privilege the human dignity and interests of victims of verifiable current abuse and inevitable future abuse (that is, the "peace camp" that tolerates amnesties for serious crimes in exceptional cases). *In both cases, it is about justice and human dignity.* As such, it is not necessarily or automatically a contradiction—in human rights terms—to be simultaneously pro-prosecutions, pro-DDR, and pro-amnesties.[147]

Second, whether an amnesty should be integrated into a DDR program, or vice versa, cannot be answered in the abstract. Sometimes it will make sense to do so, other times not. What is important is that amnesty experts and DDR experts engage in a more active dialogue at the level of both theory and practice. The stakes for the beneficiaries of transitional justice and DDR are too high to justify ongoing isolation between the fields.[148] And now that there is at least one relevant experience in which transitional justice and DDR directly coalesce (that is, the Colombian case), there is a practical starting point for greater interaction and learning across the two terrains.

Finally, because reintegration is considered the weakest link in DDR programs, further research should be done by DDR experts on the extent to which amnesty deals — and related transitional justice processes — *make* it so. It may be that the success of DDR depends mostly on the economic benefits available to ex-combatants and not on legal benefits in the form of immunity from adverse legal proceedings.[149] Alternatively, it could be that the relative gravity of the crimes committed by an ex-combatant constitutes the key determinant.[150] Only significant additional research will illuminate the reality on the ground. For now, one must simply avoid overstatements and sweeping generalizations about the importance of amnesties in relation to DDR programs.

## NOTES

1   This chapter includes sections from a forthcoming book by the same author entitled *Necessary Evils: Amnesties and the Search for Justice* (Cambridge University Press, forthcoming 2009). Many of the arguments of this chapter are examined in far greater detail in the book.

2   The author wishes to thank Dražan Djukić, ,Minna Nuclér, Laura Surano, Monica Zwaig, Jorge Errandonea, Sanne Tielemans, and Nadia Siddiqui for their valuable research assistance. Thanks are also due to Ana Patel, Pablo de Greiff, Lars Waldorf, Louise Mallinder, Laura Davis, Tyrone Savage, and Gwen K. Young for their excellent comments on earlier drafts of the chapter.

3   See Leyla Nadya Sadat, "Exile, Amnesty and International Law," *Notre Dame Law Review* 81, no. 3 (2006): 955–1036. The problem is that one could never know with certainty whether, in the amnesty's absence, there would have been more or less peace.

4   For a review of several examples of this practice, see, e.g., Mark Osiel, "Modes of Participation in Mass Atrocity," *Cornell International Law Journal* 38 (2005): 811: "Legal scholarship purporting to show that amnesties fail to advance peace and reconciliation tend to practice most flagrant selection bias.... Countries whose relevant experience of transition does not support the author's favored position on this question (such as Spain, El Salvador, Brazil, and several others) are simply ignored, like inconvenient cases that an opposing advocate can be expected to call to the court's attention. Such methods should be no more acceptable in serious legal scholarship than in social science, where

the main point is precisely to compel our confrontation of 'inconvenient facts.' " Note that the same problem repeats itself in some jurisprudence. See, e.g., *Prosecutor v. Allieu Kondewa, Decision on Lack of Jurisdiction/Abuse of Process: Amnesty Provided by the Lomé Accord Amnesty* ("Kondewa Amnesty Decision"), Decision of the Appeal Chamber, SCSL 04-14-T-128-7347, paras. 30, 31, where Justice Geoffrey Robertson of the Special Court for Sierra Leone draws conclusions about the status of the Lomé amnesty with respect to customary international law based on very few examples of state practice.

5   There is important research that is just beginning to appear on issues of cause and effect in relation to amnesties. See, e.g., Ellen Lutz and Kathryn Sikkink, "The Justice Cascade: The Evolution and Impact of Foreign Human Rights Trials in Latin America," *Chicago Journal of International Law* 2, no. 1 (2001): 1–33. The problem is that changes in the data sets, definitions, and methodologies can result in completely different sets of findings.

6   It is important to note, however, that analysis of reintegration processes appears to be in its infancy. See Macartan Humphreys and Jeremy M. Weinstein, "Demobilization and Reintegration," *Journal of Conflict Resolution* 51, no. 4 (2007): 532–33: "there have been few systematic efforts to evaluate the determinants of successful reintegration by ex-combatants after conflict.... An academic consensus appears to be emerging that these multidimensional peacekeeping operations improve the prospects for peace, democracy, and improved economic performance in the aftermath of conflict.... But the multidimensional character of these interventions makes it difficult to discern the individual contribution of specific programs to overall success. There are, quite simply, too few cases and too many confounding variables"; and Kimberly Theidon, "Transitional Subjects: The Disarmament, Demobilization and Reintegration of Former Combatants in Colombia," *International Journal of Transitional Justice* 1, no. 1 (2007): 67: "By reducing DDR [disarmament, demobilization, and reintegration] to 'dismantling the machinery of war,' these programs have failed to adequately consider how to move beyond demobilizing combatants to facilitating social reconstruction and coexistence." Theidon then discusses the phase "which has been the 'weakest link in the DDR chain'—the reintegration of former combatants into civilian life."

7   Stated differently, we might say that amnesty is generally beneficial at the "DD" phase, but much less so during the longer-term "R" phase, when people expect an end to the systematic impunity of the past—evidenced by reforms, trials, truth-seeking, and reparations. Note also that the distinction between short- and long-term peace is also sometimes expressed in the peacebuilding field as a distinction between, respectively, "negative peace" and "positive peace." Johan Galtung, "the father of peace studies," is often mentioned as the originator of this distinction.

8   This is in fact a complicated question because the "R" phase may depend as much or more on leniency. Is reintegration into society feasible when one is faced with a real threat of prosecution?

9   If a peace agreement that includes an amnesty is never implemented in legislation, it may not constitute a legal measure. It will depend on the specifics of the agreement itself. See, generally, Christine Bell, "Peace Agreements: Their Nature and Legal Status," *American Journal of International Law* 100, no. 2 (2006): 373–412.

10  See, e.g., Amnesty International USA, "Colombia: Flawed Demobilization Offers de Facto Amnesty," *AI Alert* (November 2005).

11  Note that the threshold of application of "Additional Protocol II to the Geneva Conventions" (APII) is very high. Art. 1(1) provides: "1. This Protocol, which develops and supplements common article 3 to the Geneva Conventions of 12 August 1949 without modifying its existing conditions or application, shall apply to all armed conflicts which are not covered by Article 1 of the Protocol Additional to the Geneva Conventions of 12 August 1949, and relating to the Protection of Victims of International Armed Conflicts (Protocol I) and which take place in the territory of a High Contracting Party between its armed forces and dissident armed forces or other organized armed groups which, under responsible command, exercise such control over a part of its territory as to enable them to carry out sustained and concerted military operations and to implement this Protocol." "Protocol Additional to the Geneva Conventions of 12 August 1949, and Relating to the Protection of Victims of Non-International Armed Conflicts (Protocol II) Adopted on 8 June 1977 by the Diplomatic Conference on the Reaffirmation and Development of International Humanitarian Law Applicable in Armed Conflicts."

12  Sylvie-Stoyanka Junod, "Commentary on the Protocol Additional to the Geneva Conventions of 12 August 1949 and Relating to the Protection of Victims of Non-International Armed Conflicts (Protocol II)," in *Commentary on the Additional Protocols of 8 June 1977 to the Geneva Conventions of 12 August 1949*, ed. Jean Pictet (Geneva: International Committee of the Red Cross / Martinus Nijhoff, 1987), 1402, para. 4618.

13  See, e.g., *The Azanian Peoples Organization (AZAPO) and others v. The President of the Republic of South Africa and others*, (4) SA 672 (Constitutional Court 1996), para. 53; and the Guevara Portillo Case, Sala de lo Penal de la Corte Suprema de Justica, San Salvador (August 16, 1995), in Naomi Roht-Arriaza and Lauren Gibson, "The Developing Jurisprudence on Amnesty," *Human Rights Quarterly* 20, no. 4 (1998): 849–51.

14  Jean-Marie Henckaerts and Louise Doswald-Beck, eds., *Customary International Humanitarian Law*, vol. 1, Rules (Cambridge: Cambridge University Press / International Committee of the Red Cross [ICRC], 2005), 610. The book regrettably makes claims based on small or biased case studies. Furthermore, the second volume of the study, *Practice*, examined only six treaties (APII, plus five peace treaties) that provide for amnesty, and seventeen amnesty laws from eleven states. It does look to other sources of practice, including national legal provisions governing the grant of amnesty, military manuals, national and international case law, and United Nations (UN) resolutions. However, in each case the number of sources employed is comparatively small. See Louise Mallinder,

*Amnesty, Human Rights and Political Transitions: Bridging the Peace and Justice Divide* (Oxford: Hart Publishing, 2008), 156.

15   Mallinder, *Amnesty, Human Rights and Political Transitions*, 289–90.

16   This author could not find reference to the new ICRC interpretation in any DDR manual.

17   See United Nations Security Council (UNSC), "Seventh Report of the Secretary-General on the United Nations Observer Mission in Sierra Leone," S/1999/836 (30 July 1999), para. 54; and William A. Schabas, "Amnesty, the Sierra Leone Truth and Reconciliation Commission and the Special Court for Sierra Leone," *UC Davis Journal of International Law and Policy* 12, no. 1 (2004): 145. Note that the legal consequences of this last-minute reservation are unclear and did not reflect the views of the parties to the agreement.

18   Note, however, that the UN did not need to wait until the Rome Statute of the International Criminal Court (ICC) went into effect in 2002 before adopting its new position, since earlier treaties, such as the Geneva Conventions of 1949 and the "Convention Against Torture and Other Cruel, Inhuman, and Degrading Treatment or Punishment" of 1985 already placed affirmative obligations on states to ensure criminal justice for grave breaches of international humanitarian law and torture, respectively. See Diane Orentlicher, "Settling Accounts: The Duty to Prosecute Human Rights Violations of a Prior Regime," *Yale Law Journal* 100, no. 8 (1991): 2537–2618.

19   UNSC, "Report of the Secretary-General on the Rule of Law and Transitional Justice in Conflict and Post-Conflict Societies," S/2004/616 (3 August 2004).

20   UN News Service, "Timor-Leste: UN to Boycott Truth Panel Unless It Bars Amnesty for Gross Abuses," *UN News Centre*, July 26, 2007.

21   Note, however, that the UN did not need to wait until the adoption of the Rome Statute to adopt its new position, since earlier treaties such as the 1949 Geneva Conventions and the 1985 Convention Against Torture and Other Cruel, Inhuman, and Degrading Treatment or Punishment already placed affirmative obligations on states to ensure criminal justice for grave breaches of international humanitarian law and torture, respectively. See Diane Orentlicher, "Settling Accounts: The Duty to Prosecute Human Rights Violations of a Prior Regime," *Yale Law Journal* 100, no. 8 (1991): 2537-2618.

22   See, e.g., Louis Joinet, *Study on Amnesty Laws and Their Role in the Safeguard and Promotion of Human Rights*, UN Doc. E/CN.4/Sub.2/1985/16. This was the UN's first official study on the subject of amnesty and highlights, in its very title, the generally positive view taken at the time about the utility of amnesties.

23   See, e.g., Theidon, "Transitional Subjects," 73.

24   UN negotiators must now follow the June 2006 confidential "Guidelines for United Nations Representatives on Certain Aspects of Negotiations for Conflict Resolution." Non-UN mediators are not bound by the "Guidelines" and it is possible that many of them will take a different position than the UN one.

25   Christine Bell notes that the new UN amnesty position could result in "normative-

mediator dodging parties" and risks the UN ruling itself "out of the mediation business," which is already very crowded. Although such a risk is probably low for the UN, since it is usually present in one way or another, "it would be clearly undesirable if all those who took their normative commitments seriously were ruled out of business." Christine Bell, "The 'New Land' of Transitional Justice" (paper presented at "Building a Future on Peace and Justice," Nuremberg, Germany, June 25–27, 2007), 17. Lars Kirchoff offers a different alternative: "where interests of the international community are at stake, it has to be represented at the table—but not in the role of the mediator. Therefore, in these scenarios, a representative of the international community must take part in the mediation process as an additional party to the proceedings." Lars Kirchoff, "Linking Mediation and Transitional Justice" (paper presented at "Building a Future on Peace and Justice," Nuremberg, Germany, June 25–27, 2007), 23.

26  The Sierra Leone Truth and Reconciliation Commission (SLTRC) was "unable to condemn the resort to amnesty by those who negotiated the Lomé Peace Agreement" as too high a price for peace. SLTRC, *Witness to Truth: Report of the Sierra Leone Truth and Reconciliation Commission*, vol. 3B (Accra: GPL Press, 2004), 365. See also Schabas, "Amnesty," 163–64: ". . . those who argue that peace cannot be bartered in exchange for justice, under any circumstances, must be prepared to justify the likely prolongation of an armed conflict." On the general debate about deterrence arguments in this context, see, e.g., David Wippman, "Atrocities, Deterrence, and the Limits of International Justice," *Fordham International Law Journal* 23 (1999): 473–88; and Jeremy Sarkin and Erin Daly, "Too Many Questions, Too Few Answers: Reconciliation in Transitional Societies," *Columbia Human Rights Law Review* 35 (2004): 661–728.

27  See Rodrigo Uprimny, "Transitional Justice Without Transition? Possible Lessons from the Use (and Misuse) of Transitional Justice Discourse in Colombia" (paper presented at "Building a Future on Peace and Justice," Nuremberg, Germany, June 25–27, 2007): "For instance, at the beginning the paramilitary leaders wanted straight impunity, but then they realized that in the current legal international environment, that sort of impunity was not only very difficult but even dangerous, because they risk to be subjected to the ICC or to other judicial systems, according to the principle of universal jurisdiction for some international crimes. They accepted then some form of punishment, making it easier to reach an agreement that could enhance the possibilities of a lasting and democratic peace."

28  For example, alternative but principled UN positions could be: (1) "The UN considers that amnesties for (crimes x, y, z) do not bind international, hybrid, or foreign courts"; or (2) "The UN considers that amnesties for (crimes x, y, z) are generally incompatible with international law." A completely different, and more positive, position could be the following: "The UN will proactively advocate truth, justice, reparation, and reform measures in the context of any transition-related negotiation." (Is it any wonder that

amnesty *becomes* an issue when the only overt part of current UN mediation policy is its anti-amnesty position, as opposed to its pro–transitional justice position?) The point is that there are many principled positions that could still be considered and which, in time, may *need* to be considered if it turns out that the current position is cumulatively producing more harm than good—something that has not been seriously assessed by anyone to date.

29   One must recognize, however, that mediators and negotiating parties would at most be able to offer amnesty in the form of immunity from national courts. It would be impossible, in the absence of an explicit UNSC resolution, for mediators or negotiating parties to offer or secure immunity from a foreign court, international court, or hybrid court. However, this does not change the central point about the risk of removing an important bargaining chip.

30   It is also important to take note of the true record of state practice since the adoption of the UN position. As Louise Mallinder notes in the most comprehensive study to date: "Perhaps the most significant period in the relationship between international crimes and amnesties is after the UN changed its approach to amnesty laws with the signing of the Lomé Accord on 7 July 1999. Between this date and December 2007, 34 amnesty laws have excluded some form of international crimes, which has inspired human rights activists to point to a growing trend to prohibit impunity for these crimes. This research has found, however, that during the same period, 28 amnesty laws have granted immunity to perpetrators of international crimes, and that consequently, it is too early to suggest that an international custom is developing." Mallinder, *Amnesty, Human Rights and Political Transitions*, 150.

31   See also United Nations Department of Peacekeeping Operations (DPKO), *Integrated Disarmament, Demobilization and Reintegration Standards* (IDDRS) (New York: DPKO, 2007), sec. 5.40, "Cross-Border Population Movements," para. 12.4: "Returned former combatants and their families should benefit from any amnesties in force for the population generally or for returnees specifically. Amnesties may cover, for example, matters relating to having left the country of origin and having found refuge in another country, draft evasion and desertion, as well as the act of performing military service in unrecognized armed groups. Amnesties for international crimes, such as genocide, crimes against humanity, war crimes and serious violations of international humanitarian law, are not supported by the UN. Former combatants may legitimately be prosecuted for such crimes, but they must receive a fair trial in accordance with judicial procedures."

32   Paul Seils, "The Impact of the ICC on Peace Negotiations" (paper presented at "Building a Future on Peace and Justice," Nuremberg, Germany, June 25–27, 2007): "There should be no hiding the fact that the Statute represents a seismic shift in international criminal law generally and in the context of conflict resolution in particular."

33   Paul Seils and Marieke Wierda, *The International Criminal Court and Conflict Mediation* (New

York: International Center for Transitional Justice, 2005), 19. Some seem to say that if the ICC disregards an amnesty and prosecutes someone covered under it then the amnesty becomes invalid, but this is incorrect. It is not invalidated but merely disregarded; nationally the amnesty remains intact. In addition, to suggest that amnesties that include international crimes automatically violate the Rome Statute is to suggest that government lawyers' decision *not* to include amnesty provisions in the treaty was legally irrelevant (on the basis that such amnesties are already and inherently in violation of the Rome Statute). That is surely a mistaken view. Also, contrary to the implication of Seils and Wierda's report, blanket amnesties are still widely used and accepted, and the evidence post–Rome Statute makes this abundantly clear. See Mallinder, *Amnesty, Human Rights and Political Transitions*, n. 35. (Her data shows that in sub-Saharan Africa and Asia the number of broad amnesties has been increasing since the adoption of the Rome Statute.)

34　Law on General Amnesty, *Official Gazette of the Republic of Croatia [Official Gazette]*, September 20, 1996), No. 80/96.6 of September 20, 1996, published in the *Official Gazette* on September 27, 1996.

35　Ley 46/1977 de Amnistía of October 15, 1977, published in the *Official State Gazette* on October 17, 1977, 46/1977.

36　Amnistie royale, July 1994.

37　Decreto Ley 2191, published in the *Official Gazette* on April 19, 1978.

38　Charte pour la paix et la réconciliation nationale, September 2005.

39　The Constitution of the Republic of Ghana 1992, sched. 1, art. 34, promulgated January 7, 1993, www.judicial.gov.gh/constitutio/first_schedule/page1.htm.

40　Ley de Reconciliación Nacional of December 18, 1996, Decreto No. 145-96.

41　Presidential Decree 519 of July 26, 1974, published in *Official Gazette* A 211. Amended by Constitutional Act of 3 October 1974, published in *Official Gazette* A 277.

42　Constitution of the Republic of Turkey, 1982, pt. 6, prov. art. 15, www.constitution.org/cons/turkey/part6.htm.

43　Decreto No. 128 of January 22, 2003, published in the *Official Gazette* on January 24, 2003.

44　Lomé Peace Agreement Between the Government of Sierra Leone and the Revolutionary United Front of Sierra Leone, 12 July, 1999, S/1999/777, art. IX.

45　Lei No. 11/96 of April 18, 1996.

46　La Loi No. 2003-309 du 8 août 2003 portant amnistie.

47　See, generally, Mallinder, *Amnesty, Human Rights and Political Transitions*, n. 58; and Andreas O'Shea, *Amnesty for Crime in International Law and Practice* (Berlin: Springer, 2002).

48　See, e.g., Organization for Security and Co-operation in Europe, *Handbook of Best Practices on Small Arms and Light Weapons* (Vienna: OSCE, 2003), 141.

49　General Peace Agreement for Mozambique, promulgated August 7, 1992, www.c-r.org/our-work/accord/mozambique/joint-declaration.php.

50 Loi No. 05-023 du 19 décembre 2005 portant amnistie pour faits deguerre, infractions politiques et d'opinion, published in the *Official Gazette* on December 28, 2005.

51 DPKO, *IDDRS*, sec. 4.11, "SALW Control, Security, and Development," para. 9.7: "To achieve the surrender of illegal weapons, it will be necessary to declare an amnesty for those who are returning them. In many countries, this will require a change in the law. If the open carrying of weapons is prohibited, the law also may need to be changed or suspended for the amnesty period. It will also be necessary to get the amnesty publicly declared, and information on the terms of the amnesty should be made known to all former warring factions, groups and communities. It shall also be made clear to the security forces, which may have been authorized to detain or shoot anyone openly carrying weapons. The amnesty should have a fixed time limit, to allow the declaration of penalties for owning or carrying illegal weapons after the end of the amnesty period. Extensive consultation and advice should be taken when determining the period of the amnesty. It will take time to change the attitudes and perceptions of SALW holders, as they need to be convinced that the security situation has improved so much that they will voluntarily surrender their SALW. Previous experience has shown that short amnesties of a month are rarely successful, while longer ones are more effective, resulting in large numbers of weapons being surrendered...."

52 Ron Slye coined the term "corrective amnesty." Ronald C. Slye, "The Legitimacy of Amnesties Under International Law and General Principles of Anglo-American Law: Is a Legitimate Amnesty Possible?" *Virginia Journal of International Law* 43 (2002): 243–44.

53 Human Rights Committee, Forty-Fourth Session, General Comment Number 20 (Geneva: United Nations High Commissioner for Human Rights, 1992), para. 15: "Amnesties are generally incompatible with the duty of States to investigate such acts; to guarantee freedom from such acts within their jurisdiction; and to ensure that they do not occur in the future." The right to remedy is found in many human rights treaties. See, generally, Mark Freeman and Gibran van Ert, *International Human Rights Law* (Toronto: Irwin Law, 2004), chap. 12. However, it is important to make clear that the right to remedy does not necessarily entail a right to see someone prosecuted (because that is a public right), but only a right to sue in court (because that is a private right).

54 However, it is possible that the public understands the difference between amnesties (i.e., extraordinary legal measures) and ordinary legislation. Thus, in a situation in which the government is generally decent, the public may understand that an amnesty is an exception to the ordinary rule of law and that it may have been issued in the public interest. In other words, the deterrent power of criminal law is not automatically, or even presumptively, lost because of an amnesty. O'Shea notes that in a society in transition, the general negative impact of an amnesty on the rule of law "is minimized by public knowledge of the limited nature of the digression from the rule of law." O'Shea, *Amnesty for Crime*, 84. By corollary, society's reaction would be very different in the case of a state

in the habit of granting repeated amnesties.

55 Sergio Jaramillo, Yanet Giha, and Paula Torres, "Disarmament, Demobilization and Reintegration Amidst Conflict," Country Cases (New York: International Center for Transitional Justice, 2009), http://www.ictj.org/en/research/projects/ddr/index.html.

56 Priscilla Hayner, "The Challenge of Justice in Negotiating Peace: Lessons from Liberia and Sierra Leone" (paper presented at "Building a Future on Peace and Justice," Nuremberg, Germany, June 25–27, 2007), 2. A cluster of interrelated but favorable factors resulted in an obligation by the country's transitional government merely to "give consideration to a recommendation for general amnesty to all persons and parties engaged or involved in military activities during the Liberian civil conflict." Hayner cites various factors in producing this result, including: the parties' main concern was power, not legal protection; the threat of court action was "minimal"; the public would have opposed it; and the mistaken belief that the country's planned Truth and Reconciliation Commission would give amnesty for all types of crimes. Ultimately, a TRC was established with the power to recommend amnesty for a limited set of offenses.

57 See Patricia Gossman, "Disarmament and Transitional Justice in Afghanistan," Country Cases (New York: International Center for Transitional Justice, April 2009), www.ictj.org/en/research/projects/ddr/country-cases/2376.html.

58 Ibid.

59 Jaramillo, Giha, and Torres, "Disarmament, Demobilization and Reintegration Amidst Conflict."

60 Law 782 of December 23, 2002, published in the *Official Gazette* (Colombia) on December 23, 2002.

61 See, generally, BBC, "Q & A: Trying Charles Taylor," *BBC News*, January 7, 2008, news.bbc.co.uk/2/hi/africa/4848938.stm. Another part of the "Taylor effect" may be to reduce the number of countries willing to offer asylum, as that may lead to unwelcome embarrassment or pressure if an international arrest warrant is issued by the ICC or some other competent criminal tribunal.

62 Pablo de Greiff, "Contributing to Peace and Justice—Finding a Balance between DDR and Reparations" (paper presented at "Building a Future on Peace and Justice," Nuremberg, Germany, June 25–27, 2007), 24: "Justice measures stand a better chance of being implemented after the peace is secured. This assumes, of course, that in the process of attaining peace, justice is not permanently compromised, e.g., through the granting of blanket amnesties. Hence the importance of DDR programmers improving their familiarity with the requirements of justice, so at the very least, they can display a 'do no harm' attitude and maintain the possibility of justice measures being implemented down the line."

63 See, e.g., UNSC, "Report of the Secretary-General on the Rule of Law," paras. 16, 19.

64 Patrick Vinck et al., " 'Nothing About Us, Without Us': Responding to the Needs of

Survivors of Mass Violence During and After Armed Conflicts" (paper presented at "Building a Future on Peace and Justice," Nuremberg, Germany, June 25–27, 2007), 1.

65 Ibid., 3 (emphasis in original).

66 Donors have a key role to play in this regard. See Hayner, "The Challenge of Justice," 29: "Those willing to provide funds for the talks also largely determine who can attend, and how many. Civil society groups often have to raise funding independently, in order to take part."

67 A good example of this is Uganda's Amnesty Act: "The amnesty process in Uganda was prompted by the Acholi Religious Leaders Peace Initiative (ARLPI), culminating in the Amnesty Act of 2000.... Its origins are unique compared to amnesty laws in other situations, as it is based on a consultation among victimized populations. A report by the Refugee Law Project shows that the Amnesty Act continues to enjoy broad popular support in the north, even though the process of reintegrating the perpetrators in the community is not as straightforward as sometimes claimed." Phuong Pham, Patrick Vinck, Marieke Wierda, Erica Stover, and Adrian de Giovanni, "Forgotten Voices: A Population-Based Survey of Attitudes about Peace and Justice in Northern Uganda" (New York: International Center for Transitional Justice / Human Rights Center, 2005), 46.

68 Examples of referenda on amnesties, albeit under less than free and fair conditions of public information and debate, are those of Uruguay and Algeria.

69 Key references to good faith include: *Charter of the United Nations* (1945), art. 2.2: "All Members, in order to ensure to all of them the rights and benefits resulting from membership, shall fulfill in good faith the obligations assumed by them in accordance with the present Charter"; and "Vienna Convention on the Law of Treaties (1969)," art. 26.

70 See, e.g., Carlos S. Nino, "The Duty to Punish Past Abuses of Human Rights Put into Context: The Case of Argentina," in "Symposium: International Law," *Yale Law Journal* 100, no. 8 (1991): 2639, where the author comments that "what may appear to the international community to be passivity on the part of a government may actually be the active safeguarding against future violations at the cost of forgoing prosecutions."

71 Jack Snyder and Leslie Vinjamuri, "A Midwife for Peace," *International Herald Tribune*, September 26, 2006. The reference to prosecutorial deference is probably a form of shorthand for the ICC Prosecutor. In non-ICC contexts, such political decisions might instead be taken by political leaders alone or in consultation with prosecutors.

72 Mark Osiel uses the term "symmetrical" amnesty instead. Osiel, "Modes of Participation in Mass Atrocity," 810.

73 The 1978 amnesty in Chile is often given as an example of this because there were very few opponents of the state who stood to benefit. See, generally, Robert J. Quinn, "Will the Rule of Law End? Challenging Grants of Amnesty for the Human Rights Violations of a Prior Regime: Chile's New Model," *Fordham Law Review* 62 (1994): 905–60.

74 See, generally, Slye, "The Legitimacy of Amnesties," where the author persuasively argues

that the South African amnesty process achieved an unparalleled level of accountability compared to any other amnesty process.

75   Stated more positively, sometimes amnesties are crucial to facilitating a transition in the first place. Mallinder, *Amnesty, Human Rights and Political Transitions*, 73: "The relationship between amnesty and other measures within a peace process can be sequenced to permit the amnesty to act as the starting point to enable other aspects of the agreement to occur, such as demobilisation, integration of combatants into the armed forces, or the transformation of insurgent groups into political parties that could perhaps participate in governments of national unity."

76   There are, however, cases where parties that would normally be expected to seek amnesty instead seek accountability, as, e.g., when opposing negotiating parties view accountability as a weapon they can use against the opposite side or as a tool that will vindicate their sense of being the main victim of a prior conflict or period of abuse. This appears to have been the case with the 2007 political agreements reached in Kenya following a period of intense postelection violence. See also Hayner, "The Challenge of Justice," n. 89.

77   One must bear in mind, however, that the degree to which an amnesty's scope can be limited in these ways is, in most cases, inversely related to the power of the party or parties seeking an amnesty.

78   Mallinder, Amnesty, *Human Rights and Political Transitions*, 192: "the Amnesty Law Database has shown that the majority of amnesty laws recognise the political nature of the crimes that they cover, although few attempt to define these crimes." Note, however, that according to some international treaties, certain crimes can never be characterized as "political." See, e.g., UN, "Convention Relating to the Status of Refugees," Geneva, 1951, art. 1(f)(a), which precludes the treatment of crimes against peace, crimes against humanity, or war crimes as "political" offenses.

79   Thanks to Louise Mallinder for raising this point.

80   The term "gross violations of human rights" is not a legal term; most likely it is deliberately ambiguous in order to discourage inclusion of any violations that *might* meet that description.

81   Several antiterrorism treaties set out particularly robust prosecution-related obligations on state parties. These sometimes extend beyond what is found in treaties dealing with war crimes, genocide, or crimes against humanity. See, e.g., United Nations, "International Convention for the Suppression of Acts of Nuclear Terrorism," 2005, art. 11.1: "The State Party in the territory of which the alleged offender is present shall, in cases to which article 9 applies, if it does not extradite that person, be obliged, *without exception whatsoever and whether or not the offence was committed in its territory*, to submit the case without undue delay to its competent authorities for the purpose of prosecution, through proceedings in accordance with the laws of that State. Those authorities

shall take their decision in the same manner as in the case of any other offence of a grave nature under the law of that State" (emphasis added).

82   We should be careful here, though: There could be an overlap between "economic crimes" and international crimes. For example, theft could amount to looting as a war crime. In addition, "economic crimes" could be closely related to the conflict: it could provide the means to continue the war effort.

83   See, e.g., Law on Amnesty 07-1117/1, art. 3, published in *Official Gazette* no. 18 on March 8, 2002 (Republic of Macedonia): "The provision of paragraph 1 of this Article does not apply to persons convicted of criminal acts against humanity and international law, illicit production and trafficking of narcotics, psycho-tropic substances and precursors, for enabling the use of narcotics, psycho-tropic substances and precursors as well as persons sentenced to life imprisonment."

84   Mark Freeman, "Lessons Learned from Amnesties for Human Rights Crimes," *Transparency International Newsletter* (December 2001): 3: " . . . amnesty may be more readily applied to acts of extreme terror and brutality than to acts of corruption. I think that there is an explanation for this—however, it is one that I find troubling and unpalatable. First, certain human rights violations can be rhetorically defended on the basis that they were necessary as part of a war or in pursuit of a greater cause. There is no similar justification available, however, when it comes to acts of corruption, which are only carried out for purposes of personal enrichment. Second, with crimes of corruption, the public may collectively feel that they are the victims of theft. In contrast, human rights violations generally lack this sense of collective victimization because in most cases the violations have not affected the majority of the public. If these assertions are true, this may partly explain why amnesties for high-level corruption are so rare. It may also imply that anticorruption advocates will in many cases be in a relatively strong public position to block amnesties for corruption."

85   See, e.g., Chile's Decreto Ley 2191. In some countries, the bulk of the opprobrium to certain crimes against children (e.g., recruitment of child soldiers) may come from the international community and not from the local population. Laura Davis and Priscilla Hayner, "Difficult Peace, Limited Justice: Ten years of Peacemaking in the DRC," (New York, International Center for Transitional Justice, March 2009), 31.

86   See, e.g., Lebanon's Loi d'Amnistie no. 84/91 du August 27, 1991, art. 3.

87   Jack Snyder and Leslie Vinjamuri, "Trials and Errors: Principles and Pragmatism in Strategies of International Law," *International Security* 28, no. 3 (April 2003): 13.

88   See, e.g., Chandra Lekha Sriram, "Conflict Mediation and the ICC: Challenges and Options for Pursuing Peace with Justice at the Regional Level" (paper presented at "Building a Future on Peace and Justice," Nuremberg, Germany, June 25–27, 2007), 4: "Further, many measures that may appear in direct contradiction to accountability may also be negotiated, in addition to or instead of partial or full amnesty. These may

include, inter alia, measures to integrate ex-fighters, whether state or nonstate, into the security forces, measures to allow former rebels to participate legally in the political process, and even form political parties. It may also include measures to allow all parties to a conflict (or selected ones) a portion of, or a stake in the governance of, the state's economic resources. Finally, it may include measures granting a group or groups a degree of territorial autonomy over a particular region. Given that fighting forces will most likely have been involved in some degree of violations of human rights, any such concessions have consequences not only for accountability generally, but for past and potentially future victims, but these concessions are fairly common, perhaps increasingly so."

89　Gossman, "Disarmament and Transitional Justice in Afghanistan." More generally, see Helena Cobban, *Amnesty After Atrocity? Healing Nations After Genocide and War Crimes* (Boulder: Paradigm, 2006). At page 208 she comments: "language of criminalization . . . is most often the language of political exclusion. . . . By deliberately forswearing both the language and practice of political exclusion, amnesties can make a huge contribution to the interests of long-term peacebuilding."

90　See Mohamed Gibril Sesay and Mohamed Suma, "Transitional Justice and DDR in Sierra Leone" (New York: International Center for Transitional Justice, April 2009), www.ictj.org/en/research/projects/ddr/country-cases/2383.html.

91　Paul van Zyl, "Promoting Transitional Justice in Post-Conflict Societies," in *Security Governance in Post-Conflict Peacebuilding*, ed. Alan Bryden and Heiner Hänggi (Geneva: Geneva Center for the Democratic Control of Armed Forces, 2005), 220.

92　This does not, however, diminish the concern about the current UN position, which directly threatens not only the leaders but everyone else who may have committed international crimes. It is also important to note that in practice it might be very difficult to determine who "ordered" and who "committed." This is compounded by the practice of international tribunals. Through concepts like Joint Criminal Enterprise—which is a form of "committing"—there is no clear distinction between high-ranking officials who classically "order" crimes and low-level combatants who "commit" them.

93　See, e.g., Zimbabwe's Clemency Order No. 1 of October 10, 2000 (General Amnesty for Politically Motivated Crimes), published in *Official Gazette* 457A; and Burundi's Décret-loi No. 1/034/90 du 30 août 1990 portant mesure d'amnistie en faveur de prévenues ou condamnés de certaines infractions, published in *Official Gazette* 278 (1990).

94　See, e.g., Proclamation No. 390 of September 29, 2000 (Philippines) and Decreto-Lei No. 758/76 of October 22, 1976 (Portugal).

95　See, e.g., Angola's Lei No. 7/00 of December 15, 2000, www.unhcr.org/cgi-bin/texis/vtx/refworld/rwmain?docid=3ed89ee54.

96　Also note that children and adolescents are outside the competence of the ICC. See ICC, Rome Statute of the International Criminal Court, art. 26: "The Court shall have no jurisdiction over any person who was under the age of 18 at the time of the alleged commission of a crime."

97   Examples of amnesties that are limited to immunity from prosecution (and that in some cases expressly exclude immunity from civil actions) include those of Uruguay (Ley de Caducidad de la Pretensión Punitiva del Estado No. 15.848 of December 22, 1986, published in the *Official Gazette* on December 28, 1986); Haiti (Loi relative à l'amnestie of October 6, 1994, published in the *Official Gazette* on October 10, 1994); Iran (General Amnesty Law of 1980); and Guatemala (Ley de Reconciliación Nacional of December 18, 1996, Decreto No. 145-96). See also O'Shea, *Amnesty for Crime in International Law and Practice*, 268: "I am aware of no examples of such laws that only cover civil and not criminal liability. This is understandable given that the major objectives of an amnesty law are usually to facilitate political transition and the reconciliation of the nation, the principal concern for immunity is in the criminal field. The potential deprivation of liberty and, in those states still employing the death penalty, the potential loss of life of the political offender, are the gravest consequences for—and the immediate concern of—the political offender."

98   See Mark Freeman, *Truth Commissions and Procedural Fairness* (New York: Cambridge University Press, 2006), 79, 82. Osiel argues: "To a degree little recognized or acknowledged, amnesty from prosecution is so controversial because monetary compensation, through civil recovery (for wrongful death, battery, infliction of distress, etc.) is virtually unavailable in countries where mass atrocity occurs. If civil litigation were to make such remedies practically accessible, political pressures for prosecution would much diminish, because victims are often content with (even prefer) financial and other redress." Osiel, "Modes of Participation in Mass Atrocity," 812.

99   Freeman, *Truth Commissions*, 145–46.

100  Examples of such amnesties include those of Burundi in 1993 (Décret loi du 9 septembre 1993 portant amnistie, published in *Official Gazette* 543 [1993]), in which full amnesty for less serious crimes was granted but only a sentence reduction for more serious crimes, and Algeria in 1999 (Loi relative au rétablissement de la Concorde civile of July 13, 1999), wherein those who did not murder, permanently disable, rape, commit collective massacres, or use explosives in a public place receive immunity from prosecution (whereas those who did commit certain of the enumerated acts are eligible only for probation, conditional release, reduced sentences, or exemption from the death penalty).

101  Mallinder, *Amnesty, Human Rights and Political Transitions*, 194: ". . . states are increasingly willing to make amnesty beneficiaries more accountable for the crimes by attaching conditions to the amnesty."

102  Examples include those of Uganda (Amnesty Act of 2000); Bangladesh (Peace Agreement Between the National Committee of Chittagong Hill Tracts and the Parbatya Chattagram Jana Sanghati Samity, December 2, 1997, www.radicalparty.org/humanrights/

chi_do10.htm); Solomon Islands (Townsville Peace Agreement of October 15, 2000); Guatemala (Decreto-Ley No. 89-83 of August 12, 1983, which also requires applicants to disclose locations of other arms deposits); and Angola (Lei No. 4/2002 of April 4, 2002, which as a reciprocal obligation requires the state to integrate rebels into the government army).

103  In this regard, Turkey's multiple failed amnesty efforts vis-à-vis the Kurdistan Workers' Party (PKK) come to mind. Likewise, the annual exercise in failed amnesty offers in Guatemala in the 1980s during the country's civil war. Uganda's Amnesty Commission perhaps constitutes a good contrasting example. See Amnesty Act 2000 (Uganda), art. 4.1: "A reporter shall be taken to be granted the amnesty declared under section 3 if the reporter: (i) reports to the nearest Army or Police Unit, a Chief, a member of the Executive Committee of a local government unit, a magistrate or a religious leader within the locality; (ii) renounces and abandons involvement in the war or armed rebellion; (iii) surrenders at any such place or to any such authority or person any weapons in his or her possession; and (iv) is issued with a Certificate of Amnesty as shall be prescribed in regulations to be made by the Minister"; and Ibid., art. 4.6: "The Sub-county Chief on receiving a reporter seeking amnesty, shall hand over that reporter to the Demobilization and Resettlement Team established under section 11."

104  Mallinder, *Amnesty, Human Rights and Political Transitions*, 197.

105  Ibid., 198–99: "Disarmament need not always be a pre-requisite for amnesty and on occasion, the annulment of punishment and the surrender of weapons have been treated as distinct issues. This occurred under the early release scheme in Northern Ireland, which although not included in the Amnesty Law Database, can illustrate an alternative approach to disarmament. Under this scheme, prisoners were released before their organisations had decommissioned, provided their organisations had proclaimed a ceasefire. The early release was conditional on the released individuals refraining from supporting paramilitary organisations, or becoming involved in acts which endanger the public. Furthermore, the releases were designed to occur incrementally with the possibility that they would be halted for members of individual organisations, if their organisation breached its ceasefire."

106  In Uprimny, "Transitional Justice Without Transition?" the author makes this point with particular force in regard to the DDR process for former paramilitaries: "Last but not least, the Colombian case shows another potential shortcoming of the more usual transitional justice approaches and that is the failure to take into account the differences of a peace process between the State and a guerrilla or anti-state armed actor on the one hand, and a peace process between the State and a paramilitary or friendly-state armed actor, on the other. The differences are important; for instance, when a guerrilla surrenders its arms, it gives up almost all of its power; on the contrary, a paramilitary organization can surrender its arms and retain most of its power, because this power is

linked with collusion with the authorities. Specific and more drastic measures of non repetition have to be implemented in this kind of processes." See Maria Paula Saffron and Rodrigo Uprimny, "Transitional Justice without Transition? The Colombian Case and its Challenges to the Transitional Justice Paradigm" (paper presented at the annual meeting of The Law and Society Association, Berlin, Germany, July 25, 2007).

107   Examples of such amnesties include those of Uganda 2000, Algeria 1999, Poland 1984, and Guatemala 1982.

108   See, e.g., UN, "Protocol Additional to the Geneva Conventions of 12 August 1949," arts. 32, 33. See also, by analogy, UN, "Convention on the Protection of all Persons from Enforced Disappearances" (New York, 2006), A/61/488, art. 7.2: "Each State Party may establish: (a) Mitigating circumstances, in particular for persons who, having been implicated in the commission of an enforced disappearance, effectively contribute to bringing the disappeared person forward alive or make it possible to clarify cases of enforced disappearance or to identify the perpetrators of an enforced disappearance."

109   See, e.g., Mallinder, *Amnesty, Human Rights and Political Transitions*, 200, describing the example of an amnesty in Fiji: "the negotiated Maunikau Accord 2000 required George Speight and his followers to release the hostages before benefiting from the amnesty." See also Guatemala's Ley de Amnistia, Decreto-Ley 33-82, published in the *Official Gazette* on May 28, 1982, art. 2, which makes the delivery of hostages (in good health) and the return of weapons used for their kidnapping eligibility conditions for amnesty.

110   All of this is simply a variation on the Colombian model of sentences under house arrest. The main difference is that one could follow the terms of a peace accord (perhaps supplemented by an individual written contract/undertaking), whereas the Colombian model follows the terms of a court-issued sentence.

111   Charles P. Trumbull IV, "Giving Amnesties a Second Chance," Berkeley Journal of International Law 25 (2007),325: "Jail sentences reduce the crime rate by deterring economically motivated criminals and incapacitating violent criminals. Although international prosecutions may not deter potential perpetrators of serious crimes under international law, prosecutions could still be worthwhile based on their incapacitation effect, so long as the benefit from incapacitating criminals outweighs the costs of refusing to recognize amnesties. If amnesties, however, can achieve the same incapacitation effect as prosecutions, the international community can receive the benefit of ensuring that criminals do not commit future crimes, while avoiding the costs that result from rejecting amnesties." I would not go so far because trials are about more than "incapacitation"—they also have an expressive function and contribute to the rule of law.

112   Article 13 of the Universal Declaration of Human Rights - "Everyone has the right to freedom of movement and residence within the borders of each State." Also: Article 12(2) of the International Covenant on Civil and Political Rights.

113   Examples from state practice include the Bangladesh 1973 amnesty, which requires as a

condition of amnesty that the applicant serve as a witness at the trial of another person. The Algeria 1999 amnesty is conditional on the applicant's participation in the "fight against terrorism," though it does not specify the form of that participation.

114 Examples of application-based amnesties include those of Algeria in 1999 (Loi relative au rétablissement de la concorde civile); South Africa in 1995 (Promotion of National Unity and Reconciliation Act, No. 34 of July 26, 1995, ftp.fas.org/irp/world/rsa/act95_034. htm); and the Philippines (Amnesty Proclamation No. 347 of March 25, 1994).

115 Consider this point in the context of South Africa's application-based amnesty. The fact that senior architects of apartheid crimes mostly did not come forward could be seen as a defeat for transitional justice and the TRC—as is usually the case—but it could also be seen as a victory for accountability because all those who did not apply for amnesty or who had their applications rejected *did not receive amnesty*.

116 It is, however, important to ensure the application period is neither too short (leaving insufficient time to advertise the option) nor too long (creating the incentive to continue with war for a longer period, which is in direct opposition to the purpose of the amnesty). See Mallinder, *Amnesty, Human Rights and Political Transitions*, 201. An example of an application-based amnesty that was probably too short is that of El Salvador's Ley de Amnistia para el Logro de la Reconciliación Nacional, art. 1.2, published in the *Official Gazette* on October 28, 1987, which gave only fifteen days to apply.

117 See, e.g., Ronald C. Slye, "Amnesty, Truth, and Reconciliation: Reflections on the South African Amnesty Process," in *Truth v. Justice: The Morality of Truth Commissions*, ed. Robert I. Rotberg and Dennis Thompson (Princeton: Princeton University Press, 2000), 172. Surprisingly, however, most amnesties are not explicit about precisely what kind of information and evidence must be adduced as part of a complete application (e.g., whether things within one's knowledge only, or also evidence within one's possession, whether of a physical or documentary nature).

118 Information about third parties is especially important when the conflict is ongoing. Usually, a state is seeking information less about how to prosecute others than about how to identify their whereabouts to capture them or on the details of their command and control structure. This may be different, however, when the conflict has ended. See, e.g., East Timor's UNTAET Regulation 2001/10, Part IV of July 13, 2001, which is akin to an amnesty. It provides that the Commission for Reception, Truth and Reconciliation (CRTR) in the course of a hearing may question the applicant about the identity of those who organized, planned, instigated, ordered, or participated in the commission of the disclosed crimes. Where it is of the opinion that public disclosure of such information would endanger the safety of the applicant or another person, the Commission may decide to hold a closed hearing or permit the applicant to provide the information in writing.

119 Public hearings involving full disclosures may, however, produce misplaced expectations. See, e.g., Hugo van der Merwe and Guy Lamb, "DDR and Transitional Justice in

South Africa: Lessons Learned" (New York: International Center for Transitional Justice, April 2009), www.ictj.org/en/research/projects/ddr/country-cases/2384.html: "The assumption on the part of the ex-combatants was that it would be a vehicle that would assist them with the process of reintegrating into civilian and South African life by allowing them to explain their actions and reclaim some sense of dignity while facing the victims of their actions, their communities and society at large. Instead they were subjected to intense cross-examination, which sought to portray them as criminals, questioning their political motives, the morality of their actions and their honesty. They did not feel that they were given the opportunity to explain the full context of their experience under apartheid and the reasons for their specific actions."

120  In this regard, it is worth nothing that in South Africa the option of prosecution remains available against all but the approximately 1,700 persons who applied for and received amnesty—a number representing only a fraction of the total pool of perpetrators. See also Garth Meintjes and Juan Méndez, "Reconciling Amnesties with Universal Jurisdiction," *International Law FORUM du droit international* 2, no. 2 (2000): 90: "to the extent that amnesty applicants are required expressly to acknowledge both the criminality of their actions and their culpability, it should be seen as upholding rather than denying the victims' right to justice."

121  The East Timor UNTAET Regulation 2001/10 immunity scheme provided for the possibility of requiring an applicant to make a public apology for his or her crimes as a condition of eligibility for subsequent immunity. A Community Reconciliation Process hearing panel could recommend, inter alia, a public apology and "other acts of contrition" as a required part of a Community Reconciliation Agreement.

122  I am not aware of any example of this in practice.

123  This is a feature of the amnesty-like processes adopted in East Timor and Colombia.

124  Luc Huyse and Mark Salter, eds., *Traditional Justice and Reconciliation after Violent Conflict: Learning from African Experiences* (Stockholm: International Institute for Democracy and Electoral Assistance, 2008); see also Roger Duthie, "Local Justice and Reintegration Processes as Complements to Transitional Justice and DDR," in this volume.

125  Jaramillo, Giha, and Torres, "Disarmament, Demobilization and Reintegration Amidst Conflict."

126  See, e.g., the "Helsinki Memorandum of Understanding Between the Government of Indonesia and the Free Aceh Movement," whereby a blanket amnesty apparently enabled a full DDR program to operate. The only condition was that demobilized Free Aceh Movement (GAM) combatants could not use weapons after the signing of the MoU: "Use of weapons by GAM personnel after the signature of this MoU will be regarded as a violation of the MoU and will disqualify the person from amnesty." Art. 3.1.4.

127  For example, Algeria's 1999 amnesty (Loi relative au rétablissement de la Concorde civile) expressly provides for the affirmative prosecution of the crimes that formed the

subject of the defective/deceptive application, and Portugal's 1976 amnesty (Decreto-Lei No. 825/76 of November 16, 1976) goes even further by providing that the penalty for the original infraction increases as a result of the deception.

128  See, e.g., Lebanon's Loi d'Amnistie, art. 2: "L'amnistie ne s'applique pas aux crimes cités ci-dessus, s'ils sont répétitifs et continus, ou dont les auteurs ont persisté à les commettre, ou en firent la récidive, postérieurement à la mise en vigueur de la présente loi, la poursuite reprend dans ce cas là du point où elle fut arrêtée par l'effet de ladite loi." In general, it should be precisely stated in the amnesty how many years the conditionality will stay in place, what types of new crimes will be sufficiently serious to occasion the loss of amnesty, what legal consequences may or shall ensue, and when those consequences take effect.

129  Ronald C. Slye, "The Cambodian Amnesties: Beneficiaries and the Temporal Reach of Amnesties for Gross Violations of Human Rights," *Wisconsin International Law Journal* 22, no. 1 (2004): 113.

130  See ibid., 119–20, where the author explores the idea of creating "a formal rule of international law that would allow the granting of an amnesty that would last for only five or ten years. At the end of that period, an evaluation could be made to determine if the beneficiary of the amnesty is entitled to a permanent amnesty or something less. Such a determination could be based upon the actions of the beneficiary during the 'probationary' limited amnesty period. This would create an incentive for beneficiaries (1) to show through their words and deeds that they no longer pose a threat to society; (2) to provide personal reparations not only to their immediate victims but to the larger society; and (3) to model human rights positive behavior to similarly situated individuals who might otherwise commit or sponsor gross violations of human rights. It is important that the life span of the initial amnesty be at least five years, both to provide a sweet enough 'carrot' to induce the recipient to give up power and to provide enough time for the beneficiary to demonstrate more than a superficial commitment to human rights and the rule of law. A permanent amnesty at the end of the probationary period might be rare, and could be conditioned on further demonstrations of support, such as participating in a truth commission, testifying at the trial of others, or otherwise assisting in investigations. If a permanent amnesty is not granted, the insufficient actions during the probationary period could be used in mitigation during any subsequent criminal or civil action."

131  As of this writing, the law remains in place and the commission of inquiry remains unestablished (and likely will remain so). The reference to this law is for purposes of citing an example of temporary immunity and is not meant as an endorsement of the law. For an analysis of the law and of a series of related legal measures, see S. Vandeginste, "Immunité Provisoire Et Blocage Des Négociations Entre Le Gouvernement Du Burundi Et Le Palipehutu-Fnl: Une Analyse Juridique," April 28, 2008 (copy on file with author).

132  This is analogous to "sunset" clauses or provisions used, inter alia, in modern

antiterrorism legislation. Such clauses serve to terminate all or portions of a law after a specific date, unless further legislative action is taken to extend them.

133   Slye, "The Cambodian Amnesties," 113: "Post-Franco Spain, along with post-Vichy France, post-Civil War United States, and post-Khmer Rouge Cambodia are all examples of such delayed accountability. They illustrate a trend in state practice of granting immediate impunity which, after the passage of time, gives way to accountability...."

134   Ley de Reconciliancíon Nacional, n. 66.

135   Promotion of National Unity and Reconciliation Act, n. 144. It is unfortunate that South Africans have made defending their position more difficult by not acting on what differentiated their model from a blanket amnesty—namely, the fact that individual eligibility was not automatic but had to be proved and that nonapplicants and rejected applicants would be prosecuted. Adding insult to injury, in 2008 there was an attempt at "backdoor amnesties" for these same individuals. See, generally, Graeme Simpson and Nahla Vajli, "Backroom Deals with Apartheid Perpetrators Undermined TRC Rationale," *Sunday Independent* (South Africa), July 29, 2007.

136   "Since (the) blanket amnesty was a prime factor in luring the RUF [the rebel movement Revolutionary United Front] into agreeing to a DDR, its implicit rejection by the mandate of the Special Court and the shift from amnesty to prosecution raised concerns that the fragile security situation in the country would be threatened. This posed great difficulties for the DDR process for part of the incentive for getting combatants into the DDR process was that they would not be prosecuted for crimes committed during the conflict, its removal was seen as betrayal by the combatants and created huge problems for the NCDDR [National Committee for Disarmament, Demobilization and Reintegration].... The public education campaign of SCWG [Special Court Working Group] and such other organizations as PRIDE [Post-Conflict Reintegration Initiatives for Development] however greatly enhanced understanding of the SCSL [Special Court for Sierra Leone] amongst ex-combatants and gradually increased support for the institution amongst them." See Sesay and Suma, "DDR and Transitional Justice in Sierra Leone."

137   A registration form used by Sierra Leone's National Committee on Disarmament, Demobilization and Reintegration states in its first term of acceptance that "in accordance with the Amnesty Conditions you will be exempted from criminal prosecution, with regards to any crimes committed prior to your surrender." See Roger Duthie, "Transitional Justice and Social Reintegration" (paper presented at the Stockholm Initiative on DDR Working Group 3: Reintegration and Peace Building meeting, New York, April 4–5, 2005), 17–18.

138   See, e.g., Pham et al., "Forgotten Voices," 49, discussing the case of Uganda: "There has also been much outreach to try to reassure LRA [the rebel movement Lord's Resistance Army] that they will not be the subjects of revenge killings. Returnees are often required to take part in government organized outreach events. In Gulu, Radio FM Mega runs

regular programs for returnees to call upon their former comrades to come out of the bush, and to offer reassurance that they have not been harmed."

139 See, e.g., Sesay and Suma, "DDR and Transitional Justice in Sierra Leone": "This involvement (of UNAMSIL [United Nations Mission in Sierra Leone] and the British military) greatly reduced the RUF's military strength and enhanced the government militarily and diplomatically. It was from this position that the government wrote a letter to the UN demanding the establishment of a court to try members of the RUF involved in human rights abuse."

140 Assistance with family reunification may be one of the most important components of successful reintegration. Theidon, "Transitional Subjects," 77: "Family proved to be essential, acting as the tie that connected life in the hills with their memories of civilian existence—a tie that enabled many of these former combatants to remember that they were still human beings, even out there in *el monte*."

141 See, e.g., van der Merwe and Lamb, "DDR and Transitional Justice in South Africa": "Amnesty applicants were also generally not offered psychological assistance and nothing in the way of social or economic reintegration if their amnesty resulted in release from prison. Many liberation force ex-combatants still feel resentful that they were called to account for their actions in opposing the apartheid government.…"

142 See, e.g., Lydiah Bosire, "Overpromised, Underdelivered: Transitional Justice in Sub-Saharan Africa," Occasional Paper Series (New York: International Center for Transitional Justice, 2006), 25: "In assessing DDR options for the Great Lakes region, the World Bank has cited the regional nature of the conflict involving Rwanda, Burundi, Uganda, and the DRC as particularly challenging, as it has led to a 'security dilemma' in which no government is willing to reduce its defense (both regular and irregular), thereby posing a challenge to comprehensive disarmament initiatives"; and United Nations Office of the Special Advisor on Africa, "Conference Report on Disarmament, Demobilization, Reintegration (DDR) and Stability in Africa" (Freetown: UNOAA, 2005), 27: "The presence of foreign ex-combatants in many African conflicts needs serious consideration."

143 The key is to make sure the ex-combatants will be accepted back without facing violent retaliation. Theidon, "Transitional Subjects," 83: "To assume that a change in legal status—from combatant to ex-combatant—will translate into the social sphere in the absence of any preliminary process of consultation with the host community is inherently flawed." She notes that "local initiatives and local processes play a key role in post-conflict reconciliation. Reconciliation is forged and lived locally, among families, neighbors and communities." Ibid., 88.

144 See, e.g., Eric Witte, " 'Peace vs. Justice': Understanding the Relationship Between DDR Programs and the Prosecution of International Crimes," in this volume.

145 In fact, amnesty is often a "micro" issue. The "macro" issues, on which the sustainability of many negotiated peace agreements principally and customarily rest, concern the

sharing of power and wealth.

146 DDR experts have made similar arguments in relation to DDR programs. See, e.g., United Nations Office of the Special Advisor on Africa and Government of the Republic of Sierra Leone, "DDR and Stability in Africa" (Freetown: 2006), 12: "DDR programmes should not be burdened with all post-conflict problems. Parallel programmes need to be planned and implemented, especially for vulnerable groups (including women and children). Particular emphasis should be placed on psycho-social counselling and support for women traumatized by rape and other forms of sexual violence, and children traumatized by horrific war experiences"; and ibid., 28: "DDR should always be accompanied by parallel relief, resettlement and rehabilitation efforts for all war-affected populations, especially in the context of local communities as well as by Security Sector Reform."

147 See, e.g., Moses Chrispus Okello, "The False Polarisation of Peace and Justice in Uganda" (paper presented at "Building a Future on Peace and Justice," Nuremberg, Germany, June 25–27, 2007), 2: "And, sequencing should be distinguished from prioritization. If the preferred sequencing is peace followed by justice, this in no way signals that justice is a lower priority than peace—quite the opposite, in fact. Whichever way you look at it, trying to ensure that the environment is conducive for a comprehensive pursuit of justice (i.e., that a peace deal has been struck, civilian authorities are back in place, clan structures responsible for traditional justice have re-grouped after decades of forcible dispersal, people are no longer living hand to mouth and are therefore better able to pursue justice for themselves) is definitive proof that you want real justice to be done."

148 See, in this regard, Graeme Simpson, "Transitional Justice and Peace Negotiations" (unpublished draft report, 2008), 4, describing the broader isolation between the peace-building and transitional justice fields: "The danger is not just that the lesson drawing is not reciprocal or beneficial, but that the practitioners are unfamiliar with each others' dilemmas, disciplines and opportunities."

149 Apparently, the bulk of DDR resources go to the "DD" phases, which presumably undermines the potential of a successful "R" phase. See, generally, Ernest Harsch, "Reintegration of Ex-Combatants: When Wars End: Transforming Africa's Fighters into Builders," Africa Renewal, October 2005. See also Paul Collier, "Demobilization and Insecurity: A Study in the Economics of the Transition from War to Peace," Journal of International Development 6, no. 3 (1994): 343–51.

150 See, e.g., Jeremy Weinstein and Macartan Humphreys, "Disentangling the Determinants of Successful Demobilization and Reintegration," Center for Global Development, Working Paper No. 69, September 2005: "A combatant's experience of the war—in particular, the extent to which he or she engaged in abusive practices—is the most important determinant of acceptance. Individuals who perpetrated widespread human rights abuses face significant difficulty in gaining acceptance from their families and communities after the war."

# CHAPTER 2

# Beyond "Peace versus Justice": Understanding the Relationship Between DDR Programs and the Prosecution of International Crimes

*Eric A. Witte*

## INTRODUCTION

Disarmament, demobilization, and reintegration (DDR) programs and prosecutions of international crimes have become prominent features in the landscape of postconflict states.[1] Over the past twenty years, the United Nations (UN) and other international organizations have gained experience in dismantling warring factions and promoting their reintegration into society through DDR. Meanwhile, the international community has established new international and internationalized domestic tribunals to try the perpetrators of genocide, crimes against humanity, and war crimes. These evolving DDR and prosecution mechanisms represent two important approaches to ending conflicts and consolidating peace. Some tension between them is inherent, given that DDR requires cooperation from ex-combatants, whereas prosecutions may foster resistance from ex-combatants.

Given the somewhat competing imperatives of DDR and prosecutions, it is surprising that, until recently, little attention has been paid to their interaction. In 1999, the UN Department of Peacekeeping Operations (DPKO) published guidelines for DDR processes that made no mention of prosecutions for war crimes and crimes against humanity.[2] That began to change following the UN secretary-general's August 2004 report to the Security Council on *The Rule of Law and Transitional Justice in Conflict and Post-Conflict Societies*.[3] There, Kofi Annan stated that now "the question . . . can never be whether to pursue justice and accountability, but rather when and how."[4] Subsequently, the UN's *Integrated Disarmament, Demobilization and Reintegration Standards (IDDRS)* has discussed transitional justice issues, including prosecutions, although not in much detail.[5]

In most postconflict states, DDR administrators and prosecutors have worked in isolation from each other. Throughout the patchwork approach to DDR in Bosnia, there was no integration of issues related to the prosecution of war crimes and crimes against humanity.[6] The Office of the Prosecutor at the Special Court for Sierra Leone (SCSL) had no communication with the National Commission on DDR,[7] and Sierra Leone's recently completed DDR process played no role in prosecution planning.[8] The SCSL was in full swing when the United Nations Mission in Liberia (UNMIL) launched its sensitive DDR process, yet UN officials made no attempt to discuss possible conflicts at the outset.[9]

What little interaction does exist between DDR and prosecutions is frequently premised on the assumption that prosecutions impede DDR programs. Some commentators and policy-makers are prone to framing the issue as a binary choice between peace and justice.[10] There is no doubt that prosecutions have sometimes complicated DDR (and vice versa), particularly at the earlier stages. Prosecutions can make it more difficult to coax combatants and ex-combatants into disarming and demobilizing if they think they may face legal action.[11] Nonetheless, there is compatibility in the larger, long-term goals of DDR and prosecutions: both aim at reestablishing trust among ex-combatants, victims, the broader community, and state authorities. Prosecutions may even promote successful, long-term reintegration of ex-combatants. In fact, there is no evidence that prosecutions have seriously derailed DDR or that DDR has seriously disrupted prosecutions. Thus, DDR administrators and prosecutors should abandon the unhelpful "peace versus justice" cliché and focus instead on ways to mitigate the tensions between DDR and prosecutions to the benefit of both.

This chapter will discuss the situations where DDR can complicate prosecutions, followed by those situations where prosecutions can complicate DDR. Then it will examine three areas where DDR and prosecutions share congruent interests: the removal of spoilers, the separation of perpetrators from among ex-combatants, and the lessening of victim and community resentments over reintegration packages for ex-combatants. Finally, the chapter will look at three ways in which the inherent tension between DDR and prosecutions might be mitigated through sequencing, differential treatment, and outreach.

## WHERE DDR MAY CAUSE PROBLEMS FOR PROSECUTIONS

Generally, where conflict continues, the goal of DDR creates pressure to compromise on accountability for international crimes.[12] Colombia provides a clear example of how a fragile security situation can prompt concessions on prosecutions to encourage disarmament and demobilization. The July 2005 Justice and Peace Law (Law 975) specifically targeted the demobilization of ex-combatants who had committed atrocities.[13] In exchange for disarming, demobilizing, admitting guilt, paying reparations to victims, and cooperating with authorities, perpetrators are granted reduced sentences of five to eight years, quick parole, and reinsertion benefits—regardless of the severity of their crimes. In May 2006, Colombia's Constitutional Court tightened the conditions for granting reduced sentences, but the government, which is trying to lure leftist militias into participating in DDR, has made further attempts to use the law as an incentive—for example, by easing the penalties for convicted war criminals. Progress has been made in the three years since the implementation of the Justice and Peace Law. For example, through voluntary statements, demobilized paramilitaries have confessed to more than 2,709 crimes and referred to 8,196 others. In addition, as a result of these confessions, 1,328 mass graves containing 1,698 bodies have been exhumed, 538 corpses have been preliminarily identified, and the remains of 223 have been turned over to their families.[14] In terms of victims' participation in these processes, over 155,000 victims registered with the attorney general's Justice and Peace Unit. However, implementation is lagging.[15] Many of the government bodies tasked with applying the law are overwhelmed and under-resourced. Most important, armed actors continue to commit war crimes and crimes against humanity. As a result, in parts of the country, victims continue to live in fear of armed actors, and as a consequence are hindered from participating in the Justice and Peace Law process.

In other situations, security environments are so fragile that peace negotiators are willing to grant broad amnesty to combatants or specific immunity to their leaders, even for the gravest of crimes, in order to entice them into participating in DDR.[16] Broad amnesties and specific immunity agreements were both features of Sierra Leonean peace efforts. In 1996 and 1997, amnesties were granted in conjunction with DDR programs.[17] The 1999 Lomé Peace Agreement offered a blanket amnesty to "all combatants and collaborators" for any acts committed up to that point.[18] It also included a specific "absolute and free pardon" for the Revolutionary United Front (RUF) leader Foday Sankoh.[19] Sankoh quickly reneged on the agreement and plunged the country back into war. Following British intervention in 2000, the RUF commanders who took Sankoh's place cooperated in steering RUF fighters through the DDR process despite widespread unease about the pending investigations of the Special Court for Sierra Leone.[20]

Bosnia and Kosovo both benefited from large, well-armed Western peacekeeping missions that administered disarmament and demobilization following the conflicts.[21] Yet even in those situations, policy-makers operating with weak mandates or risk-averseness still favored amnesties and immunity arrangements—something that led to substantial tension with prosecutors of international crimes. Despite an obligation under Chapter VII of the UN Charter to cooperate with the International Criminal Tribunal for the former Yugoslavia (ICTY), NATO forces made little effort early on to arrest prominent ICTY indictees, including the Bosnian Serb wartime political leader Radovan Karadžić and his military commander, Ratko Mladić.[22] Even in the absence of a formal DDR program, the United States and NATO prioritized separation of the factions and nascent disarmament and demobilization ahead of Bosnia's September 1996 election. To the extent that DDR occurred in Kosovo, the UN Mission in Kosovo (UNMIK) was jointly responsible for it in conjunction with the NATO peacekeeping mission, KFOR. Following the ICTY prosecutor's indictment of Kosovo's Prime Minister Ramush Haradinaj in March 2005, UNMIK officials blatantly acted to thwart the tribunal because they viewed Haradinaj as someone they could work with. Haradinaj, a former Kosovo Liberation Army (KLA) commander, had been involved in the militia's demobilization and transition into the civilian-controlled Kosovo Protection Corps. In June 2006, then ICTY Chief Prosecutor Carla Del Ponte told the UN Security Council: "My office has nowadays more difficulties to access documents belonging to UNMIK than in any other place in the former Yugoslavia. Furthermore, the UNMIK leadership is encouraging a climate which deters witnesses from talking to my investigators when it comes to the Albanian perpetrators."[23]

Although immunity deals for warlords and broader amnesties for ex-combatants have exacerbated tensions between DDR administrators and prosecutors during disarmament and demobilization in fragile security environments, there is good reason to believe that this will change. Prosecutors have successfully challenged the legality of immunity deals and amnesties in internationalized and national criminal tribunals. In March 2004, the SCSL Appeals Chamber refused to give legal effect to the Lomé amnesty.[24] Similarly, in 2006, the Colombian Constitutional Court ruled that several aspects of the Justice and Peace Law were too lenient on perpetrators and therefore violated Colombia's international obligations to prosecute and punish the perpetrators of atrocities.[25] These judgments may mean that amnesties and immunity deals are less likely to be offered in the future.[26] Even if they are offered, combatants may no longer trust such assurances, given the high-profile prosecutions of former Liberian president Charles Taylor. In short, DDR administrators are in the process of losing amnesties and immunity deals as potential tools for inducing combatants to disarm and demobilize. A side effect of this loss may be reduced conflict between DDR administrators and prosecutors.

## WHERE PROSECUTIONS MAY CAUSE PROBLEMS FOR DDR

Prosecutions may create difficulties for DDR with respect to perceptions of information sharing and victors' justice.

### INFORMATION SHARING

If a DDR program is sharing (or perceived to be sharing) information with prosecutors, this can heighten fears of prosecution, creating a disincentive for combatants to disarm and demobilize. In particular, commanders may be especially reluctant to allow child combatants to participate in DDR programs for fear of prosecution. In practice, however, information on specific combatants going through DDR has generally not been shared with prosecutors, largely because prosecutors never request such information. In interviews, prosecutors and former prosecutors from the ICTY, SCSL, and International Criminal Court (ICC) all stressed the limited value of DDR data for prosecutions, saying it is only useful in discovering new crime scenes or recognizing patterns in the conflict. They all stated that indictments against specific individuals must be developed through in-house investigations.[27] ICC prosecutors, for example, may seek DDR information from the UN Mission in Congo to look at broad patterns, such as the age of combatants, but they will not use that data to develop information on potential suspects.[28]

Only rarely has the non-sharing of information explicitly arisen from DDR administrators' concerns that such sharing could undermine the success of disarmament and demobilization. During the Macedonian conflict of 2001, the Chief Prosecutor at the ICTY openly criticized NATO peacekeepers conducting disarmament and demobilization for withholding information that she had requested on arms collected from Albanian rebels.[29] In Rwanda, the government has not screened demobilized ex-combatants for genocide, even though it has engaged in maximal prosecutions (including hundreds of thousands tried in community courts). Furthermore, the Rwandan government has barred International Criminal Tribunal for Rwanda (ICTR) investigators from accessing demobilization camps to interview ex-combatants about genocide crimes.[30]

While information sharing between DDR administrators and prosecutors has been limited or nonexistent in most cases, Colombia is a notable exception. Thousands of demobilized paramilitary fighters and rebel deserters are confessing to crimes in exchange for reduced sentences. In many cases, this is working as a catalyst for victims, who are then moved to report their versions of events to authorities, often for the first time.[31]

## PERCEPTIONS OF VICTORS' JUSTICE

If ex-combatants believe that prosecutions amount to an extension of the conflict by other means, they are likely to be more reluctant to disarm and demobilize, thus increasing tensions between prosecutors and DDR administrators. Perceptions of victors' justice can also hamper reintegration on the part of ex-combatants and their communities.

Where there is good reason to believe that prosecutions were designed to be unfair, disarmament and demobilization can suffer. For example, the Justice and Peace Law, which provides the legal framework for the DDR for the paramilitaries in Colombia, has failed, thus far, to lead to the prosecution of ruling politicians with links to the paramilitaries. Other armed groups continuing to operate in the country have rejected the idea of demobilization under the same legal framework, by some accounts because they perceive the prosecutions strategy to be biased.[32] Regardless, thousands of combatants from these groups have demobilized in order to take advantage of the judicial benefits, such as a reduced sentence even for international human rights crimes. At peace talks in Macedonia in 2001, the main Albanian faction, the National Liberation Army (NLA), refused to disarm while subject to Macedonian domestic prosecutions, whose fairness it distrusted. Accompanying the Ohrid Peace Agreement, NATO reached parallel agreements with the government and the NLA, leading to an amnesty law for all crimes committed during the conflict (except international crimes, which were referred to the ICTY).[33]

Less rational fears of victors' justice can also create tensions between DDR administrators and prosecutors, as happened in Bosnia. During and after the war, Bosniaks were favorably disposed to the ICTY, and Bosnian Croats were skeptical of some of its actions. But the tribunal came under frequent and persistent attack from Bosnian Serb leaders, who pointed to the disproportionate numbers of indictments against Serbs as evidence of prosecutorial bias (rather than as a reflection of the conduct of the war). For example, Radovan Karadžić, who was indicted on genocide and other charges, told a television interviewer in February 1996 that the ICTY "is not a court or a tribunal.... It is a form of lynching for the whole nation."[34] Politicians in Belgrade echoed these views even after the fall of Slobodan Milošević.

Not only victors' justice but disappointment in a lack of victors' justice can create problems for successful DDR. It can be a bitter pill for reintegrating ex-combatants from the victorious side of a conflict when they realize that prosecutions are being undertaken on the basis of how factions fought, not why. Kosovo Albanians who suffered at the hands of Serbian forces never expected their militia leaders, then in the process of demobilization and reintegration, to be subject to indictment. ICTY officials were dismayed to observe the indicted former KLA commander Fatmir Limaj parlay his war crimes indictment into enhanced political prominence at home.[35]

Finally, if ex-combatants view prosecutions as one-sided, overly harsh, or as victors' justice, then they may be more reluctant to reintegrate.[36] Likewise, communities that perceive themselves to be on the short end of victors' justice are likely to be less welcoming for the reintegration of ex-combatants from the victorious side.

## SUDAN

As of early 2009, there was little evidence that prosecutions have actually derailed DDR programs. Indeed, the contexts where DDR has failed and conflict has restarted have generally had no active prosecution efforts on the ground. Indeed, it seems more likely that where heightened attention and political will have resulted in the establishment of an internationally supported prosecution mechanism, that same attention has also led to more robust military and diplomatic measures to end the conflict. For example, DDR failures in Sierra Leone were followed by success once security improved, even as prosecutions were being added to the mix.[37] Liberia experienced a similar dynamic.[38] In Uganda, where the northern Ugandan conflict is often cited as a classic trade-off between peace and justice, it should be recalled that a DDR attempt failed before there were any ICC arrest warrants.[39] There is clearly no mono-causal connection between the prosecution of international crimes and DDR failure or continued conflict.

The ICC could offer a new test of whether DDR is more or less likely to succeed where international crimes are being prosecuted. The ICC faces pressure from critics who argue that its arrest warrant against Sudanese president Omar Hassan al-Bashir is harming prospects for ending the conflict and implementing the moribund Darfur Peace Agreement of May 2006, which included provisions for DDR.[40] ICC critics also worry about the arrest warrant's potential to derail implementation of the 2005 Comprehensive Peace Agreement (CPA) between the government and former rebels in the south, which included provisions for a DDR program that was set to begin in late 2008.

## CONGRUENCIES BETWEEN DDR AND PROSECUTIONS

### REMOVING SPOILERS

In fragile security environments, prosecutions can contribute to the success of disarmament and demobilization by physically and/or politically sidelining warlords who are bent on conflict and blocking the negotiation or implementation of peace agreements (that often include provisions for DDR). Arguably, prosecutions removed potential spoilers of DDR in Rwanda, Bosnia, Liberia, and the DRC.

Nearly all of the extremist Hutu leadership that organized the genocide of the minority Tutsi in Rwanda has been indicted by the ICTR, European courts, or Rwandan domestic courts. With the most important would-be spoilers either on the run or in jail, the pool of potential leadership for any organized destabilization of the DDR process and broader peace process was depleted. International powers achieved a similar effect in November 1995, when they convened Bosnian peace talks in Dayton, Ohio, that excluded the Bosnian Serb political leader Radovan Karadžić and his military commander, Ratko Mladić, because of their indictments on genocide and other charges at the ICTY. As a result, the Bosnian Serbs formally transferred authority to Serbian president Slobodan Milošević to negotiate at Dayton on their behalf (this occurred well before his 1999 indictment). Serb hardliners in Bosnia later complained that Milošević had made too many concessions in the resulting Dayton Peace Agreement, which paved the way for heavy peacekeeping and associated disarmament programs.

A similar dynamic took hold when the SCSL prosecutor indicted Charles Taylor in March 2003 while he was the sitting president of Liberia and Liberia was still in the midst of war. The indictment remained under seal until June 2003, when Taylor left Liberia to attend peace talks in Accra, Ghana. When the indictment was revealed Taylor rushed back to Liberia, where the war continued over the following months. At the time, the prosecutor's decision was heavily criticized amid mounting casualties.[41] Taylor, however, had a track record of deception. From the early 1990s he had signed numerous peace and cease-fire agreements and had broken all of them. He had used peace negotiations as a stalling mechanism on a number of occasions when his forces were under military pressure in order to buy time to rearm and reorganize. As with Karadžić and Mladić in Bosnia, Taylor's indictment for war crimes and crimes against humanity made continued direct diplomatic negotiations with him politically untenable for some influential countries, including the United States, and thus hastened his removal from power.

## DIFFERENTIATING AMONG PERPETRATORS

Whereas DDR administrators seek to draw a broad group of ex-combatants into their programs, prosecutors are typically only interested in a small subset of ex-combatants: those suspected of having committed war crimes and crimes against humanity, those with information on international crimes or command hierarchies implicated in such crimes, and those who are potential victim-witnesses themselves (such as forcibly recruited child soldiers).[42] Those with the most to fear from prosecution almost always constitute a small percentage of the combatants or ex-combatants. Conversely, those ex-combatants with the least to fear are more likely to shift their loyalties away from former commanders and toward DDR programs that provide them with concrete benefits. Colombia offers an important example of the nuanced treatment of ex-combatants. Through Law 975, most ex-combatants are offered amnesty and generous benefits in exchange for participation in DDR, but the worst perpetrators are punished under provisions of the same law.

Prosecuting militia leaders can help draw a distinction between those who have the greatest responsibility for international crimes and the rank-and-file ex-combatants to be reintegrated into society. The community may also gain some confidence that those who will be reintegrated are not the worst perpetrators.[43] Furthermore, findings of individual guilt may reduce the likelihood that collective guilt will be assigned by the victims and broader society, which, in turn, can aid reintegration.[44] For example, a majority of Sierra Leonean ex-combatants surveyed in 2002 supported the work of the SCSL, in part because of its promise to help sort those commanders "bearing greatest responsibility" from themselves.[45]

Prosecutors' differentiation among different degrees of perpetrators will particularly aid the reintegration of former child soldiers. The SCSL's first prosecutor pursued charges of forced recruitment of child soldiers in part to raise community awareness that child combatants—even the perpetrators among them—were also victims.[46] In November 2002, he publicly announced that although the court's statute allowed for the prosecution of anyone over the age of fifteen, he would not prosecute any children for crimes committed during the conflict.[47] As will be argued in greater detail below, these beneficial effects of differential prosecutions can only be realized if victims and the broader society are made aware of this through outreach.

### OFFSETTING RESENTMENT OVER REINTEGRATION BENEFITS

DDR programs usually include reinsertion and/or reintegration benefits for ex-combatants, which can include cash payments, travel allowances, or vocational training and employment opportunities. Such payments can cause resentment among victims and the broader public, especially given the frequent absence of reparations for victims. This, in turn, can make communities more hostile to returning ex-combatants. However, prosecuting perpetrators of international crimes among ex-combatants may serve to offset such resentment by providing a sense of accountability and reducing the impression that perpetrators are being rewarded for the crimes they have committed.[48]

In Sierra Leone there was great discontent at payments to ex-combatants,[49] and later disappointment with the government's failure to implement recommendations of the Truth and Reconciliation Commission. While many victims were also upset that prosecutions did not extend to lower-ranking perpetrators, many took some solace from the indictments of top militia leaders, and the transfer of former Liberian president Charles Taylor to the SCSL in March 2006 was widely celebrated. In Rwanda, where extensive prosecutions led to the punishment of hundreds of thousands of genocidaires, there have been few complaints from victims about reintegration benefits for ex-combatants.[50] In Colombia, the accused are simultaneously entering a DDR program and submitting to the legal process against them as a prerequisite for reduced sentencing and DDR benefits.[51] Here, to the extent that this aspect of DDR results in greater truth-telling, prosecution may enhance reintegration. These indications are anecdotal and somewhat speculative; the potential link between prosecutions and reduced community anger over reintegration benefits requires closer study.

### AMELIORATING TENSIONS BETWEEN DDR AND PROSECUTIONS

Having laid out some of the potential tensions and congruencies in the relationship between DDR and prosecutions, in this section I will now explore potential strategies for reducing tension between the two. The sequencing of

DDR and prosecutions promises no clear benefits. However, prosecutors who differentiate among perpetrators can reduce the potential for tensions with DDR administrators. And both prosecutors and DDR administrators have a shared interest in disseminating accurate information about the limited extent of prosecutions.

### SEQUENCING

DDR programs and prosecution mechanisms can be sequenced in three ways: DDR first, prosecutions first, or simultaneous efforts. Most commonly, prosecutions are an afterthought to peace negotiations and DDR planning, and prosecutors take up their work after the completion or near completion of DDR. In Sierra Leone, by the time the first SCSL staff arrived in 2002, disarmament and demobilization had been declared officially completed.[52] Similarly, the first indictments from the internationalized Kosovo tribunal were not issued until November 1999, after disarmament had begun.

In rare cases, prosecutions have predated the end of hostilities and the development of a DDR program. By the time of the November 1995 Dayton Peace Agreement that ended the war in Bosnia and established the framework for a NATO peacekeeping force that would be responsible for disarmament and demobilization, the ICTY prosecutor had already indicted fifty-two individuals. The ICTY also had immediate jurisdiction over the armed conflicts in Kosovo and Macedonia, long before those conflicts were resolved and DDR programs were even contemplated. In West Africa, the SCSL was in place before neighboring Liberia's conflict ended and had jurisdiction over Liberians who had committed war crimes and crimes against humanity in Sierra Leone. There, too, prosecutors were active to a limited degree before DDR administrators. Although prosecution before DDR has been the rarest sequencing to date, the ICC may make this more common.

DDR and prosecutions can also begin nearly at the same time, though with prosecutions occurring over a longer period of time. In Rwanda, both DDR and prosecutions were launched in the aftermath of the 1994 genocide, but DDR progressed far more quickly than prosecutions. In the most complicated cases, DDR and prosecutions have been designed and implemented simultaneously in the midst of an ongoing conflict and peace efforts. In Uganda, the Amnesty Act of 2000 offered a blanket pardon to anyone who had taken up arms against the state and was willing to lay down their weapons.[53] When the conflict in the north continued, Uganda's president referred the matter to the ICC in December 2003 in an apparent attempt to gain leverage over the Lord's

Resistance Army (LRA) insurgency.[54] The ICC issued sealed arrest warrants for five LRA leaders in July 2005 amid the ongoing conflict and efforts to broker a peace agreement just weeks following the Ugandan Amnesty Commission's DDR launch.[55]

For DDR administrators in particular, the idea of sequencing DDR and prosecutions may seem attractive. It can be argued that if a prosecution mechanism does not yet exist or is not yet being implemented, then ex-combatants are less likely to fear participating in disarmament and demobilization. Under this thinking, prosecution mechanisms should only kick in once the disarmament and demobilization phases are over. However, a glance at the various contexts in which DDR and prosecution mechanisms have been pursued together reveals no clear pattern to support this idea. Disarmament and demobilization can obviously succeed where they occur before prosecutions begin, as in Sierra Leone. Yet, DDR can also succeed where, as in Mozambique, no prosecution mechanism was ever introduced. Where prosecution mechanisms have been in place and active before DDR, each has proceeded without significant disruption from the other—for example, in Bosnia, Macedonia, Kosovo, and Liberia (after the SCSL started in neighboring Sierra Leone). By the same token, DDR without any prosecution mechanism proved unsustainable in earlier attempts in Sierra Leone and Liberia. And although Uganda is still struggling to reconcile simultaneous ICC prosecutions and DDR in the north, the DDR effort predates the ICC referral and was no more successful without it. On the contrary, some analysts have credited the ICC for pushing the rebel leaders into the 2008 Juba peace talks that included DDR.[56]

Indeed, there is the risk that deferring prosecutions could preclude the potential benefits of prosecutions for DDR implementation that were discussed above: the removal of spoilers and the differential treatment of ex-combatants. If the effect of sequencing is arguably neutral at best for the success of disarmament and demobilization, it could have decidedly negative consequences for prosecutions. Delaying prosecution activity until disarmament and demobilization are complete could mean interrupting complex investigations and risking their integrity.

## TARGETING AND DIFFERENTIAL TREATMENT

Where prosecutions and DDR have overlapped, the breadth of the prosecution mandate also determines the extent of their intersection. A prosecution focused on warlords, who may still command loyalty from ex-combatants undergoing DDR, can present different challenges for DDR administrators than does a prosecution that extends to greater numbers of low-level perpetrators, who may be going through DDR themselves. At one end of the spectrum, the SCSL prosecutor indicted only thirteen individuals under its mandate to try "persons who bear the greatest responsibility for serious violations of international humanitarian law."[57] Subsequently, three of the accused have died and one is missing and presumed dead. At the other end, Rwanda has tried over a million cases related to the 1994 genocide.[58]

Where DDR administrators and prosecutors think in terms of differential treatment for different categories of ex-combatants, they may be less likely to perceive conflict between their approaches during the disarmament and demobilization phases. From a DDR administrator's viewpoint, inducements for the mass of low-level ex-combatants are rightly regarded as a valuable tool in shifting their loyalty away from wartime commanders. In similar fashion, DDR administrators should more readily acknowledge that in many contexts prosecution mechanisms can serve this same end by demonstrating to the bulk of ex-combatants that wartime commanders have no viable future on the battlefield. Prosecutors and the policy-makers who design their mandates also share responsibility for differentiating among various categories of ex-combatants to reduce conflicts with DDR programs. There is usually a strong bias toward narrow prosecution mandates simply due to the lack of resources to pursue all perpetrators. As discussed next, outreach plays a pivotal role in making affected societies aware of the differentiation.

## OUTREACH

Some of the factors that exacerbate tensions between DDR programs and prosecutions of international crimes involve misunderstandings and misconceptions among combatants and ex-combatants related to the scope of prosecution and whether DDR information is being shared with prosecutors. Such misconceptions can lead ex-combatants to have exaggerated fears of prosecution, thereby hindering their willingness to disarm and demobilize. In Sierra Leone, a lack of information about the SCSL's mandate among the general public and ex-combatants increased concerns that extensive prosecutions might upset the peace process and squander the progress made in DDR implementation. A 2002 survey by the Post-Conflict Reintegration Initiative for Development and Empowerment (PRIDE) found that nearly a third of all ex-combatants expected the SCSL to try all perpetrators.[59] The survey also found that sensitization exercises about the Special Court markedly increased support among ex-combatants.

In 2004, SCSL officials grew concerned about reports from Liberia that much of the Liberian public, and many ex-combatants, falsely believed the court's mandate applied to crimes in Liberia and low-level Liberian perpetrators of crimes in Sierra Leone. Reports indicated that anxiousness about the court was being fueled by statements from allies of former president Charles Taylor.[60] In June 2004 the SCSL and UNMIL arranged for a high-profile outreach visit by court staff to Monrovia in order to counter widespread misunderstandings in Liberia regarding the SCSL mandate. Through community meetings and a press conference, court staff were able to address Liberians' concerns about the SCSL's effect on Liberian stability and emphasize that the court was only interested in those "bearing the greatest responsibility" for crimes committed in Sierra Leone.[61] Following the visit, Radio UNMIL conducted several follow-up interviews with court staff that provided additional opportunities to reach Liberians with accurate information about the court's mandate and activities.

## CONCLUSION

Transitional justice and DDR share the same overall goals: "the reestablishment of trust and the rebuilding of social capital between individuals, groups, communities, and institutions in war-torn societies."[62] The complex narrower relationship between the prosecution of international crimes and DDR programs generally has been marked by greater tensions during the disarmament and demobilization phases and greater harmony during the reintegration phase. But overall, the two approaches have not been as mutually disruptive as often assumed.

This chapter has outlined some practical steps to reduce tensions during disarmament and demobilization, and to take advantage of the greater synergy during reintegration. There are no magic formulas, but some lessons of a general nature can be identified. Although there has been little discernible advantage to sequencing DDR and prosecutions to date, prosecutors may nevertheless consider focusing on the most responsible perpetrators first. If lower-level perpetrators fall within the court's mandate, their prosecution should wait until DDR is well under way or even finished in order to prevent possible disruptions.[63] Where commanders are fully cooperative in DDR, prosecutors should also hold off on indicting them until disarmament and demobilization is complete; here communication between DDR officials and prosecutors could be especially helpful in determining which commanders are spoilers and which are being cooperative. In the course of this communication, it is important that policy-makers and DDR administrators resist temptations to set a low bar for the determination of senior perpetrators' cooperation out of hope or fear of worse; otherwise they risk becoming de facto advocates for commanders seeking to stave off prosecution.

Given the limited value of sharing DDR information with prosecutors and the risks to DDR implementation, administrators should generally err on the side of caution and only share broad data with prosecutors, not specific statements or names. Prosecutors and DDR administrators working in the same conflict or postconflict countries can benefit through communication. Openly discussing their mutual concerns can help in mapping a strategy through which both mandates can best be fulfilled. Potential attempts by militia leaders to play one goal against the other can be avoided, and information on the perceptions of ex-combatants, victims, and the general population regarding prosecutions can be shared.

Where the use of child combatants characterizes a conflict, prosecutors should pursue charges of forced recruitment of child soldiers as a war crime. This may aid in their reintegration by further bolstering the notion that they too were victims of the most responsible perpetrators. For the same reason, prosecutors should forgo the prosecution of children for war crimes.[64] DDR administrators should heed the *IDDRS*: "Combatants, ex-combatants and their commanders should be sensitized and informed, whether during the time they spend in demobilization sites or before their integration into new security forces, of protection measures and the prosecution of anyone who violates children's rights."[65]

Prosecutors can cause problems for DDR if they are perceived to be using DDR information to target suspects or undertaking biased prosecutions. For the benefit of both, DDR programs and prosecutors should effectively disseminate accurate information about prosecution mandates. Effective outreach programs can help to blunt the factors that most antagonize the relationship between prosecutions and DDR. Prosecutions introduce a volatile element into the DDR process, and if prosecution intentions are left open to interpretation by militia leaders and ex-combatants, the result will diminish support for both prosecutions and DDR among ex-combatants themselves. Support for prosecutions also will suffer among the broader affected population and among the diplomatic community, both of which will fear a resumption of conflict. Outreach can stem misinformation campaigns and eliminate fears of destabilizing mass arrests. Clarity regarding the prosecution mandate can serve to deter new violence that would disrupt the DDR process.

## NOTES

1    Unless otherwise indicated, this chapter will use the terms "international crimes" or "war crimes and crimes against humanity" as shorthand to refer to genocide and all violations of international humanitarian law. "International crimes" is admittedly over-inclusive, as it includes the (as-yet undefined) crime of aggression under the Rome Statute of the International Criminal Court.

2    United Nations Department of Peacekeeping Operations (DPKO), *Disarmament, Demobilization and Reintegration of Ex-Combatants in a Peacekeeping Environment: Principles and Guidelines* (New York: United Nations Department of Peacekeeping Operations, 1999).

3    See United Nations, Report of the Secretary-General, *The Rule of Law and Transitional Justice in Conflict and Post-Conflict Societies*, S/2004/616, August 23, 2004.

4    Ibid., para. 21.

5    United Nations Department of Peacekeeping Operations (DPKO), *Integrated Disarmament, Demobilization and Reintegration Standards (IDDRS)* (New York: United Nations Department of Peacekeeping Operations, 2006). *IDDRS* modules are periodically updated and available at www.unddr.org/iddrs/framework.php.

6    See Massimo Moratti and Amra Sabic-El-Rayess, "Missing Link Between Disarmament, Demobilization, and Reintegration and Transitional Justice: The Case of Bosnia and Herzegovina," Country Cases (New York: International Center for Transitional Justice, 2009), www.ictj.org/en/research/projects/ddr/country-cases/2377.html. Various studies of DDR in Bosnia make no mention of the war crimes issue as a factor for DDR. See Jeremy King, *Building Peace in Bosnia: Lessons Learned in Disarmament, Demobilization, Reintegration and Civilian Police Capacity-Building* (Ottawa: International Security Research and Outreach Programme / International Security Bureau / Canadian Department of Foreign Affairs and International Trade, 2001); Jeremy King, A. Walter Dorn, and Matthew Hodes, *An Unprecedented Experiment: Security Sector Reform in Bosnia and Herzegovina* (Bonn: Bonn International Center for Conversion, 2002); and Tobias Pietz and Shay Duffy, *Turning Soldiers into a Work Force: Demobilization and Reintegration in Post-Dayton Bosnia and Herzegovina*, Brief No. 27 (Bonn: Bonn International Center for Conversion, 2003).

7    A former staff member of the SCSL's Office of the Prosecutor, interview by the author, New York, May 14, 2007.

8    David Crane, former SCSL Prosecutor, telephone interview by the author, May 11, 2007.

9    Ibid. As will be discussed below, UNMIL and the SCSL later did cooperate on outreach to counter misconceptions about the court's mandate among Liberian ex-combatants.

10   See, e.g., Refugee Law Project, *Whose Justice? Perceptions of Uganda's Amnesty Act 2000: The Potential for Conflict Resolution and Long-Term Reconciliation*, Working Paper No. 15 (Kampala: Refugee Law Project, 2005).

11　Swedish Ministry for Foreign Affairs, *Stockholm Initiative on Disarmament Demobilisation Reintegration: Background Studies* (Stockholm: Ministry for Foreign Affairs, 2006), 76.

12　For an interesting exception to that general rule, see the discussion of Rwanda in Lars Waldorf, "Transitional Justice and DDR in Post-Genocide Rwanda," Country Cases (New York: International Center for Transitional Justice, 2009), http://www.ictj.org/en/research/projects/ddr/index.html

13　Sergio Jaramillo, Yanet Giha, and Paula Torres, "Disarmament, Demobilization and Reintegration Amidst Conflict," Country Cases (New York: International Center for Transitional Justice, 2009), http://www.ictj.org/en/research/projects/ddr/index.html

14　Organization of American States, Mission to Support the Peace Process in Colombia, "Twelfth Quarterly Report of the Secretary General to the Permanent Council on the Mission to Support the Peace Process in Colombia," February 9, 2009, 2–3, www.mapp-oea.org/sites/default/files/images/twelfthquarterlyreport%20mapp.pdf.

15　International Crisis Group, "Correcting Course: Victims and the Justice and Peace Law in Colombia," Latin American Report No. 29 (October 30, 2008).

16　For a more detailed discussion of amnesties, see Mark Freeman, "Amnesties and DDR Programs," in this volume.

17　See Peace Agreement Between the Government of the Republic of Sierra Leone and the Revolutionary United Front of Sierra Leone, 1996, www.usip.org/library/pa/sl/sierra_leone_11301996.html (hereafter Abidjan Peace Agreement). In October 1997, representatives of the Sierra Leonean government-in-exile and the ruling Armed Forces Revolutionary Council/Revolutionary United Front (AFRC/RUF) junta agreed to a peace plan put forward by the Economic Community of West African States, which provided for DDR and full amnesty for those involved in the junta's coup. See the Economic Community of West African States Six-Month Peace Plan for Sierra Leone, 1998, www.usip.org/library/pa/sl/sl_ecowas_10231997.html.

18　Peace Agreement Between the Government of Sierra Leone and the Revolutionary United Front of Sierra Leone, 1999, art. 9, www.sierra-leone.org/lomeaccord.html (hereafter Lomé Peace Agreement). During the DDR process in Sierra Leone, the registration form for ex-combatants stated: "In accordance with the Amnesty Conditions you will be exempted from criminal prosecution, with regards to any crimes committed prior to your surrender." See DPKO, *Disarmament, Demobilization and Reintegration*, 109.

19　Lomé Peace Agreement, art. 9.1.

20　Thokozani Thusi and Sarah Meek, "Disarmament and Demobilisation in Sierra Leone," in *Sierra Leone: Building the Road to Recovery*, Monograph 80 (Pretoria: Institute for Security Studies, 2003), 23–38.

21　A U.S.-led NATO intervention in Bosnia, conducted in parallel with Croatian and Bosnian Federation army advances in 1995, forced the Bosnian Serb army and sponsoring Serbian government to agree to the Dayton Peace Agreement. The Dayton Peace

Agreement that ended the war failed to include any comprehensive plan for DDR, ignoring lessons learned through UN DDR programs elsewhere in the early 1990s. See King, *Building Peace in Bosnia*, 5. However, the agreement did create space for ad hoc disarmament carried out by NATO peacekeepers (numbering 60,000 at the outset), as well as later rounds of DDR programs. In Kosovo, NATO forces in conjunction with the Kosovo Liberation Army (KLA) defeated the Yugoslav army and other Serbian security services. Just days after the victory in June 1999, NATO signed an agreement with the KLA on its disarmament and transformation into a civilian protection force. Approximately 50,000 soldiers (mostly from NATO) patrolled Kosovo's small territory.

22  Whether Karadžić received a formal guarantee of immunity, as he claimed in court following his eventual July 2008 arrest, there is no denying that he lived openly in the town of Pale during the first six months of the NATO peacekeeping deployment in Bosnia, giving media interviews and attending political meetings. He and other ICTY indictees passed through American and other NATO checkpoints without facing arrest. One U.S. soldier told the *Washington Post*, "War criminals are something we don't even look for…. All they told us in training was: It's not your job." See Christine Spolar, "Karadzic, Mladic: Unfamiliar Faces; NATO Checkpoints Don't Recognize Bosnian War Crimes Suspects," *Washington Post*, February 17, 1996; and John Pomfret, "Bosnian Serbs' Leader Stages Show of Defiance; Karadzic Tour Ends Months of Seclusion," *Washington Post*, February 10, 1996. U.S. ambassador-at-large Robert Gallucci made clear, "The apprehension of indicted war criminals is not a mission requirement." See "NATO Alters Tactics in Pursuit of War Criminals," Reuters, February 15, 1996.

23  "Statement by Tribunal's Prosecutor Carla Del Ponte to the Security Council 7 June 2006," UN ICTY Press Release, www.un.org/icty/pressreal/2006/p1085e-annex.htm (accessed October 19, 2008). ICTY trial judges acquitted Haradinaj and one co-accused in April 2008 amid prosecution complaints over witness intimidation. See Tracy Wilkinson, "UN War Crimes Tribunal Acquits Kosovo Rebel Leader," *Los Angeles Times*, April 4, 2008.

24  *Prosecutor v. Kallon and Kamara, Decision on Challenge to Jurisdiction: Lomé Accord Amnesty*, SCSL-04-15-PT-060, Appeals Chamber of the Special Court for Sierra Leone, http://www.scsl.org/CASES/RevolutionaryUnitedFrontTrialRUF/AppealsChamberDecisions/tabid/195/Default.aspx

25  Jaramillo, Giha, and Torres, "Disarmament, Demobilization and Reintegration Amidst Conflict."

26  Over time, it may also reduce the incidence of amnesties and immunity agreements offered at the national level. Countries wishing to avoid ICC assertion of jurisdiction under the Rome Statute—where applicable—may seek to maintain at least an appearance of accountability for international crimes at the national level.

27  Interviews, May and June 2007.

28  Staff member of the ICC Office of the Prosecutor, interview by the author, The Hague, June 2007.

29  Peter Bouckaert, "The Macedonian Tribunal," Institute for War and Peace Reporting, September 12, 2001, www.iwpr.net/?p=tri&s=f&o=164478&apc_state=hsritri2001.

30  Waldorf, "Transitional Justice and DDR in Post-Genocide Rwanda."

31  Sibylla Brodzinsky, "To Go Forward, Colombia Looks Back," *Christian Science Monitor*, October 17, 2008, www.csmonitor.com/2008/1017/p01s02-woam.html.

32  Statement of the Revolutionary Armed Forces of Colombia [*Fuerzas Armadas Revolucionarias de Colombia*] (FARC), "Las Farc se pronuncian sobre los dos gestures," ANNOCOL, April 4, 2009, anncol.eu/index.php?option=com_content&task=view&id=1953&Itemid=9.

33  International Crisis Group, "Macedonia: Wobbling Toward Europe," Europe Briefing No. 41 (Brussels: International Crisis Group, 2006), 2–4.

34  Pomfret, "Bosnian Serbs' Leader Stages Show of Defiance."

35  ICTY Registry official, interview by the author, The Hague, June 6, 2007.

36  Swedish Ministry for Foreign Affairs, *Background Studies*, 64, 82.

37  Beginning in 1998, Sierra Leone saw repeated efforts to implement DDR during its conflict. In May 2000, after the rebel RUF and AFRC had reneged on the 1999 Lomé Peace Agreement, which also included DDR provisions, Sierra Leone's civil society confronted the RUF leader Foday Sankoh, leading to his arrest; the rebels' transgressions also led to British intervention and a more robust military stance by the United Nations Mission in Sierra Leone (UNAMSIL) that fundamentally weakened the RUF and AFRC. This created an environment in which DDR could succeed, even as RUF and allied ex-combatants were wary about the looming establishment of the SCSL.

38  Liberian DDR failed during the 1990s and conflict continued until a peace agreement and successful DDR could be implemented in 2003, in parallel with the fully functional SCSL that had indicted the Liberian leader Charles Taylor and made many of his armed faction wary of possible indictment.

39  By itself the Amnesty Act of 2000 failed to lure the Lord's Resistance Army (LRA) into DDR and the conflict continued. The Ugandan government only referred the case to the ICC in 2003. The LRA leader Joseph Kony subsequently emerged from hiding and came to the negotiating table, by some accounts in reaction to the ICC investigation. Peace negotiations remain difficult and the ICC arrest warrants for five LRA officials (two of whom have since died) are certainly a complicating factor in the effort to end the conflict and implement DDR. In April 2008, Kony failed to appear at the scheduled signing of a peace agreement—reportedly out of fear of the ICC indictment. See "Uganda: Optimism Prevails, Despite Setbacks in Peace Talks," IRIN News, April 18, 2008.

40  See Stephen Rademaker, "Unwitting Party to Genocide: The International Criminal Court Is Complicating Efforts to Save Darfur," *Washington Post*, January 11, 2007. The

Darfur Peace Agreement is available at www.unmis.org/English/2006Docs/DPA_ABUJA-5-05-06-withSignatures.pdf.

41   See, e.g., Steven Edwards, "Indicted Leader of Liberia Flees Peace Talks: 'We may have lost a chance to persuade President Taylor to stand down peacefully,'" *National Post* (Canada), June 6, 2003; and Bernard Otabil, "UN Indictment of Taylor Blamed for 'Bloodbath,'" *Inter Press Service*, July 23, 2003.

42   In Sierra Leone, most ex-combatants received such benefits as vocational training through participation in DDR, while the SCSL mandate restricted its prosecutions to those "bearing greatest responsibility" for war crimes and crimes against humanity—in the end deemed by the prosecution to include only thirteen individuals.

43   Swedish Ministry for Foreign Affairs, "Stockholm Initiative on Disarmament Demobilisation Reintegration: Final Report" (Stockholm: Swedish Ministry for Foregin Affairs, 2006), 30.

44   Swedish Ministry for Foreign Affairs, *Background Studies*, 63.

45   PRIDE and ICTJ, "Ex-Combatant Views of the Truth and Reconciliation Commission," September 12, 2002, 16–17, www.ictj.org/images/content/0/9/090.pdf.

46   Former SCSL Chief Prosecutor David Crane, telephone interview by the author, May 11, 2007.

47   SCSL press release, "Special Court Prosecutor Says He Will Not Prosecute Children," November 2, 2002, www.sc-sl.org/LinkClick.aspx?fileticket=XRwCUe%2BaVhw%3D&tabid=196.

48   See Pablo de Greiff, "Establishing Links Between DDR and Reparations," in this volume.

49   Jeremy Ginifer, "Reintegration of Ex-Combatants," in *Sierra Leone: Building the Road to Recovery*, 39–52.

50   Waldorf, "Transitional Justice and DDR in Post-Genocide Rwanda."

51   Jaramillo, Giha, and Torres, "Disarmament, Demobilization and Reintegration Amidst Conflict."

52   However, at the time of the SCSL's first indictments in March 2003, the UN secretary-general reported concern that the Civil Defense Force still retained its structure, which "may undermine not only the credibility of the demobilization process, but also the long-term stability of the country." See United Nations Security Council, *Seventeenth Report of the Secretary-General on the United Nations Mission in Sierra Leone*, S/2003/321, para. 72.

53   Tim Allen, *Trial Justice: The International Criminal Court and the Lord's Resistance Army* (New York: Zed Books, 2006); and Refugee Law Project, *Whose Justice?*

54   International Crisis Group, "Building a Comprehensive Peace Strategy for Northern Uganda," African Briefing No. 27 (Brussels: International Crisis Group, 2005), 8–10.

55   These were announced publicly in October 2005. One of the indictees, Raska Lukwiya, was subsequently killed in combat in 2006, and another, Vincent Otti, was reportedly

killed in 2007. The LRA leader Joseph Kony remains at large, together with co-accused Okot Odhiambo and Dominic Ongwen.

56  Nick Grono and Adam O'Brien, "Justice in Conflict? The ICC and Peace Processes," in *Courting Conflict? Justice, Peace and the ICC in Africa*, ed. Nicholas Waddell and Phil Clark (London: Royal African Society, March 2008), 13–20.

57  Special Court for Sierra Leone Statute, art. 1, www.sc-sl.org/LinkClick.aspx?fileticket=u Clnd1MJeEw=&tabid=200. The court's first prosecutor further narrowed the mandate by using his discretion to forgo prosecutions based on national law.

58  Waldorf, "Transitional Justice and DDR in Post-Genocide Rwanda."

59  PRIDE and ICTJ, *Ex-Combatant Views of the Truth and Reconciliation Commission*, 16.

60  The author was one of the concerned officials. In January 2008, the first insider witness to appear in the trial of Charles Taylor, Varmuyan Sherif, testified that Taylor lieutenant (and current Liberian senator) Roland Duoh had deliberately spread fear about the Special Court among Taylor's associates. Speaking of SCSL investigators, Sherif stated, "I was skeptical. I never knew what their mission was, because the information that Roland Duoh gave us moved most of us into fright. So he said they were calling people on their phones telling them that we are the people working from the Special Court and we want to talk to you, but before that time Roland Duoh had frightened so many people already, so most people were just running helter-skelter, moving from one place to another. And most people in fact changed their SIM cards." Varmuyan Sherif, testifying before the Special Court for Sierra Leone on January 11, 2008, Case No. SCSL-2003-01-T, transcript, 1067-1068, www.sc-sl.org/LinkClick.aspx?fileticket=pgvZzXGR9GQ=&tabi d=160.

61  The author was the SCSL prosecution representative on the trip, which was led by Registrar Robin Vincent and organized by the court's outreach section in coordination with UNMIL.

62  Swedish Ministry for Foreign Affairs, *Background Studies*, 81.

63  Ibid., 82.

64  There are other reasons to forgo the prosecution of child perpetrators, but also strong arguments for developing alternative forms of accountability for them. See Roger Duthie and Irma Specht, "DDR, Transitional Justice, and the Reintegration of Former Child Combatants," in this volume.

65  DPKO, *IDDRS*, sec. 5.30, para. 7.3.

# CHAPTER 3

# Ex-Combatants and Truth Commissions

*Lars Waldorf*

## INTRODUCTION

Truth-seeking is a key element of most transitional justice mechanisms: prosecutions, local justice processes, lustrations, and, of course, truth commissions. Done well, truth commissions may contribute to both accountability and redress.[1] Truth commissions can reveal the specifics of individual cases, the scope and systematic nature of abuses, and the complicity of key actors and institutions. At a minimum, they can help debunk myths and misperceptions while creating a more accurate historical accounting: as Michael Ignatieff puts it, "[a]ll that a truth commission can achieve is to reduce the number of lies that can be circulated unchallenged in public discourse."[2]

For the most part, disarmament, demobilization, and reintegration (DDR) programs and truth commissions have operated independently of one another. This has resulted in missed opportunities for strengthening both DDR and truth commissions. DDR's reintegration aims may be furthered by increased truth-telling: ex-combatants may reintegrate more easily if they have a forum where they can tell the truth, apologize to victims and communities, and explain their actions (including possible forced participation). In addition, truth commissions may help victims and communities individualize guilt by differentiating between those combatants who perpetrated international crimes or gross human rights abuses and those who did not. From the perspective of truth commissions, ex-combatants are often key witnesses for uncovering international crimes, command responsibility, and joint criminal enterprises. Aggregated data from DDR programs can also aid in documenting the larger causes and patterns of violence.

This chapter begins with a brief discussion of the right to truth before providing an overview of truth commissions. It then moves on to consider the experiences of ex-combatants in truth commissions in South Africa, Sierra Leone, Timor-Leste, and in Indonesia and Timor-Leste. Finally, the chapter will look at the benefits to both DDR programs and truth commissions of making links between the two.

## THE RIGHT TO TRUTH

Truth commissions are premised on the right to truth—a right whose legal recognition they also helped spur.[3] Over the past twenty years, a growing body of international and regional human rights law has recognized a right to truth about international crimes (genocide, crimes against humanity, and war crimes) and gross human rights violations (such as torture, disappearances, and extrajudicial executions).[4] What started off as a state duty to investigate and remedy human rights abuses has evolved into a freestanding and non-derogable right to truth about such gross violations. This right is closely linked to the right not to be subjected to torture or ill treatment, the right to family life, the right to a hearing by a competent, independent, and impartial tribunal, and the right to an effective judicial remedy. The right to truth has both individual and collective dimensions. The UN Principles on combating impunity, for example, declares that "every people has the inalienable right to know the truth about past events concerning the perpetration of heinous crimes and about the circumstances and reasons that led, through massive or systematic violations, to the perpetration of those crimes."[5]

In 2006, the UN High Commissioner for Human Rights affirmed a broad right to truth:

> The right to truth implies knowing the full and complete truth as to the events that transpired, their specific circumstances, and who participated in them, including knowing the circumstances in which the violations took place, as well as the reasons for them.[6]

Importantly, this right means that victims, their families, and society at large should know the identities of suspected perpetrators (consistent, of course, with the suspects' rights).[7] The High Commissioner justified the right to truth on both Kantian and consequentialist grounds: that truth is fundamental to human dignity, and that truth will help eradicate impunity, remedy past abuses, and prevent future abuses.[8]

The right to truth has links to armed conflict and DDR programs. First, the right to truth is rooted in international humanitarian law. Additional Protocol I of the Geneva Conventions imposes obligations on belligerents to account for missing combatants and civilians.[9] The International Committee of the Red Cross (ICRC) has stated that the right to truth is now a norm of customary international law, which applies in both international and non-international conflicts: "each party to the conflict must take all feasible measures to account for persons reported missing as a result of armed conflict and must provide their family members with any information it has on their fate."[10] Second, the UN High Commissioner for Human Rights has approvingly noted that "the legal framework governing the disarmament, demobilization and reintegration process of illegal armed groups should guarantee the rights to truth, justice and reparations."[11]

Yet, in practice, truth-telling by ex-combatants about international crimes and gross human rights abuses has not played much of a role in most DDR programs. DDR programs usually collect information from ex-combatants, provide them with psychosocial counseling, and help trace their family members (particularly in the case of former child combatants). While all these activities are implicitly truth-seeking, they only touch indirectly on the right to truth, if at all. The obvious reason why the right to truth is largely absent from DDR programs is the worry that it will create disincentives for combatants to disarm and demobilize.

## TRUTH COMMISSIONS

Of all transitional justice mechanisms, truth commissions are the most explicitly concerned with truth-seeking and truth-telling. Prosecutions focus narrowly on the guilt or innocence of specific perpetrators. Local justice mechanisms often elevate remorse, forgiveness, community "harmony," and performative rituals over truth-telling.[12] By contrast, truth commissions are concerned with giving voice to victims, explaining the root causes of violence, constructing historical narratives, and issuing policy recommendations for redress and future prevention.[13] They also may offer (de jure or de facto) amnesties to perpetrators in exchange for truth-telling.[14] While some are more successful than others, truth commissions have provided a measure of accountability and reparations for large numbers of victims in numerous post-authoritarian and postconflict states.[15]

Three main criticisms are often leveled at truth commissions: they fail to reveal the full truth, they do not promote reconciliation, and they may be culturally inappropriate. First, there is considerable debate over whether truth commissions have lived up to their promise of generating "truth." This raises the obvious questions: Which truth? and Whose truth? Truth, of course, is an inherently slippery and contentious concept, with much made of the seeming distinction between empirical truth(s) and politico-moral truth(s). The South African Truth and Reconciliation Commission identified what it called "four notions of truth": (1) forensic truth based on objective facts and verifiable evidence; (2) personal, narrated truth grounded in individual subjectivity; (3) social truth achieved through intersubjective dialogue and debate; and (4) healing truth, or the state's public acknowledgment of past human rights violations.[16] Sierra Leone's Truth and Reconciliation Commission adopted these same four categories, though it recognized they were "probably not exhaustive."[17] Peru's Truth and Reconciliation Commission also struggled with these often competing notions of truth: "The tension between explaining what happened and finding legal evidence of what happened was never adequately solved, and ended up with the creation of parallel investigative units" — the Legal Team, the National Processes Team, the In-Depth Studies Area, and the Regional Histories Area.[18] Still, for all their recognition of such multiplicity, these truth commissions largely wound up privileging forensic truth.[19]

The truthfulness of the testimonies given in statements to and hearings before a truth commission is open to question. Survivor and victim testimonies are often fragmented and incomplete, and are inevitably shaped by trauma and the passage of time. On the other hand, perpetrators have incentives to deny or minimize their responsibility, particularly in the absence of credible threats of prosecutions.[20] As Leigh Payne observes:

> These [perpetrator] confessions, however, do not necessarily disclose truths about the past. They are merely accounts, explanations, and justifications for deviant behaviour or personal accounts of a past. As such, they unsettle, or compel, audiences of victims, survivors, and human-rights activists to assert their own, often contending, interpretations of the past.[21]

As truth commissions operate without a trial's evidentiary rules (such as hearsay) and practices (such as cross-examination), they are not well suited to uncover (intentionally or unintentionally) false testimonies. Furthermore, truth commissions often stitch together competing interpretations of the past into a meta-narrative that pares away much of the contestation and inconvenient facts to create a "shared history" and renewed national identity.[22] As a result, some victims, like one widow in Sierra Leone, find that "testifying did not consist of replacing silence with voice, but of being silenced by the TRC's model of redemptive memory."[23]

Second, several critics have challenged the more grandiose claims that "revealing is healing" and that truth commissions promote reconciliation. Some victims who testify in truth commissions may not find the experience therapeutic.[24] Also, truth commissions may, at least in the short term, contribute to a worsening of social relations.[25] Where truth commission hearings have achieved some measure of reconciliation, this may be more the result of staged rituals than truth-telling.[26] According to Payne, the clash of competing interpretations in truth commissions creates "contentious coexistence."[27] While that falls well short of the lofty rhetoric of reconciliation, it is still, in the end, nonviolent coexistence.

Finally, some critics express concern that truth commissions have been imposed on local communities without paying sufficient attention to their needs and cultural practices. Truth-telling processes may be less appropriate after conflicts characterized by violence among neighbors and intimates, where perpetrators, survivors, bystanders, and former combatants all have to find a way to live together in mutual insecurity.[28] In Sierra Leone, for example, the anthropologist Rosalind Shaw argues that the TRC "set itself in opposition to widespread local practices of social reconstruction as forgetting."[29] Others have pointed out how that TRC neglected important social practices like jokes, oaths, and cleansing rituals.[30] Shaw also has shown how local actors sometimes reshaped and reappropriated the TRC's techniques: "from the very beginning their truth-telling diverged from that of a simple duplication of TRC ideals: transformed by its context, truth telling became a new technique of forgetting."[31]

In the end, these critiques are not arguments against truth commissions per se; rather, they raise concerns about how specific truth commissions were created, implemented, and oversold. To help minimize future problems, the Office of the High Commissioner for Human Rights has issued a set of guidelines for truth commissions, which summarizes best practices and lessons learned. Those guidelines caution against creating unreasonable expectations of what truth commissions can achieve in the way of truth and especially reconciliation:

> While some countries have constructed a truth commission around the notion of advancing reconciliation—or have seen such a commission as a tool that would naturally do this—it should not be assumed that such an inquiry will directly result in reconciliation either in the community or in the national or political sphere…experience shows that many individual victims and communities may require more than the truth in order to forgive.[32]

Those guidelines also recognize that truth commissions should only be established after consulting victims and survivors and after taking account of national and local circumstances.[33]

## EX-COMBATANTS' EXPERIENCES IN TRUTH COMMISSIONS

It is often assumed that ex-combatants will be reluctant to participate in truth-telling processes for fear that their testimonies could be used against them in future prosecutions (particularly if there are concurrent internationalized tribunals, as was the case in Sierra Leone and Timor-Leste). However, there is some (very limited) empirical evidence suggesting that combatants and ex-combatants may be more willing to participate than supposed; for example, a large majority of ex-combatants surveyed in Sierra Leone expressed support for that country's TRC.[34] In fact, ex-combatants have testified in several truth commissions. In this section, we look at the involvement of ex-combatants in truth commissions in South Africa, Sierra Leone, Timor-Leste, and Indonesia and Timor-Leste.

### SOUTH AFRICA

South African ex-combatants expressed very divergent attitudes toward the TRC, depending on which side they had fought on.[35] As one study found, those who worked for the apartheid regime's security forces felt the TRC had excluded and stigmatized them. One respondent argued that the TRC "is nothing more than an ANC [African National Congress] orchestrated witch-hunt."[36] Not surprisingly, then, none of those respondents had participated in the TRC. By contrast, ex-combatants from the various liberation movements were largely positive toward the TRC, though many complained they had not received enough attention from the TRC. The minority who had applied for amnesty stated they were both relieved and fearful:

> In the TRC I testified that I was the one to give an order to this guy so that he would kill this one. So [now] it's free for me because I'm relieved you know...I can take out [of me] the thing which is not good.... On another side, I'm not relieved...I told them what I did, and there are people who hate me now....[37]

Another study respondent stated: "[I]f I killed your brother and went to TRC, well—[it] doesn't count that I went to TRC.... It can lead you to hurt me because now you know what I did to your brother."[38]

The South African TRC missed several opportunities when it came to those ex-combatants who did testify at hearings. First, it failed to ask questions about chains of command that could have helped document broader patterns of abuse.[39] Second, it focused on noncombatant victims, while treating ex-combatants as perpetrators and criminals:

> Ex-combatants [on the government side] did not feel that they were given the opportunity to explain the full context of their experience under apartheid and the reasons for their specific actions.... Even those who were granted amnesty felt that the process itself was one that at times contributed to their stigmatization.... Many liberation force ex-combatants still feel resentful about the fact that they were called to account for their actions in opposing the apartheid government....[40]

Having categorized participants as either victims or perpetrators, the TRC "[left] 'ordinary' soldier experiences largely invisible."[41] Finally, by treating combatants as perpetrators or "wishing them away," it made their reintegration more difficult.[42]

## SIERRA LEONE

A Sierra Leonean NGO, Post-Conflict Reintegration Initiatives for Development (PRIDE), found that a majority of ex-combatants (across all factions) expressed willingness to give statements to the TRC.[43] Interestingly, a majority stated they would still offer statements even if that information were to be shared with the Special Court for Sierra Leone[44]—perhaps because only 15 percent of ex-combatants felt they had done anything wrong[45] and because many considered themselves victims, too.[46] Overall, PRIDE concluded that "ex-combatants are willing and eager to participate in the TRC because they believe the TRC will facilitate reintegration into their former communities."[47]

In the end, however, few ex-combatants submitted statements to the TRC: less than 1 percent of the 7,706 statements came from direct perpetrators.[48] Ex-combatants were also conspicuously absent from several district hearings.[49] This may reflect several factors. First, there are obvious methodological difficulties with conducting attitudinal surveys among populations that are highly traumatized, but also highly skilled at giving strategic answers to patrons, government officials, and NGOs.[50] The authors of the PRIDE survey recognized "the possibility that some ex-combatants may have formulated their answers according to what they thought we wanted to hear."[51] Elsewhere, the authors note that the "focus groups lead us to believe that many of the [rebel Revolutionary United Front] respondents were not being honest in their response [that is, expressing support for the Special Court]."[52] Second, the PRIDE survey was conducted in mid-2002, just a few months after the creation of the Special Court. The survey authors acknowledged that ex-combatants' support for the TRC "may change considerably once the Special Court starts its indictment procedures."[53] Unfortunately, there have been no follow-up attitudinal surveys of ex-combatants' attitudes toward the TRC. Nevertheless, anecdotal and ethnographic evidence suggests that ex-combatants came to see the TRC as an investigative arm of the Special Court—notwithstanding statements, sensitizations, and outreach from the TRC, Special Court, and NGOs.[54]

Even when ex-combatants did testify, their testimony was sometimes less than truthful. Tim Kelsall, who attended district hearings in Tonkolili, concluded that "[t]he principal function of the first four days was not to elicit the truth, but to psychologically pressure and prepare perpetrators [all of whom were ex-combatants] to show remorse and to be symbolically reintegrated into the community."[55] Shaw also found that participants appropriated the TRC's district-level hearings for their own reintegration rituals, which emphasized the (re)subordination of ex-combatant youth to male elites—rather than truth-telling.[56]

### TIMOR-LESTE

Many participants in Timor-Leste's truth commission (known by its Portuguese acronym, CAVR) were ex-combatants who had been forcibly recruited into the pro-Indonesian militias during the period surrounding the 1999 independence referendum.[57] Most of them had only played support roles or engaged in lesser acts of violence.[58] There were two reasons for this. First, the pro-Indonesian militia members responsible for serious acts of violence (including the leadership) had fled to West Timor and Indonesia and were either too unrepentant or too fearful to return. Second, the truth commission only had "jurisdiction" over minor criminal offenses: "theft, minor assault, arson (other than that resulting in death or injury), the killing of livestock or destruction of crops."[59] All "serious crimes" had to be referred to the Special Panel for Serious Crimes (SPSC) for possible prosecution.[60] As a result, the truth commission's hearings dealt mostly with the events of 1999, even though its temporal mandate extended back to the civil war and Indonesian invasion in 1975.[61]

The CAVR established the innovative Community Reconciliation Process (CRP) to hold local truth and reconciliation hearings. The CRP was mostly driven by perpetrators requesting hearings to recount their actions.[62] Even though many ex-militia members had self-demobilized and already returned to their communities before the CAVR began, they sought CRP hearings to reduce their stigma, avoid retribution, and achieve legal finality.[63] They first had to submit written statements admitting responsibility for their actions and naming their accomplices and superiors.[64] In total, the Commission received statements from 1,541 perpetrators and held CRP hearings for 1,371 of them.[65]

Many, but not all, CRP hearings were adaptations of a customary reconciliation ceremony, *nahe biti boot* ("unfolding the mat," where reconciliation traditionally took place).[66] At the end of the hearings, perpetrators signed Community Reconciliation Agreements, which, among other things, included: "(a) a description of the acts disclosed; (b) a record of the Deponent's acceptance of responsibility for such acts, and the Deponent's apology for the acts disclosed; (c) the agreed upon act of reconciliation for the acts disclosed...."[67] Importantly, the victims' consent was not required, though their input was often sought.[68]

Many ex-militia members were fairly perfunctory when it came to truth-telling in their statements and in CRP hearings. As Piers Pigou explained:

> The quality of the disclosures was often very limited, which may reflect the fact that there is simply not much to say. Many Timorese were simply press-ganged into the lowest rungs of the militia structures, where they fulfilled basic roles such as guard duty, or were forced to attend meetings, where they literally made up the numbers.[69]

Not surprisingly, then, many blamed their actions on higher-level militia members, many of whom were still in exile in West Timor and Indonesia.[70] As CRP hearings were not adversarial in nature, ex-combatants were not pushed to reveal more than they did:

> Although the [perpetrators] are required to make a full disclosure, and the Panel is empowered to ask specific details on command structures and details on others who were involved, many Panels upheld an unwritten rule that these processes were not meant to be interrogative or designed to catch-out [perpetrators] who preferred to tailor their disclosures by being economical with the truth.[71]

In the end, then, many CRP hearings produced a less-than-full accounting.

Nonetheless, CRP hearings provided some measure of shaming and reintegration: "In a number of hearings it was evident the [perpetrators] were 'lowering themselves' before their communities, and that the hearing was at one level a public process of shaming, that concluded with the official re-admittance of the [perpetrators] back into the family."[72] Anecdotal evidence suggests that the CRP hearings have helped some low-level ex-combatants reintegrate into their communities.[73] In one small study, a number of ex-militia "felt that community members were no longer suspicious of them or called them 'militia.'"[74]

In the end, though, Timor-Leste is an anomalous case in two respects. First, perpetrators of international crimes and gross human rights abuses were specifically excluded from testifying in the truth commission's local hearings.

Second, and as a consequence, most of the ex-combatants who participated were low-level, forcibly recruited, self-demobilized, and did not commit crimes more serious than assault. Thus, Timor-Leste's experience offers somewhat limited guidance for future truth commissions. Still, it does demonstrate how truth commissions can help reintegrate low-level ex-combatants back into their local communities.

## INDONESIA AND TIMOR-LESTE

In March 2005, Timor-Leste and Indonesia established a bilateral truth commission, whose name made its political goal clear: the Commission for Truth and Friendship (CTF).[75] The Commission was meant to establish "the conclusive truth" regarding the events and abuses of 1999.[76] To accomplish that goal, the CTF reviewed documents compiled by the CAVR, SPSC, and two other investigative bodies. It also conducted limited fact-finding through six public hearings in 2007, as well as through statements and interviews (involving a total of 147 witnesses).[77] Thirteen members of the Indonesian military and twelve former militia members testified in the public hearings (out of fifty-six witnesses).[78]

As an exercise in truth-seeking, the hearings failed miserably. Worse than that, they gave a public platform to alleged perpetrators to engage in lies, disinformation, and denial. Megan Hirst ruefully concludes (*pace* Michael Ignatieff) that "the CTF's public hearings may have *increased* the number of lies that can be circulated unchallenged in Indonesian public discourse regarding the events of 1999 in East Timor."[79] This occurred for several reasons. First, some of the Commissioners did not see the public hearings as a truth-seeking exercise.[80] Not surprisingly, then, the questioning from Commissioners was mostly inept.[81] Second, perpetrators had no real incentive to tell the truth, as there was no guarantee of amnesty and no threat of prosecution.[82] At the same time, they had good reason to "protect their own reputation, job or personal security, to avoid institutional retribution, or to uphold their loyalty to their institution and commanders."[83] In addition, there was insufficient witness protection for those who might have been inclined to speak out. In one hearing, a militia commander reneged on his earlier commitment to publicly disclose his militia's links to the Indonesian military: "But since this is only a public hearing I can't tell you much...if I tell you too much I will face difficulties, I will be in trouble...."[84]

The lack of truth-telling in the public hearings, as well as other problems with the Commission's mandate and operations,[85] augured poorly for the

Commission's final report. To the surprise of many, however, the Commission issued a report in July 2008 finding that the Indonesian military and the pro-Indonesian militias were responsible for crimes against humanity in 1999.[86] The report also concluded that the Indonesian military had directly supported the militias with money and weapons, though it left open the question of whether the military had created and controlled them.[87] The report also raised serious doubts about the credibility of two militia leaders who testified in the public hearings.[88]

## LINKING DDR AND TRUTH COMMISSIONS

As the previous section indicates, it is difficult to generalize about the experiences of ex-combatants in truth commissions. This is partly because of the variation among the different truth commissions. Some emphasized truth-seeking, while others privileged community reconciliation. Some provided meaningful incentives for ex-combatants to testify truthfully and others gave ex-combatants a public platform to spin lies. What all four commissions had in common was their lack of coordination with DDR programs. I am not arguing that coordination would have made the commissions more successful (that is, after all, a counterfactual). Nonetheless, in the remainder of this chapter, I want to consider the possibilities for linkages that could benefit *both* DDR and truth commissions.

### BENEFITS FOR DDR PROGRAMS: STRENGTHENING SOCIAL REINTEGRATION

Truth-telling could be useful to DDR at both a programmatic and an individual (ex-combatant) level. DDR programs have a clear interest in ex-combatants telling the truth. First, they have to screen out fraudulent claims for DDR benefits — not just for budgetary reasons, but, more important, to avoid discrediting the programs. Proper screening may require "[d]etailed cross-examination of DDR candidates' knowledge of key battles, commanders and armed force or group structure."[89] In other words, DDR benefits are already conditioned on truth-telling (at least as regards eligibility). Second, DDR practitioners need to collect truthful personal information from ex-combatants if they are to provide them with appropriate services (such as psychosocial counseling, family tracing, and so on). Third, for DDR programs to be successful, practitioners need to learn ex-combatants' true motivations for joining armed groups and for later demobilizing. Such information is not only useful to improve outreach and programming, but can also help prevent future remobilization.[90] The UN's integrated standards recommend that DDR practitioners conduct a "conflict and security analysis" in which they look at the root causes of conflict.[91] One obvious resource for such an analysis is the ex-combatants themselves. Finally, and more broadly, DDR programs may better achieve the goal of social reintegration if different parties to a conflict (particularly those who have never been heard) have a forum where they can articulate their grievances and claims, and thus begin to recover a sense of agency and recognition.

At an individual level, ex-combatants may benefit from truth commissions. First, they may use them to "make sense of the war" and perhaps ease their own trauma, guilt, shame, or fear.[92] Second, ex-combatants may want an opportunity to explain that they too were victimized (particularly if they were forcibly recruited) or to distance themselves from those who committed international crimes or gross human rights abuses. Third, ex-combatants, and especially the perpetrators among them, may want the chance to apologize or show contrition in order to ease their reintegration back into communities they had victimized. As a former combatant in Sierra Leone explained, the truth "will help families and victims forgive us."[93]

Still, ex-combatant perpetrators may be unwilling to testify in truth commissions for fear that such information could lead to their own prosecution or that of their comrades or commanders. As one Liberian ex-combatant put it, "If I committed a crime, I will not go testify to the TRC because this government will hand me over to a war crimes court."[94] Such fears are magnified when a truth commission operates concurrently with internationalized tribunals (especially when there is insufficient outreach to clarify how the two bodies will share information). Ex-combatants also may fear that if they confess their crimes, it will make their communities more afraid or more vengeful, and actually inhibit their reintegration.

### BENEFITS FOR TRUTH COMMISSIONS: INFORMATION SHARING

Truth commissions can benefit enormously from former combatants telling the truth about international crimes and gross human rights abuses that they perpetrated or witnessed. Such testimony can help locate victims' remains, identify beneficiaries for reparations, prompt security sector reforms, and construct more honest accounts of the past. In fact, a major weakness of many truth commissions is their overreliance on victim statements—for the obvious reason that perpetrators are reluctant to come forward even when promised amnesty. Most noncombatant victims simply do not possess useful information about military orders, command structures, and the larger patterns and practices of conflict. Such information can only come from combatants or former combatants willing to provide it.

The South African TRC illustrates the difficulties that truth commissions face in obtaining such information. The apartheid regime's military forces denied any role in human rights abuses and refused to provide information and documentation to the Commission.[95] Only 31 of the 256 members of the regime's security forces who applied for amnesty had served in the military.[96] Those few who did appear before the Amnesty Committee were not asked about their military history or lines of command.[97]

The main way to enhance coordination and cooperation between DDR programs and truth commissions is for them to share information.[98] DDR programs are generally reticent about sharing personal details of individual ex-combatants.[99] There is good reason for this: ex-combatants, especially those responsible for recruiting or using child soldiers, may fear their information could eventually wind up in the hands of prosecutors.[100] In Sierra Leone, for example, some ex-combatants believed that the national commission for DDR was sharing their photographs with the TRC and the Special Court.[101]

The more likely prospect for information sharing is for truth commissions to request, and DDR programs to provide, aggregated data on armed groups, such as their size, arms, movements, territory, recruitment methods, command structures, and the like. Such information would be particularly useful for truth commissions in documenting the patterns of armed conflict and accompanying human rights abuses.[102] Sharing such aggregated data would not create disincentives for ex-combatants to participate in DDR programs. Still, care would need to be taken to ensure that reliance on such information does not skew a truth commission's final report, say, in terms of underestimating the role played by women combatants and girl soldiers (as they are more likely to self-demobilize than go through DDR programs).

There appears to be very limited precedent for such information sharing. Sierra Leone's National Committee for Disarmament, Demobilisation and Reintegration (NCDDR) made three submissions to the TRC in 2003.[103] Those submissions comprised fairly superficial (and, at times, self-congratulatory) summaries of the DDR program accompanied by basic statistics on numbers disarmed and demobilized.[104] More interestingly, the NCDDR submitted short profiles of how the three main armed groups behaved during the demobilization process, along with summary demographics of all ex-combatants.[105] This sort of information, if fleshed out in considerably more detail, could have helped the TRC. Overall, though, the NCDDR conceived its workings as separate from and parallel to that of the TRC.[106] A more substantive form of cooperation could have involved targeting TRC hearings for local communities that were receiving sizable numbers of demobilized combatants.

## CONCLUSION

DDR programs and truth commissions generally work in isolation from one another. This is partly based on the assumption that ex-combatants would not cooperate with truth commissions and that closer links between the two mechanisms might dissuade combatants from disarming and demobilizing. In fact, ex-combatants have submitted statements and testified in several truth commissions. There were rumors in Sierra Leone that the DDR program was sharing photos with both the TRC and the Special Court, but it is unclear whether those rumors actually dissuaded any combatants from participating in the DDR program.

DDR programs should want more truth-telling, both for programmatic reasons and to give individual ex-combatants a broader range of reintegration options. Some ex-combatants may have an easier time reintegrating into their local communities if they have a forum where they can tell the truth, apologize to victims and communities, and explain their actions (including forced participation). This may persuade victims and communities to differentiate between ex-combatants who perpetrated gross human rights abuses and those who did not. East Timor provides an example of how this might work in practice (at least for low-level and [largely] forcibly conscripted ex-combatants). On the other hand, truth commissions should request aggregated data from DDR programs on armed groups—such as their size, arms, movements, territory, recruitment methods, command structures, and so on—to aid in documenting the larger causes and patterns of violence.

We want to stress that what we are proposing are "external" links between DDR programs and truth commissions. We would reject making more "internal" links, such as conditioning ex-combatants' DDR benefits on their cooperation with truth commissions. Such a scheme would raise a host of problems. For one, it would only work if a truth commission was collecting information at the same time that a DDR program was paying out benefits—an unlikely confluence of events. In addition, it would likely result in truth commissions receiving thousands of self-serving statements from ex-combatants. More fundamentally, DDR officials would probably oppose such conditionality for fear it would jeopardize DDR programs—either by discouraging combatants from disarming and demobilizing up front or by reducing the chances for successful reintegration down the road. Instead, our aim in this chapter has been to sketch some pragmatic and achievable ways that DDR and truth commissions could benefit from one another.

## NOTES

1   I deliberately avoid making the claim that truth commissions contribute to reconciliation because reconciliation is a deeply problematic term and because causation is difficult to prove.

2   Michael Ignatieff, "Articles of Faith," *Index on Censorship* 5 (1996): 113.

3   UN Commission on Human Rights (UNCHR), "Study on the Right to the Truth, Report of the Office of the United Nations High Commissioner for Human Rights, 8 February 2006," E/CN.4/2006/91, paras. 15, 16.

4   See Yasmin Naqvi, "The Right to the Truth in International Law: Fact or Fiction?" *International Review of the Red Cross* 88, no. 862 (June 2006): 245–73; and Mark Freeman, *Truth Commissions and Procedural Fairness* (Cambridge: Cambridge University Press, 2006), 6–9. See also Juan E. Mendez, "The Human Right to Truth: Lessons Learned from Latin American Experiences with Truth Telling," in *Telling the Truths: Truth Telling and Peace Building in Post-Conflict Societies*, ed. Tristan Anne Borer (Notre Dame: University of Notre Dame Press, 2006), 115–50.

5   United Nations, "Updated Set of Principles for the Protection and Promotion of Human Rights Through Action to Combat Impunity," February 8, 2005, E/CN.4/2005/102/Add.1, Principle 2. The UN Principles on reparations for victims of gross human rights violations sets forth that reparations includes "[v]erification of the facts and full and *public* disclosure of the truth" (emphasis added). United Nations, "Basic Principles and Guidelines on the Right to a Remedy and Reparation for Victims of Gross Violations of International Human Rights Law and Serious Violations of International Humanitarian Law," December 16, 2005, A/Res/60/147, 20(b).

6   UNCHR, "Right to the Truth," para. 58.

7   Ibid., para. 39.

8   Ibid., paras. 57, 58, 60.

9   See, e.g., Protocol Additional to the Geneva Conventions of 12 August 1949, and relating to the Protection of Victims of International Armed Conflicts (Protocol I), 8 June 1977, arts. 32 and 33.

10  UNHCR, "Right to the Truth," para. 7.

11  Ibid., para. 16 and n. 28.

12  See, e.g., Thomas Harlacher, et al., *Traditional Ways of Coping in Acholi: Cultural Provisions for Reconciliation and Healing from War* (Kampala: Caritas Gulu Archdiocese, 2006); Luc

Huyse and Mark Salter, eds., *Traditional Justice and Reconciliation after Violence: Learning from African Experiences* (Stockholm: International Institute for Democracy and Electoral Assistance [IDEA], 2008); Sally Falk Moore, "Treating Law as Knowledge: Telling Colonial Officers What to Say to Africans About Running 'Their Own' Native Courts," *Law and Society Review*, vol. 42 (1992), 42.

13    The ur-text on truth commissions is Priscilla Hayner, *Unspeakable Truths: Confronting State Terror and Atrocity* (New York: Routledge, 2001). Mark Freeman has usefully updated and refined Hayner's definition of truth commissions. See Freeman, *Truth Commissions and Procedural Fairness*, 12–22. There is now an enormous literature on truth commissions. See, generally, Teresa Godwin Phelps, *Shattered Voices: Language, Violence, and the Work of Truth Commissions* (Philadelphia: University of Pennsylvania Press, 2004); and Robert I. Rotberg and Dennis Thompson, eds., *Truth v. Justice: The Morality of Truth Commissions* (Princeton: Princeton University Press, 2000).

14    The South African TRC was best known for its exchange of amnesty for truth.

15    Truth commissions are also starting to be used in nonconflict and non-transitional settings, though this is still the exception. The two most recent examples are the truth commissions in Greensboro, North Carolina, and Canada. See, e.g., Lisa Magarrell and Joya Wesley, *Learning from Greensboro: Truth and Reconciliation in the United States* (Philadelphia: University of Pennsylvania Press, 2008).

16    South African Truth and Reconciliation Commission, *South African Truth and Reconciliation Commission: Final Report*, vol. 1, ch. 5, paras. 29–45. As Deborah Posel rightly observed, this schema misleadingly suggests that the "notions" are mutually exclusive and can be pursued separately without fear of contradiction. Deborah Posel, "The TRC Report: What Kind of History? What Kind of Truth?" in *Commissioning the Past: Understanding South Africa's Truth and Reconciliation Commission*, ed. Deborah Posel and Graeme Simpson (Johannesburg: University of the Witwatersrand Press, 2001), 155–56.

17    Sierra Leone Truth and Reconciliation Commission, *Sierra Leone Truth and Reconciliation Commission Final Report*, vol. 1, chap. 3, para. 21.

18    Eduardo Gonzalez Cueva, "The Peruvian Truth and Reconciliation Commission and the Challenge of Impunity," in *Transitional Justice in the Twenty-First Century*, ed. Naomi Roht-Arriaza and Javier Mariezcurrena (Cambridge: Cambridge University Press, 2006), 79–80.

19    Richard Wilson critiqued the South African TRC for its bureaucratic production of positivistic truth. Richard A. Wilson, *The Politics of Truth and Reconciliation in South Africa: Legitimizing the Post-Apartheid State* (Cambridge: Cambridge University Press, 2001), 34.

20    See, e.g., Tim Kelsall, "Truth, Lies, Ritual: Preliminary Reflections on the Truth and Reconciliation Commission in Sierra Leone," *Human Rights Quarterly* 27 (2005): 361–91, esp. 371–72; and Rosalind Shaw, "Linking Justice with Reintegration? Ex-Combatants and the Sierra Leone Experiment," in *Localizing Transitional Justice: Interventions and Priorities After*

*Mass Violence*, ed. Rosalind Shaw and Lars Waldorf (Palo Alto: Stanford University Press, forthcoming).

21 Leigh Payne, *Unsettling Accounts: Neither Truth Nor Reconciliation in Confessions of State Violence* (Durham, NC: Duke University Press, 2008), 2.

22 See Wilson, *The Politics of Truth and Reconciliation in South Africa*, 13–17.

23 Rosalind Shaw, "Memory Frictions: Localizing the Truth and Reconciliation Commission in Sierra Leone," *International Journal of Transitional Justice* 1, no. 2 (2007): 202.

24 One study found no significant correlation between participation in the South African TRC and psychiatric health or attitudes of forgiveness. Debra Kaminer, et al., "The Truth and Reconciliation Commission in South Africa: Relation to the Psychiatric Status and Forgiveness among Survivors of Human Rights Abuses," *British Journal of Psychiatry* (2001), 373-377.

25 Polls showed that the South African TRC had worsened relations between blacks and whites. Hayner, *Unspeakable Truths*, 156. Richard Wilson found that the South African TRC had little impact in reducing vengeance in black urban townships. Wilson, *The Politics of Truth and Reconciliation in South Africa*, 227. By contrast, Paul Gibson found that the TRC had a long-term positive impact on reconciliation. James L. Gibson, *Overcoming Apartheid: Can Truth Reconcile a Divided Nation?* (New York: Russell Sage Foundation: 2004), chap. 4.

26 Kelsall, "Truth, Lies, Ritual," 363.

27 Payne, *Unsettling Accounts*, 3.

28 See, e.g., Rosalind Shaw, "Rethinking Truth and Reconciliation Commissions: Lessons from Sierra Leone" (Washington, D.C.: United States Institute of Peace, February 2005), 12; Kimberly Theidon, "Intimate Enemies: Toward a Social Psychology of Reconciliation," in *The Psychology of Resolving Global Conflicts*, vol. 2, ed. Mari Fitzduff and Chris E. Stout (London: Praeger Security International, 2005); Peter Uvin, *Ex-combatants in Burundi: Why They Joined, Why They Left, How They Fared* (Washington, DC: The World Bank Multi-Country Demobilization and Reintegration Program, October 2007); and Lars Waldorf, "Transitional Justice and DDR in Post-Genocide Rwanda" (New York: International Center for Transitional Justice, 2009).

29 Shaw, "Linking Justice with Reintegration?" in *Localizing Transitional Justice*.

30 Kelsall, "Truth, Lies, Ritual," 385; and Mohammed Gibril Sesay and Mohamed Suma, "DDR and Transitional Justice in Sierra Leone" (New York: International Center for Transitional Justice, 2009), 56.

31 Shaw, "Memory Frictions," 207. Kimberly Theidon's research in Peru has yielded similar findings. See, e.g., Theidon, "Intimate Enemies," 220.

32 Office of the United Nations High Commissioner for Human Rights (OHCHR), "Rule-of-Law Tools for Post-Conflict States: Truth Commissions," HR/PUB/06/1 (2006), 2. The High Commissioner's report further observes that "Reconciliation is usually a very long

and slow process, and the work of a truth commission may be only a part of what is required." Ibid. Priscilla Hayner authored this document.

33   Ibid., 3–6.

34   Post-Conflict Reintegration Initiatives for Development (PRIDE) and ICTJ, "Ex-Combatant Views of the Truth and Reconciliation Commission," September 12, 2002, 6, http://www.ictj.org/images/content/0/9/090.pdf.

35   This is consistent with James Gibson's finding that "Generally, whites are displeased with the TRC; blacks are relatively happy with its performance." James L. Gibson, "The Truth about Truth and Reconciliation in South Africa," *International Political Science Review* 26, no. 4 (2006), 345.

36   Sasha Gear, "Wishing Us Away: Challenges Facing Ex-Combatants in the 'New' South Africa" (Johannesburg: Centre for the Study of Violence and Reconciliation, 2002), http://www.csvr.org.za/wits/papers/papvtp8a.htm.

37   Ibid.

38   Ibid.

39   Hugo van der Merwe and Guy Lamb, "DDR and TJ in South Africa: Lessons Learned" (New York: International Center for Transitional Justice, 2009), 30.

40   Ibid., 48.

41   Gear, "Wishing Us Away"; Van der Merwe and Lamb, "DDR and TJ in South Africa," 53.

42   Gear, "Wishing Us Away."

43   PRIDE and ICTJ, "Ex-Combatant Views of the Truth and Reconciliation Commission," 6.

44   Ibid., 7

45   Ibid., 8.

46   Ibid., 13.

47   Ibid., 5.

48   Richard Conibere et al., "Statistical Appendix to the Report of the Truth and Reconciliation Commission of Sierra Leone," Report by the Benetech Human Rights Data Analysis Group, October 2004, http://www.trcsierraleone.org/pdf/APPENDICES/Appendix%201 %20-%20Statistical%20Report.pdf. However, some "ex-combatants explained that their ability to testify against their commanders is limited by their continuing lack of economic independence. Several participants urged the TRC to recommend job-creation programs that would liberate ex-combatants to speak out against their leaders in their communities. . . . " PRIDE and ICTJ, "Ex-Combatant Views of the Truth and Reconciliation Commission," 8–9.

49   Shaw, "Linking Justice with Reintegration?" in *Localizing Transitional Justice.*

50   See, e.g., Shaw, "Linking Justice with Reintegration?" in *Localizing Transitional Justice*; and Susan Shepler, "The Rites of the Child: Global Discourses of Youth and Reintegrating Child Soldiers in Sierra Leone," *Journal of Human Rights*, vol. 4 (2005) 197-211.

51   PRIDE and ICTJ, "Ex-Combatant Views of the Truth and Reconciliation Commission,"
     17.

52   Ibid., 29. See Shaw, "Linking Justice with Reintegration?" in *Localizing Transitional Justice.*

53   PRIDE and ICTJ, "Ex-Combatant Views of the Truth and Reconciliation Commission,"
     17.

54   Kelsall, "Truth, Lies, Ritual," 381; and Shaw, "Linking Justice with Reintegration?" in
     *Localizing Transitional Justice.*

55   Kelsall, "Truth, Lies, Ritual," 386. Kelsall reported that only two of the eight ex-combatant
     perpetrators admitted any involvement in atrocities, but they provided few details. The
     remaining six, including the commander, denied even witnessing atrocities. Audience
     members expressed disbelief, unhappiness, and occasional outrage with those testimo-
     nies. Ibid., 371-373, 377-378.

56   Shaw, "Linking Justice with Reintegration?" in *Localizing Transitional Justice.*

57   See Piers Pigou, "The Community Reconciliation Process of the Commission for Recep-
     tion, Truth and Reconciliation" (United Nations Development Programme Timor-Leste,
     2004), 10, 79.

58   The CAVR found that these militias had committed approximately 70 percent of the
     documented property and economic violations. Commission for Reception, Truth and
     Reconciliation in East Timor (CAVR), *Chega! [Enough!]: Final Report* (2005), 6.3.3, para.
     125.

59   United Nations Transitional Administration in East Timor (UNTAET), Reg. No. 2001/10
     "On the Establishment of a Commission for Reception, Truth and Reconciliation in East
     Timor," UNTAET/REG/2001/10 (July 13, 2001), sched. 1.

60   UNTAET set up a dual system to ensure accountability for the political violence com-
     mitted from 1974 to 1999: a mixed national-international tribunal (the SPSC) to prosecute
     "serious crimes" and a truth and reconciliation commission (CAVR) to hear less serious
     crimes. Serious crimes were defined as genocide, crimes against humanity, war crimes,
     murder, attempted murder, torture, and sexual offenses. UNTAET, Reg. No 2000/15 "On
     the Establishment of Panels with Exclusive Jurisdiction over Serious Criminal Offences,"
     UNTAET/REG/2000/15 (June 6, 2000), sec. 1.3. Less serious crimes were described in
     the UNTAET regulations establishing the CAVR. UNTAET, Reg. No. 2001/10, sched. 1.
     When it closed in May 2005, the SPSC had tried only 87 of 391 indicted suspects, as the
     vast majority were located outside the court's jurisdiction in West Timor and Indonesia.
     Caitlin Reiger, "Hybrid Attempts at Accountability for Serious Crimes in Timor Leste,"
     in *Transitional Justice in the Twenty-First Century*, 151. For critiques of the SPSC, see, e.g.,
     Reiger, "Hybrid Attempts at Accountability," 143–70; Megan Hirst and Howard Varney,
     *Justice Abandoned? An Account of the Serious Crimes Process in East Timor* (New York: Inter-
     national Center for Transitional Justice, 2005); and David Cohen, "Seeking Justice on the
     Cheap: Is the East Timor Tribunal Really a Model for the Future?" *AsiaPacific Issues* 61

(Honolulu: East-West Center, 2002).

61 The CAVR and Benetech's Human Rights Data Analysis Group estimated 102,800 civilian deaths from conflict in the period from 1974 to 1999, with most occurring in the late 1970s and 1980s. Commission for Reception, Truth and Reconciliation in East Timor (CAVR), "Conflict-Related Deaths in Timor-Leste 1974–1999: The Findings of the CAVR Report Chega!" http://www.cavr-timorleste.org/updateFiles/english/ CONFLICT-RELATED%20DEATHS.pdf. They attributed approximately 18,600 of those deaths to killings or disappearances. A comparatively small number of conflict-related deaths—from 1,200 to 1,500—occurred during the 1999 violence. The 1999 violence was marked by the widespread and systematic forced displacement of approximately 400,000 people and the destruction of about 70 percent of the country's buildings. Megan Hirst, "Too Much Friendship, Too Little Truth: Monitoring Report on the Commission of Truth and Friendship in Indonesia and Timor-Leste" (New York: International Center for Transitional Justice, January 2008), 6.

62 In some cases, the community pressured perpetrators into making those requests. Judicial System Monitoring Programme (JSMP), "Unfulfilled Expectations: Community Views on CAVR's Community Reconciliation Process" (JSMP, 2004), 17.

63 Pigou, "The Community Reconciliation Process," 50, 76–78.

64 The statement had to provide a "full" description of their actions and its association to Timor-Leste's political conflicts as well as "a renunciation of the use of violence to achieve political objectives." UNTAET, Reg. No. 2001/10, sec. 23.1. See Pigou, "The Community Reconciliation Process," 50 (describing as "particularly problematic" the requirement that deponents disclose the names of accomplices or persons with command responsibility). Deponents also had to give informed consent that the Office of General Prosecutor would review their statements and could use the contents against them in future prosecutions. UNTAET, Reg. No. 2001/10, sec. 23.3.

65 CAVR, *Chega!* pt. 9.4.1. In addition, the CAVR collected 7,927 statements from victims, held fifty-two public hearings for victims, and conducted fifty-two community mapping exercises. Patrick Burgess, "A New Approach to Restorative Justice—East Timor's Community Reconciliation Processes," in *Transitional Justice in the Twenty-First Century*, 197.

66 For descriptions of these hearings, see, e.g., Burgess, "A New Approach to Restorative Justice," 188–93; and Pigou, "The Community Reconciliation Process," 29-31, 64-75.

67 UNTAET, Reg. No. 2001/10, sec. 27.8. The acts of reconciliation could include "community service; reparation; public apology; and/or other act[s] of contrition." Ibid., sec. 27.7. The Agreements received legal imprimatur from the formal justice system: district courts registered the Agreements, thereby making them court orders. Ibid., sec. 28.2. Once a deponent fully complied with the Agreement's obligations, he received immunity from criminal and civil liability for his confessed actions. Ibid., sec. 32.1.

68   Ibid., secs. 32.1, 32.2.

69   Pigou, "The Community Reconciliation Process," 73.

70   See ibid., 81; JSMP, "Unfulfilled Expectations," 11; and Zifcak, *Restorative Justice in East Timor*, 21.

71   Pigou, "The Community Reconciliation Process," 67.

72   Pigou, "The Community Reconciliation Process," 66; see Spencer Zifcak, "Restorative Justice in Timor-Leste: The Truth and Reconciliation Commission," *Development Bulletin* (October 2005): 54. Kelsall and Shaw made similar observations about local TRC hearings in Sierra Leone. Kelsall, "Truth, Lies, Ritual," 379-380; and Shaw, "Linking Justice with Reintegration?" in *Localizing Transitional Justice*.

73   Pigou, "The Community Reconciliation Process," 81. Pigou discusses the case of a female ex-militia member (a local treasurer). Ibid., 77–78.

74   JSMP, "Unfulfilled Expectations," 12.

75   The political leadership of the newly independent, but devastated and impoverished, Timor-Leste sought diplomatic rapprochement with its economically and militarily powerful neighbor.

76   Commission for Truth and Friendship (CTF), "Per Memoriam Ad Spem: The Final Report of the Commission of Truth and Friendship" (March 31, 2008), i.

77   Megan Hirst, "An Unfinished Truth: An Analysis of the Commission of Truth and Friendship's Final Report on the 1999 Atrocities in East Timor" (New York: International Center for Transitional Justice, March 2009), 14.

78   Hirst, "Too Much Friendship," 28.

79   Ibid., 34.

80   Some saw it primarily as publicity for the Commission. Hirst, "Too Much Friendship," 24.

81   Ibid., 31–32. This was not just due to the Commissioners' poor skills, insufficient preparation, and perhaps political biases. It also resulted from the institutional design of the hearings. Ibid.

82   Ibid., 28–31.

83   Ibid., 28.

84   Ibid., 33. He subsequently requested a closed hearing, where he reportedly provided useful information. Ibid.

85   See Hirst, "Too Much Friendship," 14–23.

86   See Hirst, "An Unfinished Truth," 15–17.

87   Ibid., 17–19.

88   Ibid., 21.

89   United Nations, *Operational Guide to the IDDRS*, 2.30, 45.

90   For example, the World Bank's Multi-Country Demobilization and Reintegration Program commissioned independent studies on the motivations of ex-combatants

in Burundi and foreign combatants in the eastern Democratic Republic of Congo. See Uvin, "Ex-combatants in Burundi"; and Hans Romkema, "Opportunities and Constraints for the Disarmament and Repatriation of Foreign Armed Groups in the Democratic Republic of Congo" (Washington, DC: The World Bank Multi-Country Demobilization and Reintegration Program, June 2007).

91　United Nations Department of Peacekeeping Operations (DPKO), *Integrated Disarmament, Demobilization and Reintegration Standards (IDDRS)* (New York: DPKO, 2006), sec. 4.30, 7–8.

92　PRIDE and ICTJ, "Ex-Combatant Views of the Truth and Reconciliation Commission," 2.

93　Ibid., 12.

94　Quoted in Thomas Jaye, "DDR and Transitional Justice in Liberia" (New York: International Center for Transitional Justice, 2009), 36.

95　Van der Merwe & Lamb, "DDR and TJ in South Africa," 46. The Commission decided not to exercise its search and seizure powers. Ibid.

96　Ibid., 46. By contrast, nearly 1,000 amnesty applications came from ex-combatants affiliated with the ANC. Ibid.

97　Ibid., 30.

98　Realistically, though, any information sharing is more likely to be one-way than reciprocal, simply because DDR programs are usually winding down as truth commissions get started.

99　For example, Rwanda's demobilization commission refused to share information with national and international prosecutors. See Waldorf, "Transitional Justice and DDR in Post-Genocide Rwanda."

100　Interestingly, prosecutors may not find information from DDR all that useful. See Eric A. Witte, "Beyond 'Peace vs. Justice': Understanding the Relationship Between DDR Programs and the Prosecution of International Crimes," in this volume.

101　Shaw, "Linking Justice with Reintegration?" in *Localizing Transitional Justice*; Chris Coulter, "Reconciliation or Revenge: Narratives of Fear and Shame among Female Ex-combatants in Sierra Leone" (Uppsala: Department of Cultural Anthropology and Ethnology, 2006).

102　Roger Duthie, "Transitional Justice and Social Reintegration," in Stockholm Initiative on Disarmament Demobilisation Reintegration, *Background Studies* (Stockholm: Ministry for Foreign Affairs, 2005), 78–79, 83. Less realistically, Duthie suggests that "[i]nformation gathered during a DDR process concerning the crimes committed by ex-combatants,then, could be provided to a truth commission without the names of the perpetrators." Ibid., 78. DDR programs rarely, if ever, collect information about international crimes and gross human rights abuses. Although the initial World Bank Multi-Country Demobilization and Reintegration Program recommended screening ex-combatants in the Democratic Republic of Congo for war crimes, this was never implemented. World Bank, "Greater Great Lakes Regional Strategy for Demobilization and Reintegration" (Washington, DC: World Bank, 2002), 20; and Waldorf, "Transitional Justice and DDR in Post-Genocide Rwanda."

103 National Committee for Disarmament, Demobilisation and Reintegration (NCDDR), "Submission from the CDDR to the Truth and Reconciliation Commission (TRC)" (March 2003); NCDDR, "Presentation on Militias and Armed Groups to the Truth and Reconciliation Commission (TRC)" (June 2003); and NCDDR, "Promoting Reconciliation and National Integration (Role of NCDDR) at the Truth and Reconciliation Commission" (August 4, 2003).

104 The statistics are contained in NCDDR, "Submission" and NCDDR, "Promoting Reconciliation."

105 NCDDR, "Presentation on Militias."

106 The NCDDR wrote:

The role of local actors and community organisations in explaining the function of the TRC as a societal healing mechanism is vital. NCDDR as part of its social reintegration mandate has worked very closely with such local actors, CBOs and communities at large to promote reconciliation between ex-combatants and the wider civilian communities. This is in line with efforts being pursued by the TRC to consolidate the ongoing peace process. (NCDDR, "Submission.")

# CHAPTER 4

# Establishing Links Between DDR and Reparations

*Pablo de Greiff*

## INTRODUCTION

It is obvious that one stands in new territory when the first task of a chapter's introduction is to explain the very choice of topics. What is the point of writing about disarmament, demobilization, and reintegration programs (DDR) and reparations programs in the same chapter? After all, aren't these very different programs serving different constituencies, and, most important, different ends? Isn't it the case that DDR programs are part of the tool boxes of peacemakers and peacebuilders and of development practitioners, whereas reparations programs can be located (when they are implemented at all) in that the world of justice or human rights practitioners? In actual fact, DDR programs have traditionally been designed and implemented in total isolation from transitional justice measures, of which reparations for victims is one kind. Indeed, it is only recently that the traditional approach that considers DDR as essentially a technical issue to be decided exclusively on the basis of military and security concerns with no regard for political or justice considerations has begun to be questioned. While there are now a few documents that argue for the introduction of justice-related considerations into DDR programming, these are still not just few in number but also tentative in nature.[1]

The incentives to try to bring the worlds of the peacemaker and of the justice and human rights promoter together are manifold. In the first place, it should be acknowledged that the international legal domain has changed in the recent past. The two most visible manifestations of this change are, perhaps, the (new) disposition to act in accordance with (an older) prohibition against granting amnesties for war crimes and crimes against humanity, and the not unrelated establishment of the International Criminal Court, which will now make the effects of any national amnesty for such crimes internationally moot, at least in theory. Peacemaking, then, now has to be practiced in a way that accommodates, at the very least, these broad justice concerns.[2]

Aside from these legal considerations, there has of course been an extended discussion within the peacebuilding and even the peacemaking arenas about the role of justice. The long negative versus positive peace debate is at least partly about this.[3] Since I have never taken this debate to be about whether negative peace is the best that can be hoped for, but rather about what we ought to be prepared to pay in order to get it, so that then other more substantive goals can be pursued, this means that there are incentives for thinking about the relationship between peace and justice internal to the sphere of peace itself (just as, of course, justice and human rights promoters have a reason to take peace considerations seriously, for war is one of the conditions least conducive to respect for justice and rights).

Although this chapter is written from the standpoint of someone who works in the field of transitional justice, its general aim is to construct an argument about the advisability of drawing some links—to be specified—between DDR and reparations programs, but not just because this is better from the standpoint of justice; the argument is that this may help DDR programs as well. From the standpoint of justice, the strong support in circles where DDR is discussed for the idea that each and every ex-combatant should be a beneficiary of a DDR program[4] jars with the absence of a similar commitment in either the national or international sphere to the idea that each and every victim of conflict should be made a beneficiary of a reparations program.[5] In fact, the international community provides much more support for peace and security issues than for justice issues.[6] As disturbing as this might be (again, from the standpoint of justice), ultimately, in this chapter I explore the possibility of deploying justice considerations not primarily in the interest of justice (a commitment to which cannot be taken for granted), but in the interest of peace. If the argument I make here is correct, the security-related aims of DDR are facilitated by establishing links between these programs and justice measures. This is part of what it means to think that there is an internal relationship between peace and justice.

Now, more specifically, the chapter will proceed as follows. In section 1, I will outline some of the fundamental challenges faced by DDR and reparations programs, respectively. In section 2, I will present conceptions of transitional justice and of DDR that facilitate seeing why implementing a DDR program but no reparations program is problematic. The argument will capitalize on and reinforce the trust-inducing potential of both DDR and transitional justice measures, which I explore in more detail in section 3. If the argument is correct, a successful linkage of these measures will strengthen both DDR and transitional justice programs. Focusing on DDR programs, one of the main advantages this linkage offers is that it would help them mitigate one of the fundamental criticisms to which they have been subject—namely, that they reward bad behavior. My hope is that by showing a potential synergy between a peace and security measure on the one hand and a justice measure on the other, the paper will contribute to a more sophisticated understanding of the complex relationship between peace and justice.

## THE MAIN CHALLENGES FACED BY DDR AND BY REPARATIONS PROGRAMS

Establishing DDR and reparations programs is an immense undertaking in any context, let alone precisely in the situations in which they most need to be established—namely, postconflict or post-authoritarian societies, which are marked by profound political divisions; weak, ineffective, or mistrusted institutions; and usually deep scarcity as well. The challenges are of various sorts, running the gamut from the design to the implementation stages. Within the domains of design and implementation, of course, multiple factors that generate difficulties are usually at play, and these also cover a broad spectrum that includes a lack of expertise, poor funding, weak political commitment, and severe coordination problems among the many actors that are (or ought to be) involved at each step of the way if these programs are to be set up and achieve their goals.

That both reparations and DDR initiatives have been marred by implementation problems there can be no doubt. In this chapter, however, I will not focus on these, for, in principle, implementation problems are avoidable. I will concentrate instead on design challenges, at least in part because they apply across the board, independently of contextual considerations, and are, in this sense, more revealing.[7]

### SOME CHALLENGES FACED BY REPARATIONS PROGRAMS

#### HOW TO DEFINE VICTIMS AND BENEFICIARIES

It makes sense to think about reparations, at least ideally, as a three-term relationship in which links are established between the members of a set defined as "victims" (at least for the purposes of the program) and the members of a set defined as "beneficiaries." In this relationship, the links take the form, precisely, of the benefits distributed by the program. The ideal behind a reparations program, then, is to make sure that at least every victim is a beneficiary; that is, that he or she receives something from the program.[8] If this helps to clarify, at least abstractly, how reparations are supposed to work, it also clarifies one of the fundamental challenges faced by reparations programs—namely, how to define "victims" and "beneficiaries," and how to craft an effective package of benefits.

The real challenge these days concerning the notion of victim, given developments in international law, is not so much with a choice of a general definition,[9] but with a fundamental question that all reparations programs face: how to select the rights whose violation will trigger access to benefits. In order for a reparations program to satisfy the ideal of making sure that every victim is a beneficiary, it would have to extend benefits to the victims of the same broad range of violations that may have taken place during the conflict or repression.[10] Now, no program has achieved this type of total comprehensiveness. Most programs have actually provided reparations for a rather limited and traditional list of rights violations, concentrating heavily on the more fundamental civil and political rights, leaving the violations of other rights largely unrepaired.[11]

While it makes sense, particularly under conditions of scarcity, to concentrate on what are perceived to be the worst forms of abuse, it remains true that no program to date has worried about articulating the principles behind why it chooses to provide benefits for the violations of some rights and not others. One of the predictable consequences of this omission is that violations that affect mainly or predominantly marginalized groups have rarely led to reparations benefits. This has had a nefarious effect on the way that women, for example, have been dealt with by reparations programs.[12] The mere demand that those in charge of designing reparations programs articulate the grounds on which they choose the catalogue of violations that the programs will provide benefits for will have a salutary effect.

Rather than offering a solution to this challenge, I am interested here in highlighting this as one of the crucial challenges that reparations programs always face. In situations of limited resources, choosing a very extensive list of rights violations will inevitably lead to the dilution of the benefits. On the other hand, choosing a very narrow list will leave out of consideration entire categories of deserving victims, which means not just that important claims to justice will be left unaddressed by the program—making it less effective than it could be—but also, since people tend to persist in their struggles for justice, that the issue of reparations will remain a contested one on the political agenda.

## HOW TO DEFINE THE BENEFITS TO BE DISTRIBUTED BY THE PROGRAM

The term "reparations" in international law is a broad notion closely related to the concept of "legal remedy," and therefore includes measures of restitution, compensation, rehabilitation, satisfaction, and guarantees of nonrepetition.[13] No reparations program to date has assumed the responsibility for undertaking measures of all these kinds. For purposes of simplicity, in the domain of the design of reparations programs more narrowly conceived, the measures that programs typically distribute can be organized around two fundamental distinctions, one between material and symbolic reparations, and the other between the individual and the collective distribution of either kind. Material and symbolic reparations can take different forms. Material reparations may assume the form of compensation; that is, of payments either in cash or negotiable instruments, or of service packages, which may in turn include provisions for education, health, housing, and so on. Symbolic reparations may include, for instance, official apologies, the change of names of public spaces, the establishment of days of commemoration, the creation of museums and parks dedicated to the memory of victims, rehabilitation measures, such as restoring the good name of victims, and so on. These symbolic measures would fall under the category of "satisfaction" used in the "Basic Principles."

The combination of different kinds of benefits is what the term "complexity" seeks to capture. A reparations program is more complex if it distributes benefits of more distinct types, and in more distinct ways, than its alternatives. There are at least two fundamental reasons for crafting complex reparations programs that combine measures of different kinds. The first has to do with the maximization of resources; programs that combine a variety of benefit types, ranging from the material to the symbolic, and each distributed both individually and collectively, may cover a larger portion of the universe of victims than programs that concentrate on the distribution of material benefits alone, and thus make the program more complete. Since victims of different categories of violations need not receive exactly the same kinds of benefits, having a broader variety of benefits makes this task feasible. Just as important, this broader variety of benefits allows for a better response to the fact that a particular violation can generate harms of different types, and having a range of reparatory measures makes it more likely that these harms can, to some degree, be redressed.

Reparations programs, then, can range from the very simple—that is, from programs that behave as mere compensation procedures, distributing money alone—to the highly complex, which distribute monetary compensation but also health care, educational and housing support, and so forth, in addition to both individual and collective symbolic measures. In general, since there are certain things that money cannot buy (and there are certain things for which there is no money), complexity brings with it the possibility of providing benefits to a larger number of victims[14] and of targeting benefits flexibly so as to respond to a variety of victims' needs. All other things being equal, then, complexity is a desirable characteristic in a reparations program. Of course, in most cases not all things remain equal. There are some costs to increased complexity that may make it undesirable beyond a certain threshold.

Now, it is unlikely that complexity, in the sense of the distribution of a variety of types of benefits, will be effective on its own. The types of benefits, ideally, must reinforce one another, making a coherent whole, giving the program "internal coherence."[15] Thus, a packet of mutually reinforcing benefits is more likely to satisfy victims than a random assortment of goods. Deliberate planning about the interrelationships between the different types of benefits is called for.

### HOW TO DEFINE THE GOALS OF THE PROGRAM

In isolated civil cases of reparations before courts, the fundamental aim of the proceedings is quite clear: to make each victim whole; that is, to the extent possible, to return him or her to the status quo ante, to the situation the person was in before his or her rights were violated. This is done, to the extent possible, by providing compensation in proportion to the harm suffered—that is, technically, by satisfying the criterion of *restitutio in integrum*. This is an unimpeachable criterion for the individual case, for its main motivation is, on the side of the victim, to neutralize as far as possible the consequences of the violation suffered, and, on the side of the violator, to prevent him or her from enjoying the benefits of crime.

The problem, however, is that there is no massive reparations program that has even approached the satisfaction of this criterion. Typically, the compensation victims receive by way of reparations programs is only a fraction of what the harm caused by the rights violations (for example, disappearance, extrajudicial execution, illegal detention—in general, severe violations of the right to freedom and against bodily harm) would suggest they should receive.

This generates at least two challenges. First, given that the judicial criterion of compensation in proportion to harm is both perfectly familiar from its application both in national and regional courts as well as intuitively attractive, victims' expectations are set around this notion. How to manage these expectations by reparations bodies that in all likelihood cannot meet this criterion of justice is a serious challenge. The second, related problem is how to define the aim(s) of the program in the face of the impossibility of satisfying the criterion of justice around which the point of reparations, in general, has traditionally been conceived. If reparations programs cannot make victims whole, what are they trying to do? Are they the same thing as victims' assistance programs? Is the frequent move on the part of governments faced by reparations claims—namely, to argue that since reparations are too expensive they would rather either do development or do reparations by means of development programs—a legitimate one? To these questions we must certainly return. To anticipate, however, the mediate aims of a reparations program, arguably, are to provide recognition to victims and to foster a minimal sense of civic trust. These aims, which reparations programs can be thought to share with other transitional justice measures, partly explain why it is important for programs to be not merely internally coherent, in that they provide a variety of benefits that reinforce one another, but also *externally* coherent—that is, that they bear significant relationships with other justice initiatives, such as truth-telling, prosecutions, or institutional reform.

## SOME CHALLENGES FACED BY DDR PROGRAMS

### HOW TO DEFINE THE BENEFICIARIES

Despite the fact that on the face of it the question of who the beneficiaries of a DDR program should be seems to have a ready answer—namely, "ex-combatants"—it is clear that this does not begin to settle the question, for even in the case of conventional conflicts with well-organized armies, the boundary between combatants and noncombatants is porous.[16] This is even more so in the case of nonconventional conflicts whose forces are characterized by a great deal of circulation between civilian and conflict-related activities of different kinds. Furthermore, however stable (or not) combat functions and positions may be, there is always a large contingent of people in support positions of different types without which combatants could not play their roles, and it is not clear that these people should be left out of DDR programming. Even if a security-oriented conception of DDR is adopted (about which more will be said), in contexts in which arms are easily available, leaving out of DDR programs large groups of people who have played important support positions, and, moreover, who likely circulated between combat and noncombat roles, does not serve security interests very effectively.

The challenge of defining who is eligible for benefits is multidimensional; that it is also pervasive and unavoidable does not mean that ready answers have been found. How "beneficiaries" are defined has an impact on the design of procedures for accessing the benefits, and it has a very significant impact on women and children. To illustrate, a good number of the earlier programs made benefits conditional on turning in weapons, in effect defining beneficiaries as those who bear arms. One can of course see why this was at some point considered an attractive alternative: being an incentive for disarming, it was thought to kill two birds with one stone. However, the simplicity of this approach failed to take into account not just that particularly among insurgent forces there are typically more combatants than arms, but that this would by definition exclude from benefits the bulk of women and children in support roles who had no arms to turn in.[17] Variations to this approach, such as the one tried in Sierra Leone, which required not turning in a weapon but demonstrating the ability to assemble and disassemble one, were rapidly met by the sudden availability in the streets of instructions on how to do that.[18] An entirely different approach—namely, to allow commanders of the forces to be demobilized to define the beneficiaries of the DDR programs by providing lists of names—has also encountered difficulties; particularly in the early stages of the process, when confidence levels are low, this procedure lends itself to easy manipulation, and has frequently led to massive overreporting—not surprisingly, however, overreporting of women and children, who are not well served by this procedure, either.[19]

In summary, then, all DDR programs face a challenge in defining the beneficiaries (as well as in establishing verification procedures) in a way that avoids both the exclusions that predictably come about as the result of narrow definitions and demanding procedures, as well as the over-inclusiveness (with the consequent increase of costs and the potential resentment and friction) that comes from loose definitions and lax procedures. Since two notoriously vulnerable groups, women and children, stand to lose more than others from mistakes, it is imperative to exercise utmost care in establishing these definitions and the attendant verification procedures.

### HOW TO DEFINE A SENSIBLE PACKET OF BENEFITS

We are used to speaking about DDR programs as if each one of them were a single program. In reality, of course, each DDR program is a complex set of (ideally integrated) initiatives, each one of them serving its own ends; thus, for example, reinsertion measures have specific ends that are distinct from the ends of reintegration programs. This alone explains part of the difficulties that characterize the effort to put together a sensible packet of benefits. Since the ends of both reinsertion and reintegration can be conceived differently, this only increases the complications.[20]

Even if there is consensus about what the proper way of understanding these goals might be, there is no single way of pursuing or achieving them. Even the relatively modest goal of reinsertion can be served in many ways. Regarding the more ambitious goal of social reintegration, this is more so. Considering that these decisions are made under conditions of scarcity, in contexts in which markets for both labor and goods are partially functioning at best, in which civil society has been disarticulated under the pressure of authoritarianism or conflict, targeting a universe of beneficiaries who in many cases have no skills other than those of waging war and little formal education, and that these decisions are often made by people—including donors—with little familiarity with the local context, it is not surprising that there are so many stories of poorly conceived benefit packages, in particular skills-training courses. Benefits drawn with the participation of recipients, and on the basis of labor market analyses, increase the likelihood that beneficiaries will not only be recipients but that they will actually benefit from the goods and services provided by the program.[21]

### HOW TO DEFINE THE GOALS OF THE PROGRAM

Once again, it may be surprising that programs that were traditionally conceived in narrow, technical terms have ended up encountering difficulties defining their goals. Why this has come about, however, is easier to understand by keeping in mind one inherent and one extrinsic feature of DDR programs. First, "reintegration," one of the dimensions (and goals) of these programs, is a broad notion, whose satisfaction potentially makes reference to and calls for myriad, sustained, and long-term interventions in a variety of areas. Second, as if this internal factor did not provide a sufficient incentive for the proliferation of aims to be pursued by DDR programs, in the early stages of a postconflict process DDR programming is frequently the only source of access to international funds; this has turned these programs into the means to attain the various goals pursued by the myriad projects that get their funding via DDR programs, including, in some cases, both services and infrastructure.[22]

Thus, all DDR programs face a challenge in defining the goals that can be legitimately pursued through initiatives of this sort. As usual, there are pitfalls to be avoided both on the side of conceptual parsimony as well as profligacy; among other problems, a very narrow understanding of DDR may strengthen the tendency to think about it as an exclusively technical issue to be addressed solely in military- or security-related terms, ignoring thereby the crucially important *political* dimensions of DDR and weakening the incentive for consultation and participation—which will undermine the sense of ownership over the programs, making them in turn more difficult to implement and less sustainable. On the other hand, conceptual profligacy in the definition of the goals of DDR can easily generate expectations—and not just on the part of beneficiaries—that are impossible to satisfy, weakening also the sustainability of the programs. Assigning DDR programs the responsibility to, say, make a significant contribution to economic development and then criticizing the program for failing to achieve this goal is an example of how conceptual profligacy with the goals of DDR programs may discredit them in general.

But the challenge of clearly defining and articulating the goals of DDR programs is important for reasons that go well beyond narrow matters of implementation. It is through the definition of the goals of the program that we can begin to answer the fundamental challenge that all DDR programs face—namely, the charge that these programs reward bad behavior. Particularly in contexts of deep economic scarcity and weak or uneven state presence, the establishment of programs to benefit ex-combatants has often led others to conclude that apparently the only way to get the attention of the state is to bear and use arms.[23]

## CONCEPTUALIZING DDR AND REPARATIONS

I have argued that one of the main challenges that both DDR and reparations programs face is to define the goals that can legitimately be sought through them. In this section, after offering an account of a holistic transitional justice policy and adopting an account of DDR, I argue that a proper conceptualization of these goals helps to explain why it makes sense to think about establishing links between the two types of programs. I will also defend the view that establishing these links helps DDR fend off the objection that it rewards "belligerents." The section begins with a brief account of a holistic conception of transitional justice and of a comparatively narrow, security-oriented conception of DDR. It then tries to show how even this narrow understanding creates a sufficiently rich conceptual overlap to warrant thinking about the relationship between reparations and DDR. Finally, it will show how establishing these links helps DDR programs meet one of the frequent objections raised against them.

### TRANSITIONAL JUSTICE

I think of reparations as one element of a holistic conception of transitional justice that includes as some of its other elements criminal prosecutions, truth-telling, and institutional reform. While this list need not be thought to exhaust the elements of a comprehensive transitional justice policy, what is important if this is going to be part of a holistic conception is that the list be more than a random assortment of measures—in other words, that the close relationship among its different elements be articulated. I will do so by means of two arguments.[24]

The first argument focuses on the relations of complementarity that the measures arguably have in practice. I will illustrate the point by reference to reparations measures. The general argument is that reparations in the absence of other transitional justice measures are more likely to be seen by victims as "compensatory" measures that lack the proper connections to justice, connections without which compensation can hardly be seen as *reparations*. A society that responds to norm breaking exclusively by compensating the victims for the costs that the norm breaching may have caused them is one that fails to understand that there are dimensions of corrective justice that go beyond the obligation to try to restore victims to their economic status quo ante. A good illustration of this unsatisfactorily narrow approach is that of the Japanese reaction to the euphemistically called "comfort women," the majority of whom have not accepted the benefits offered through a Japanese foundation established to compensate them, for the benefits not only come from private funds but are unaccompanied by an explicit recognition of fault from the Japanese government.[25] Similarly, and in the opposite direction, a society that responds to crime without redressing victims at all would fail to understand that when violations occur it is not just norms that are broken but lives as well.

Thus, to be more concrete, reparations in the absence of truth-telling can be seen by beneficiaries as the attempt, on the part of the state, to buy the silence or acquiescence of victims and their families, turning the benefits into "blood money." But the relation holds in the opposite direction as well: truth-telling in the absence of reparations can be seen by victims as an empty gesture, as cheap talk. The same bidirectional relationship links criminal justice and reparations: from the standpoint of victims, especially once a possible moment of satisfaction derived from the punishment of perpetrators has passed, the punishment of a few perpetrators without any effective effort to positively redress victims could be easily seen by victims as a form of more or less inconsequential revanchism. But reparations without criminal justice can easily be seen by victims as something akin to the payments of a crime insurance scheme, which does not necessarily involve the assumption of responsibility on the part of anyone, including the state. The same tight and bidirectional relationship may be observed between reparations and institutional reform, since a democratic reform that is not accompanied by any attempt to dignify citizens who were victimized can hardly be legitimate. By the same token, reparative benefits in the absence of reforms that diminish the probability of the repetition of violence are nothing more than payments whose utility and, again, legitimacy are questionable.

The second argument to explain the holistic dimension of a comprehensive transitional justice policy acknowledges that each of the measures that forms a part of such a policy—criminal prosecutions, truth-telling, reparations, and institutional reform (of which vetting is one modality[26])—has its own specific goals, but points out that they share two mediate goals:[27] it can be argued that the different elements of a comprehensive transitional justice policy are meant to provide recognition to victims and to foster civic trust. Very briefly, the various transitional measures can be interpreted as efforts to institutionalize the recognition of individuals as rights bearers. Criminal justice can be interpreted as an attempt to reestablish the equality of rights between the criminal and his or her victim, after the criminal severed that relationship with an act that suggested his superiority over the victim. Truth-telling provides recognition in ways that are perfectly familiar, and that are still probably best articulated by the old difference proposed by Thomas Nagel between knowledge and acknowledgment, when he argued that although truth commissions rarely disclose facts that were previously unknown, they still make an indispensable contribution in acknowledging these facts.[28] The acknowledgment is important precisely because it constitutes a form of recognizing the significance and value of persons—again, as individuals, as citizens, and as victims. Reparations are the material form of the recognition *owed* to fellow citizens whose fundamental rights have been violated, manifesting that the state has taken to heart the interests of those whose rights went previously unrecognized.[29] Finally, institutional reform is guided by the ideal of guaranteeing the conditions under which citizens can relate to one another and to the authorities as equals.

The other aim that, arguably, the different elements of transitional justice share is the promotion of trust among citizens and among them and their institutions.[30] The sense of trust at issue here is not the thick form of trust characteristic of relations between intimates, but rather a thin disposition between strangers that can be characterized initially as a nonhostile disposition that contrasts not just with its direct opposite but with one that puts a premium on surveillance and the threat of sanctions.

At the most general level, the point can be put in the following terms: Law both presupposes and catalyzes trust among individuals and trust between them and their institutions. It can help generate trust between citizens by stabilizing expectations and thus diminishing the risks of trusting others. Similarly, law helps generate trust in institutions (including the institutions of law themselves), among other ways by accumulating a record of reliably solving conflicts. But the accomplishment of these goals naturally presupposes the effectiveness of the law, and in a world of less than generalized spontaneous compliance this means that law, although rational, must also be coercive. And this coercive character at the limit entails criminal punishment.

Truth-telling can foster civic trust in different ways. Among those who were directly affected by the violence—whose trust is obviously particularly difficult to recover—we will concentrate here on those who are fearful that the past might repeat itself, whose confidence was shattered by experiences of violence and abuse. Their specific fear might be that the political identity of (some) citizens has been shaped around values that made the abuses possible. So, members of minority groups in different contexts fear that majorities have internalized values, dispositions, and attitudes that might lead to violence again. How can trust be fostered among citizens of whom some suspect that others still carry dispositions that, either due to their outright wickedness or to their weakness, made terror possible and are likely to make it possible again?

Truth-telling, remembering the past in public ways, can be regarded, precisely, as the beginning of the effort to satisfy the requirements of civic trust; we give those who worry about our political identity as well as those who worry about whether they can rely on people who may still be the carriers of dubious dispositions and attitudes reasons to participate in a common political project if we are willing to reflect upon the constitution of our identity and the character of our dispositions. An institutionalized effort to confront the past might be seen by those who were formerly on the receiving end of violence as a good faith effort to come clean, to understand long-term patterns of socialization, and, in this sense, to initiate a new political project.

Reparations foster civic trust by signaling for victims the seriousness of the state and of their fellow citizens in their efforts to reestablish relations of equality and respect. In the absence of reparations, victims will always have reasons to suspect that even if the other transitional mechanisms are applied with some degree of sincerity, the "new" democratic society is being constructed on their shoulders, ignoring their justified claims. By contrast, if even under conditions of scarcity funds are allocated for former victims, a strong message is sent to them and others about their (perhaps new) inclusion in the political community. Former victims of abuse are given a material manifestation of the fact that they are now living among a group of fellow citizens and under institutions that aspire to be trustworthy. Reparations, in summary, can be seen as a method to achieve one of the aims of a just state—namely, inclusiveness, in the sense that all citizens are equal participants in a common political project.

Finally, most post-transitional institutional reform is motivated not just by the aims of increasing the efficiency of state institutions—understanding efficiency simply in terms of quantifiable output—but by the richer goals of relegitimizing the state and of preventing the recurrence of violence. The achievement of these goals provides reasons to individuals for trusting one another and their institutions.

These two arguments, one centering on the relationships of complementarity between the different transitional justice measures, and the other focusing on the goals that the different measures arguably share, are part of the explanation of the holistic character of a transitional justice policy. My interest here, however, is not simply explanatory or conceptual, but practical. These arguments also provide a motivation to make sure that each of the measures is implemented in an externally coherent manner—that is, in a way that reinforces, precisely, the relationship between each of the measures and other initiatives that seek to provide recognition, and, for the purposes of this chapter, most relevantly, civic trust.

### DDR

The UN's recently completed *Integrated Disarmament, Demobilization and Reintegration Standards* (IDDRS) represents, perhaps, the most sophisticated understanding of DDR. One reason it is so sophisticated is that it certainly makes an effort to go well beyond the (excessively) narrow focus on disarmament and demobilization that has characterized if not the thinking, at least the practice of DDR for so long. As the document puts it, "Integrated DDR places great emphasis on the long-term humanitarian and developmental impact of sustainable reintegration processes and the effects these have in consolidating long-lasting peace and security."[31] While this is certainly a measure of great progress, the text is sufficiently ambiguous as to allow for different readings of what it really intends to say about the relationship between DDR and development. To claim that the *IDDRS* places emphasis on the developmental impact of reintegration is not the same thing as saying that development is one of the goals of, let alone the responsibilities it attributes to, DDR programs. To illustrate the ambiguity again, the text argues that DDR is "a process that helps to promote both security and development." However, the same sentence argues that DDR "is just one of several post-conflict recovery strategies" and that "it must work together with other comprehensive peace-building strategies including socio-economic recovery programmes...."[32] What DDR's contribution to (and responsibility for) development might be, exactly, the text does not make explicit. On a charitable reading of the text, one may argue that the contribution that it assigns to DDR is to promote the economic development not of society, generally, but of the program's own beneficiaries. This is plausible but (1) it would be slightly odd to talk about development in such a circumscribed manner,[33] and (2) it may clash with the document's injunctions against "turning [ex-combatants] into a privileged group within the community" and its explicit statement that DDR programs seek only to fulfill their "essential needs," which is not a big developmental aim.[34] It is in these more careful contexts where the *IDDRS* trims its sails and returns to what may be a less ambitious but nevertheless more defensible position that recognizes that "DDR is carried out primarily to improve security";[35] more boldly, that it is precisely because returning ex-combatants are potential "spoilers" of peace that we provide them benefits through DDR programs even though other war-affected groups may be larger,[36] and where it shifts the main responsibility for developmental tasks to the other, broader "post-conflict recovery strategies" (insisting, nevertheless, on the importance of coordinating these various programs).

This is not the place to engage in a detailed exegesis of the *IDDRS*, for that is not my point. In this chapter I explicitly adopt a narrower understanding of the goals of DDR (at least narrower than the widest but still plausible reading of the *IDDRS*). That is, I adopt an interpretation of the goals of DDR programs that is more focused on the security-enhancement aim of DDR. I do so not only because I think this is more realistic (and avoiding defeated expectations in a postconflict setting in which institutions have both a low level of credibility and a low capacity to deliver is crucial, in my opinion), but also because I do not want my argument to turn on nothing more than definitional fiat; obviously, the possibility of finding interesting overlaps between transitional justice measures in general and reparations in particular, on the one hand, and DDR programs, on the other, increases if one adopts an expansive understanding of DDR. But that would be uninteresting. I would rather take the hardest case, because if it can be shown that even a narrower understanding of DDR is one that relates in interesting and significant ways with transitional justice measures, then this will be even more so for the broader conceptions of DDR.

I will therefore concentrate here on a conception according to which, as the "Final Report of the Stockholm Initiative on DDR" (SIDDR) is not shy to recognize, "the primary aim of DDR is to contribute to a secure and stable environment in which the overall peace process and transition can be sustained."[37] This understanding of the basic goal of DDR programs is not indifferent at all to further developmental aims, but it explicitly takes DDR processes to be, at best, *enabling conditions*[38] rather than direct *causal contributions* to development. The way the SIDDR "Final Report" puts it dovetails with the *IDDRS* when the latter is at its most cautious; the point is not to go back to a conception of DDR that concentrates exclusively on disarmament and demobilization, but to argue that the more ambitious dimensions of reintegration should be carried out by means of *coordination with other programs* rather than being the responsibility and parts of the DDR program:

> The SIDDR, on the one hand, sets the boundaries of DDR programmes based on the goals of security and stability — and therefore does not encourage thinking that these programmes alone can achieve either a rapid or comprehensive transformation of societal structures. On the other hand, to the extent that the SIDDR promotes the idea that DDR programmes ought to be designed and implemented as part of a comprehensive peace-building framework, it provides an incentive to think about the many ways in which DDR programmes need to be linked with other interventions if they are to support the long-term goals of a larger peace process.[39]

## THE OVERLAP BETWEEN DDR AND TRANSITIONAL JUSTICE

So, now, why does this conceptual work matter? In a nutshell, this is the argument: It is significant that both DDR and transitional justice measures can be seen to be intended to promote trust. I have already sketched the ways in which transitional justice measures can be thought to have as one of their fundamental goals the promotion of civic trust, and, in particular, trust in institutions. The point is that even a narrow understanding of DDR programs attributes to them a confidence-building role. The aim of disarming and demobilizing is both to demonstrate and to cultivate confidence in the prospects of peace and a minimal sense of trust in one's partners in the process.

Of course, it could be argued that the objects of trust at issue for DDR and for transitional justice measures are not the same: DDR, it could be said, can reasonably be thought to foster trust initially in *partners* in a peace process, whereas transitional justice measures aspire to making a contribution to the trustworthiness of institutions, largely by reaffirming the importance of foundational *norms* and *values*. While the objection is generally valid, it must also be kept in mind that a norm-based account of trust suggests that trusting individuals is a function of certain convictions of the norms and values on which these individuals act; in other words, partners in peace processes trust one another only to the extent that they have reliable convictions that the other parties will have as one of their reasons for acting certain norms and values.[40]

## DDR AND REPARATIONS

Now, how does finding this functional and conceptual overlap between DDR programs and transitional justice measures help, concretely? Returning to one of the topics in the introduction to this chapter, my interest here, at least at first, is to deploy justice-related arguments in the interest of security. The general point is the following: If the primary goal of DDR programs is to enhance security by preventing the marginalization of potential spoilers of the peace process, then the goal is better achieved by means of processes that contribute to the reintegration of the ex-combatants. And the rub is that justice-enhancing measures may facilitate this process. Although it is difficult to generalize conclusively on the basis of a single case and a relatively small sample of participants in that case, evidence seems to support the case I am making here. A recent study of the DDR program in Sierra Leone suggests that the single most important factor in the reintegration of ex-combatants is the reputation of the unit to which the ex-combatants belonged: those who belonged to the units that allegedly perpetrated the greatest abuses have had a harder time reintegrating. This is true regardless of whether the individuals in question participated in the DDR programs or not.[41] The argument that I have offered here provides an explanation for these results: to the extent that successful reintegration is not simply a matter of the ex-combatants' disposition but *also* of the attitudes and reactions of the receiving communities, DDR programs that are completely devoid of any justice component are less likely to facilitate reintegration.[42] By contrast, DDR programs (in association with other initiatives) that provide to receiving communities, for example, some certainty that those whom they are expected to readmit are not the worst offenders, or that make a contribution to the clarification of the abuses through, say, creative ways of making information available for truth-telling purposes,[43] or that include safeguards against "recycling" human rights abusers by making them part of new or reformed security forces, may contribute to the reintegration of ex-combatants.[44]

Before closing this section, however, I would like to consider how this general argument plays itself out with respect to reparations, for, as I have said, one of the frequent charges that are brought against DDR programs is that while these programs distribute benefits to ex-combatants, victims, by contrast, receive nothing. In virtually all countries where DDR programs have ever been established, the charge has come up. In Sierra Leone, for example, a victim put the point as follows: "those who have ruined us are being given the chance to become better persons financially, academically and skills-wise."[45] In Rwanda, the chairman of the RDRC acknowledged that this disparity in the treatment of ex-combatants versus victims upsets some survivors who feel "you recompense killers but you forget the victims."[46] The basic point is the same: resistance on the part of receiving communities, particularly victims, may diminish if they are given reasons to think that they will also be attended to. DDR programs have taken this presumption on board, and hence the *IDDRS*, for example, emphasizes the importance of "balancing equity with security," of making sure that "reintegration support for ex-combatants is not...regarded as special treatment for ex-combatants, but rather as an investment in security for the *population as a whole*,"[47] and ultimately by arguing that "*all war-affected populations... should be given equal access to reintegration opportunities*."[48] But this is not enough; victims call for measures that not only improve their security to the extent that everyone's security improves, or for measures that benefit them alongside everyone else. After all, while it is true that under conflict or authoritarianism everyone suffers, the suffering of victims is special and calls for special recognition; the point is not mainly psychological, but normative. The fact that victims have their fundamental rights violated, and violated in particularly serious ways, must make some difference at the moment of redress, on pains of making the system of rights meaningless. Providing benefits to ex-combatants without attending to the claims of victims not only leaves victims at a comparative disadvantage but gives rise to new grievances, which may exacerbate their resistance against returning ex-combatants. By contrast, guaranteeing that the claims of victims will be addressed may diminish such resistance. This is the argument for establishing links between DDR and reparations programs.

## CONCLUDING CONSIDERATIONS

The point of the argument that links ought to be drawn between DDR and reparations programs is *not* that DDR and reparations programs should be folded into one, for despite the fact that both programs overlap around the notion of trust, it is still the case that their immediate goals differ. The urgent security needs that motivate DDR programs guide the design of such programs by considerations having to do, at least initially, with estimates of what is sufficient to avert the risks posed by potential spoilers. The considerations that should guide the design of reparations programs are, by contrast, related to an understanding of what justice requires in situations of massive human rights violations. Although this is not an argument against making some of the benefits distributed through DDR programs available to victims and to the community at large, the element of recognition that is part and parcel of reparations, and that makes them different from mere compensatory schemes, will typically require targeting victims for special treatment. This is part of what it means to give them recognition, and part of the reason that transitional institutions can give them to motivate their trust. So, rather than dissolving reparations programs into DDR programs, this is an argument for some type of coordination between them, for a particularly broad type of external coherence between programs that have heretofore never been thought of in relation to one another. Ultimately, because it is not just that these programs serve different constituencies and pursue different immediate aims, but also because they typically move in accordance with very different calendars, one way of putting the point is that what needs to be coordinated is not so much the programs but the commitments; although time after time victims have shown themselves reasonable enough to understand the importance of security and are willing to countenance the provision of benefits to those who may thwart a peace process, they need reasons to think that this does not amount to surrendering their claims to justice. Were they to be given assurances that this will not happen, these justice-based reasons may facilitate the achievement of security aims.

## NOTES

1    Perhaps the "Final Report of the Stockholm Initiative on DDR" [hereafter "SIDDR Report"] goes farther in this direction than any. See sec. 3.5 of the " SIDDR Report." In a more tentative vein, see Sarah Meek and Mark Malan, eds., "Identifying Lessons from DDR Experiences in Africa: Workshop Report," Institute for Security Studies, Monograph No. 106, October 2004, which talks about "the need to move towards a new DDR framework that is based on human rights," vii.

2    See Mark Freeman's chapter in this volume, "Amnesties and DDR Programs," which reviews recent developments regarding amnesties for massive human rights violations and their relevance for DDR.

3    See some of the papers in David Barash, ed., *Approaches to Peace* (Oxford: Oxford University Press, 1999).

4    See, e.g., the statement by the head of Rwanda's Demobilization and Reintegration Commission (RDRC), which is not atypical: "Our mission is to ensure that *all* ex combatants are socially and economically reintegrated in their communities...." See RDRC, "Demobilization and Reintegration" (n.d.), available on the MDRP's Web site at www.mdrp.org/rwanda.htm, 2

5    An asymmetry that can be observed from the fact that of the twenty-two countries with ongoing DDR programs in a recent global study, programs involving 1.25 million beneficiaries and the expenditure of more than $2 billion, only a few have discussed the possibility of establishing reparations programs, but none of these countries has implemented one. See Escola de Cultura de Pau (ECP), "Analysis of the Disarmament, Demobilisation and Reintegration Programs Existing in the World During 2006," Barcelona, March 2007 (hereafter ECP Analysis).

6    For example, in the eleven-year period from 1995 to 2005, of the US$2.686 billion in aid given to Rwanda by fifteen donors, only $111 million (4.1 percent) was allocated to transitional justice measures. In the same period, Guatemala received $2.143 billion, and allocated $140 million (6.5 percent) to transitional justice measures. For my purposes the figures are even more striking, for in the rubric of transitional justice measures the authors of the international aid paper include support for security sector reform, to which in fact roughly half of the total transitional justice budget in each country was devoted. See Stina Petersen, Ingrid Samset, and Vibeke Wang, "Aid to Transitional Justice in Rwanda and Guatemala 1995–2005," in *Building a Future on Peace and Justice: Studies on Transitional Justice, Peace and Development*, eds. Kai Ambos, Judith Large, and Marieke Wierda (Berlin: Springer, 2009), 441, 443, 449-450.

7    As will become obvious, some of the challenges are shared. I derive no special significance from this fact; these are some of the challenges inherent to the design of distributive procedures. My argument about the importance of establishing links between DDR

and reparations programs therefore does not rest on the observation that these programs face some common challenges.

8   This is nothing more than a heuristic; on the one hand, the ideal is indeed more demanding than this suggests, for reparations programs usually provide benefits to a set of people larger than the set of victims (think about family members who have not been the direct victims of the violations that trigger access to reparations benefits). On the other hand, however, programs usually fail to provide benefits to all victims (e.g., the many victims of violations of the type of rights that are frequently abused in situations of conflict or authoritarianism but that have never been triggers of reparations through a massive reparations program. In situations of conflict, rights to free association or speech are often violated, but no massive reparations program has sought to redress these kinds of abuses. There are also many people who are victims of the very violations that the program is supposed to provide benefits for who nevertheless never receive any). To use the vocabulary that the author developed for the Office of the UN High Commissioner for Human Rights (OHCHR), "Rule-of-Law Tools for Post-Conflict States: Reparations Programmes" (New York and Geneva: United Nations, 2008), the former is a problem of lack of "comprehensiveness" in the reparations program, the latter of "incompleteness."

9   For instance, the "Basic Principles and Guidelines on the Right to a Remedy and Reparation for Victims of Gross Violations of International Human Rights Law and Serious Violations of International Humanitarian Law" offers a general definition of "victims" that is likely to be adopted by most reparations programs in the near future:

Victims are persons who individually or collectively suffered harm, including physical or mental injury, emotional suffering, economic loss or substantial impairment of their fundamental rights, through acts or omissions that constitute gross violations of international human rights law, or serious violations of international humanitarian law. Where appropriate, and in accordance with domestic law, the term "victim" also includes the immediate family or dependants of the direct victim and persons who have suffered harm in intervening to assist victims in distress or to prevent victimization. A person shall be considered a victim regardless of whether the perpetrator of the violation is identified, apprehended, prosecuted, or convicted and regardless of the familial relationship between the perpetrator and the victim. A/RES/60/147, March 21, 2006, at 5 (hereafter "Basic Principles").

10   If it did that, the program would be "comprehensive" in the technical sense defined in the OHCHR, "Rule-of-Law Tools: Reparations."

11   For a review of the many types of rights violations that different reparations programs have left unaddressed, see Pablo de Greiff, "Addressing the Past: Reparations for Gross Human Rights Abuses," in *Civil War and the Rule of Law: Security, Development, Human Rights*, ed. Agnés Hurwits and Reyko Huang (Boulder: Lynne Rienner Publishers, 2007).

12  On this topic, see the introduction in Ruth Rubio-Marín, ed., *What Happened to the Women? Gender and Reparations for Human Rights Violations* (New York: Social Science Research Council, 2006).

13  See "Basic Principles."

14  And, particularly in the case of collective symbolic measures, such as public apologies and sites of memory, to non-victims as well.

15  See, e.g., OHCHR, "Rule-of-Law Tools: Reparations," sec. IV.

16  United Nations Department of Peacekeeping Operations (DPKO), *Integrated Disarmament, Demobilization and Reintegration Standards (IDDRS)* (New York: DPKO, 2006), module 2.30, sec. 5.1.

17  The following chart clearly shows that only exceptionally is there a close to one-to-one relationship between demobilized ex-combatants and recovered arms. So, if returning arms is chosen as a criterion of accessing the program, lots of ex-combatants will be left out.

*Weapons handed in per demobilised combatant in selected countries*

| COUNTRY | PEOPLE DEMOBILISED | WEAPONS HANDED IN | WEAPONS PER PERSON | YEARS |
|---|---|---|---|---|
| Afghanistan | 62,000 | 48,919 | 0.78 | 2003–06 |
| Angola | 97,115 | 33,000 | 0.34 | 2002–06 |
| Burundi | 21,769 | 26,295 | 1.2 | 2004–06 |
| Colombia | 31,761 | 18,051 | 0.57 | 2004–06 |
| Côte d'Ivoire | 981 | 110 | 0.11 | 2006 |
| Indonesia (Aceh) | 3,000 | 840 | 0.28 | 2005 |
| Liberia | 101,405 | 28,364 | 0.28 | 2005 |
| Republic Congo | 17,400 | 11,776 | 0.68 | 2000–06 |
| El Salvador (FMLN) | 11,000 | 10,200 | 0.93 | 1992 |
| Guatemala (URNG) | 3,000 | 1,824 | 0.61 | 1997 |
| **TOTAL** | **335,521** | **167,525** | **.49** | |

Source: ECP Analysis, 30.

18  See Jeremy Ginifer, "Reintegration of Ex-Combatants," in *Sierra Leone: Building the Road to Recovery*, ed. Sarah Meek et al. (Pretoria: Institute for Security Studies, 2003).

19  The *IDDRS* has come down in favor of tests to determine an individual's membership in an armed force or group, but adds that "[a]ll those who are found to be members of an

armed force or group, whether they were involved in active combat or in support roles (such as cooks, porters, messengers, administrators, sex slaves and 'war wives') shall be considered part of the armed force or group and therefore shall be included in the DDR programme." DPKO, *IDDRS*, 2.30, sec. 5.1, 2.

20  See, for example, the definitions of "reinsertion" and "reintegration" in DPKO, *IDDRS*:

Reinsertion is the assistance offered to ex-combatants during demobilization but prior to the longer-term process of reintegration. Reinsertion is a form of transitional assistance to help cover the basic needs of ex-combatants and their families and can include transitional safety allowances, food, clothes, shelter, medical services, short-term education, training, employment and tools. While reintegration is a long-term, continuous social and economic process of development, reinsertion is short-term material and/or financial assistance to meet immediate needs, and can last up to one year. Reintegration is the process by which ex-combatants acquire civilian status and gain sustainable employment and income. Reintegration is essentially a social and economic process with an open time-frame, primarily taking place in communities at the local level. It is part of the general development of a country and a national responsibility, and often necessitates long-term external assistance.

DPKO, *IDDRS*, 2.10, -. 5.

21  How to institutionalize the participation of civil society and other stakeholders in both reparations and DDR programs is another critical challenge. For reparations programs, see OHCHR, "Rule-of-Law Tools: Reparations," sec. IV; for DDR programs, see DPKO, *IDDRS*, 2.30 and 3.30.

22  "SIDDR Report," 10.

23  This is a challenge that these programs cannot afford not to meet, and therefore I will return to this issue below. The charges are an important aspect of the debates about DDR in Colombia at present.

24  See Pablo de Greiff, "Justice and Reparations," in *The Handbook of Reparations*, ed. Pablo de Greiff (New York: Oxford University Press, 2006), for an elaboration of these arguments.

25  See, e.g., Yoshiaki Yoshimi, *Comfort Women: Sexual Slavery in the Japanese Military During World War II* (New York: Columbia University Press, 2002); and Margaret Stetz and Bonnie C. Oh, eds., *Legacies of the Comfort Women of World War II* (New York: ME Sharpe, 2001).

26  I am following Alexander Mayer-Rieckh in thinking about vetting as a form of institutional reform, without rehearsing his argument. See Alexander Mayer-Rieckh, "On Preventing Abuse," in *Justice as Prevention: Vetting Public Employees in Transitional Societies*, ed. Alexander Mayer-Rieckh and Pablo de Greiff (New York: Social Science Research Council, 2007).

27 They also share two long-term goals—namely, democratization and reconciliation, but I cannot address these here.

28 Thomas Nagel argues that there is "a difference between knowledge and *acknowledg-ment*. It is what happens and can only happen to knowledge when it becomes officially sanctioned, when it is made part of the public cognitive scene." Quoted in Lawrence Weschler, "Afterword," in *State Crimes: Punishment or Pardon*, Aspen Institute Report (Washington, DC, 1989).

29 For a full elaboration of this argument, see de Greiff, "Justice and Reparations."

30 I have worked out in detail the relationship between reparations and civic trust in de Greiff, "Justice and Reparations"; between truth-telling and civic trust in Pablo de Greiff, "Truth-telling and the Rule of Law," in *Telling the Truths*, ed. Tristan Anne Borer (South Bend: University of Notre Dame Press, 2005); between vetting and civic trust in Pablo de Greiff, "Vetting and Transitional Justice," in *Justice as Prevention*; and between reconcilia-tion and civic trust in Pablo de Greiff, "The Role of Apologies in National Reconciliation Processes: On Making Trustworthy Institutions Trusted," in in *The Age of Apology. Fac-ing up to the Past*, Mark Gibney, Rhoda E. Howard-Hassmann, Jean-Marc Coicaud and Niklaus Steiner, eds., (Philadelphia, PA: University of Pennsylvania Press, 2007).

31 DPKO, *IDDRS*, 2.10, 1.

32 Ibid., 2.20, 1.

33 Particularly given the insistence on the importance of making sure that DDR benefits not just ex-combatants but also communities. See, e.g., ibid., 2.30, 6.

34 Ibid., 4.30, 3.

35 Ibid., 4.30, 6.

36 Ibid., 4.30, 3. Of course, size is not the relevant consideration, *desert* is. But these are waters in which the *IDDRS* chooses not to wade.

37 "SIDDR Report," 14.

38 Ibid., 23.

39 Ibid., 19.

40 For the norm-based account of trust on which this argument relies, see de Greiff, "The Role of Apologies in National Reconciliation Processes."

41 Jeremy Weinstein and Macartan Humphreys, "Disentangling the Determinants of Suc-cessful Demobilization and Reintegration," Center for Global Development, Working Paper 69, September 2005.

42 In this sense, the argument does not depend on thinking that the reputation of the unit to which ex-combatants belong is the single most important factor for their reintegra-tion *in all cases*. To the extent that successful reintegration depends, to some degree, on the attitudes of receiving communities, making sure that DDR programs are linked with justice measures provides a reason for the attitudinal changes on the part of receiving communities that facilitate the process.

43   This need not be thought of in terms of sharing information that may compromise individuals, and therefore increase the resistance on the part of ex-combatants to participate in DDR programs to begin with, but might consist exclusively of information about the more "structural" dimensions of the parties to the conflict.

44   Notice the modality. They *may*. Whether they do in fact is an empirical issue that depends on many factors, including highly contextual considerations, among which a sense of whether returning ex-combatants are "our boys (and girls)" or not is an important one. The strength of the tendency to forgive "our boys" for what they have done to *others* should not be underestimated.

45   Cited by Ginifer in "Reintegration of Ex-combatants," 46.

46   See Lars Waldorf, "Transitional Justice and DDR in Post-Genocide Rwanda" (New York: International Center for Transitional Justice, 2009), 26.

47   DPKO, *IDDRS*, 4.30, 6 (emphasis added).

48   Ibid. (emphasis added).

# CHAPTER 5

# Transitional Justice and Female Ex-Combatants: Lessons Learned from International Experience[1]

*Luisa Maria Dietrich Ortega*

Over the past decade practitioners, academics, and policy-makers have focused greater attention on the role of women in conflict prevention and transformation, the impact of women and their organizations on peace negotiations, and the involvement of women in political, economic, and social postconflict reconstruction.

The increased recognition of, and response to, women's experiences led to the United Nations (UN) Security Council Resolution (SCR) 1325 on Women, Peace and Security, which was adopted unanimously in 2000.[2] This is the first UN Resolution to explicitly recognize women's multiple roles and experiences of conflict and peacemaking. It demands protection for women and the inclusion of women in peace-related processes. It urges those involved in the planning and implementation of disarmament, demobilization, and reintegration (DDR) programs to "consider the different needs of female and male ex-combatants and . . . take into account the needs of their dependents."[3] Moreover, it calls on all actors to ensure that women's rights are addressed in the context of postconflict reconstruction, including in processes related to the reform of the constitution, the judiciary, and the police. It also addresses the vast and often invisible challenge of gender-based violence.[4]

UNSCR 1325 also opens the door to broader discussions about women's roles in and experiences of DDR and transitional justice measures. Transitional justice (TJ) refers to a range of measures that societies use to confront past atrocities and human rights abuse. Such initiatives often include trials, truth-seeking initiatives, reparations for victims, and institutional reform. One result of gender advocacy in this field has been the increase of the number of women in transitional justice institutions as commissioners, judges, and technical staff within courts and truth commissions (hereafter truth commissions or TCs).[5] The creation of gender units or gender focal points within international, ad hoc, and hybrid tribunals, as well as TCs, indicates a growing commitment to gender mainstreaming and to addressing women-specific issues.

In spite of these important advances, the relationship between female ex-combatants, DDR, and transitional justice measures has been overlooked. Women comprise between 10 and 30 percent of armed opposition groups,[6] in nonfighting roles and as active combatants and commanders, yet female ex-combatants have often been excluded and marginalized in post-hostilities settings, and particularly in DDR programs. This may be a consequence of the portrayal of women as nurturers of life and as "positive" social actors who support violence reduction and peace—an image that encourages greater acceptance of the idea of women as victims of armed conflict rather than as perpetrators of violence.[7] Similarly, transitional justice has had limited engagement with female ex-combatants, a gap that may be exacerbated by stereotypical gendered notions about women, based on traditional concepts of what is female and what is male.[8] Female ex-combatants, by transgressing common gender roles, challenge those assumptions.

Acknowledging the range of female ex-combatants' experiences in war and peace and recognizing women's potential for complicity and agency in organized violence is an important step toward deconstructing commonly held stereotypes of gender-appropriate behavior.[9] The creation of TJ bodies in which women, too, are held accountable for crimes committed during a conflict period has important implications for the long-term success of demilitarization and peacebuilding.[10] Initial analysis of ex-combatant engagement with transitional justice measures finds that women are mostly disregarded, and provides some evidence of complex power dynamics in which female ex-combatants in particular have not been a primary focus of attention.[11] Prosecutions in many places, for example, have focused on a very limited number of high-ranking commanders considered to be the most responsible for atrocities, who are predominantly male.[12] In those few cases in which women face prosecutions, they are not combatants, but politicians. Such are the cases of Biljana Plavsic, a member of the presidency of the Republika Srpska, and Pauline Nyiramasuhuko, a former Rwandan minister for the Family and the Advancement of Women. Both were tried for genocide and genocidal rape before, respectively, the International Criminal Tribunal for the former Yugoslavia and the International Criminal Tribunal for Rwanda.[13] Reparations programs have not formally considered offering benefits to ex-combatants who can also claim to be victims. Furthermore, security sector reform has tended to operate under a gender-blind efficiency rationale, which has created barriers to female entry or relegated women to administrative tasks.[14] There are nonetheless a few interesting examples of TCs' engagement with female ex-combatants, specifically in Peru, Sierra Leone, and South Africa, that may be analyzed in order to facilitate further participation of women ex-combatants in transitional justice initiatives.

This chapter thus examines the relationship between female ex-combatants, DDR, and transitional justice, with a particular focus on TCs. It argues that the potential of TCs to recognize women's multiple and contradictory roles during armed conflict and to publicly acknowledge their agency and experience can contribute to a reconsideration of postconflict gender relations. The chapter is based on the author's work with and participation in research projects on female ex-combatants in Colombia and Peru, as well as a review of relevant literature and TC documentation. Given the scarcity of empirical research on female ex-combatants and their engagement with TCs, the ideas set out in this chapter are of a provisional nature. The chapter aims to encourage more work in this area, rather than offer final conclusions.

The first section presents a general overview of the situation of female combatants. It draws attention to the gendered dimensions of their experiences from mobilization and recruitment, through conflict, war termination, and negotiations, to DDR, and finally to the postconflict period. The second section explores the limited experiences of TC engagement with female ex-combatants. It focuses on mandate and design, statement taking, women-specific and thematic hearings, gender-specific submissions, reconciliation activities undertaken by TCs, and final reports. The third section identifies opportunities for collaboration between DDR programs and TCs in terms of addressing and engaging with female ex-combatants. The final section draws conclusions from this developing analysis: it finds that both DDR programs and TCs tend to base their assumptions on rigid, gendered stereotypes of women. Both, for different reasons, fail to address the specific needs and capacities of female ex-combatants, thus missing an opportunity to ensure their meaningful participation in postconflict situations.

## OVERVIEW OF THE SITUATION OF FEMALE EX-COMBATANTS

Women fighting in armed conflicts are a diverse group, both within the same armed groups as well as across regions and cultural contexts. As such, comparative analysis without overgeneralization is a challenge. For example, female ex-combatants may differ in terms of the circumstances of their mobilization, age at recruitment, class, ethnic and religious background, type of military or political engagement, and command levels achieved. It is difficult to bridge the gap between female "freedom fighters," political and military commanders, and full-fledged combatants on the one hand, and female labor forces, "bush-wives," and "camp-followers" on the other.

Female combatants continue to be perceived as an exception in the male-dominated sphere of warfare. International experience indicates that women combatants' multiple forms of engagement in armed opposition groups, such as in military intelligence missions, weapons training, and combat, tend to be downplayed and trivialized in both official and popular accounts of war.[15] Consequently, female ex-combatants may be marginalized, stigmatized, and excluded in different ways, not just with respect to their experiences in armed groups, negotiations, and DDR, but also with respect to transitional justice measures.[16]

What do we know about female combatants? Female combatants are still a minority in armed groups. Researchers have estimated that women represent from 10 to 30 percent of members of armed groups.[17] Second, women fulfill multiple—and sometimes contradictory—roles within armed groups, as combatants, commanders, porters, sex workers, cooks, spies or intelligence officers, communications officers, and community outreach workers, and may shift between political and military roles.[18] Participation in any of those roles is often related to a woman's educational background, certain personal conditions (such as motherhood), and the organizational structures of the group. Third, although armed groups may, in some cases, provide opportunities for women to access leadership roles, the majority of women combatants are to be found in the rank-and-file segments, not at the command level.[19]

Discourses claiming the empowerment of female ex-combatants through their involvement in armed groups need to be critically assessed. Participation in armed groups has not necessarily provided women a means of achieving upward social mobility. Instead, female ex-combatants tend to leave the armed groups and return to their previous socioeconomic level.[20] Women do, however, acknowledge acquiring important personal developments and achievements through their association with armed groups, such as the acquisition of decision-making skills, more positive self-perception, and increased self-esteem. In some cases, women have acquired skills in community organization and mass organization.[21] Often identification with an armed group replaces previous family bonds, and is strengthened by the purpose of struggle and sense of belonging to an important social project. The experience of participation in an armed group can also result in positive breaks with traditional or cultural socialization, evident in increased levels of gender equality within some armed groups, and expressed by shared work, more open sexual prac-tices, and the presence of women in previously male-reserved spaces, such as combat.[22] In these situations, combatants may view their experiences posi-tively and, as a consequence, see peace as a disappointment because of the loss of these individual and group aspects of their service.[23]

Apart from possible empowering factors, there may also be factors that constitute sources of disempowerment for female combatants. Women may be disappointed, for example, when they find that the reality of daily life in an armed group contradicts the egalitarian opportunities promised to them during their recruitment. Exploitative gender relations is another such source, which can result in women being stripped of the control of their bodies and subject to forced contraception, forced abortion, or forced sexual relations.[24] This point is especially relevant for those women who were abducted, who were victims of forced recruitment, or who were lured in by false promises of recruiters. Another source of disempowerment reported by women is the experience of leaving their children behind, as well as the denial of maternity that may be enforced by the armed group.[25] Similarly, female combatants are disempowered when they fall into enemy hands and are forced to endure tor-ture or sexual and gender-based violence.

## FEMALE (EX-)COMBATANTS IN NEGOTIATION PROCESSES

Experiences of disempowerment and marginalization often increase for women combatants as conflict comes to an end. It begins with the negotiation process.

There is a tendency across different negotiation processes involving armed opposition groups to exclude women, regardless of whether they achieved leadership positions in armed groups.[26] Women's absence from formal negoti-ation tables as well as from other informal preparatory activities, such as stra-tegic planning sessions and consultations with civil society, has far-reaching consequences. One of the results is that women's voices are sidelined from decision-making on DDR processes, as well as in other areas of postconflict reconstruction and peacebuilding.

In the limited cases where women have participated, researchers have high-lighted that it was not in chief negotiating positions but often as spokespersons or in other support roles—meaning that women have lacked direct influence in the project of identifying priorities for reconstruction that are usually part of a peace agreement.[27] Although the inclusion of women in peace negotiations is no guarantee of the adoption of gender-responsive approaches, researchers have argued that the participation of women has made a difference in some cases. In El Salvador, for example, the participation of high-ranking female political and military commanders in the different stages of the peace negotiations influenced the adoption of gender-responsive measures for the DDR program.[28]

## FEMALE EX-COMBATANTS AND DDR PROCESSES

Over the past decade, the mechanisms of exclusion of female ex-combatants, as well as the failure of DDR programs to address their gender-specific needs, have been documented extensively.[29] A study conducted by Geneva Call argues that the majority of women and girls in the African context have been excluded from DDR programs.[30] Other researchers have established that often women actively choose to abstain from registering with DDR programs. They may feel that they have nothing to gain, that the costs of stigmatization override the potential benefits, that participation in DDR may even be counterproductive to their reintegration, that they simply have other priorities at that time, or that they no longer want to be connected with armed forces.[31]

Whether excluded or willingly abstaining from DDR programs, women's consequent self-demobilization has a powerful impact on the success of their reintegration. While some women will quietly drift back into their families or communities, others may seek anonymity in big towns, practically "disappearing."[32] While this secrecy protects them, it also conceals their need for support. Often poverty, a lack or resources and access to networks, and their condition as mothers or heads of households pushes women to engage in undesirable coping strategies, such as "transactional sex" or other exploitative situations, effectively hindering their reintegration.[33] Women are therefore not likely to publicly acknowledge their participation in armed groups, talk openly about their experiences, or engage easily in "social and political" activities, and even less so if the activities are perceived to be potentially stigmatizing. These factors are also significant for the participation of women combatants in TCs and other transitional justice measures.

Female ex-combatants registered officially in a DDR program face different obstacles created by gender-blind DDR processes. The first set of obstacles is related to the lack of adequate consideration of women's specific needs and capacities in DDR program planning and implementation. For example, the provision of sexual and reproductive health care, maternal health care, hygienic needs related to menstruation, and specialized psychosocial assistance in confidential, secure, and violence-free environments is rarely provided to women combatants in DDR programs.[34]

The second set of obstacles is related to factors that deter female ex-combatants from taking full advantage of DDR program benefits and services. In general terms, DDR processes operate in accordance with structural constraints that often result in disadvantages for women, such as male land tenure, traditional inheritance rights that exclude women, and restrictive traditional roles for women that relegate them to the domestic and reproductive sphere, rather than empower them to engage in the public sphere.[35] In Sierra Leone, a female applicant for loans provided by the DDR program must be present with a "husband" willing to identify her as his wife. Women could not claim benefits alone regardless of the number of children they cared for.[36] Such obstacles can play a role in contributing to the feminization of poverty in the postconflict period.[37]

Further, DDR programs often promote a traditional sexual division of labor by offering training for female combatants in "female" skills, such as cooking, tailoring, and mat weaving, that support the "return" of women into the domestic and private sphere. Recent DDR programs have addressed a series of these shortcomings. In the Democratic Republic of the Congo (DRC), for example, the UN-sponsored DDR program developed women's informal or formal skills, including computer or nursing/medical skills. Yet women-centered initiatives, such as collective income-generating projects and microcredit schemes, tend to be relatively small and poorly funded. In this sense, the relatively flexible gender roles and broadened spaces for engagement open to women during their participation in armed groups is rarely translated into postconflict gains, especially because the passage to civilian life tends to be framed as a "return to normalcy," meaning a return of women ex-combatants to the domestic and reproductive spheres. [38] In 1993, a study of 1,100 female members of the Farabundo Martí National Liberation Front (FMLN) armed group in El Salvador showed that 57 percent of the women had primarily worked in the household before the war, while barely a year after the peace accords 95 percent said that they were engaged in domestic work.[39]

A third set of obstacles for women in DDR processes is related to the breakup of chains of command and the disintegration of collective group identity in favor of individual identity. Recent studies have highlighted the positive effects on female ex-combatant reintegration of support networks, peer assistance, and self-help groups based on former group alliances.[40] In Liberia, the Liberians United for Reconciliation and Democracy maintained female fighting units, called Women's Artillery Commandoes, which were headed by women. Female commanders often establish quasi-maternal relationships with girls and women under their command, resulting in strong bonds of solidarity and dependence of girls and women with their commanders. Although these relationships are not always in the best interest of girl or women combatants, there are still grounds to rethink the DDR objectives of breaking these chains of command, since in some contexts close ties with commanders may function as a viable support network furthering the reintegration of female combatants.[41] One reason is that when girls and women can no longer rely on their parents, they may be able to rely on their former commanders for protection and survival. Another is that collective demobilization may contribute to the continued political and social activism of female combatants, as was the case with female ex-combatants in Guatemala after the peace agreements. Research by Wenche Hauge finds that, for at least two communities of female ex-combatants, collective demobilization allowed women, including women of lower educational levels, to continue to play active political roles because of the significant number of former female fighters who remained active in the decision-making spaces of cooperatives. In addition, Hauge finds that these cooperatives allowed women to advance positive gender dynamics that were present in the armed groups during the conflict, and that women who participated in them experienced lower levels of domestic violence and had increased opportunities to be politically active through the provision of appropriate child-care facilities. [42]

Finally, there are obstacles related to the stigmatization of female ex-combatants—an issue that is often cited as a hindrance to women's reintegration and that similarly constitutes a deterrent for women's engagement in voluntary transitional justice initiatives. Stigmatization in the context of demobilization relates to a strong social disapproval of female ex-combatants by their partners, family, and community, often based on oversimplified perceptions of past behavior. As a multilayered phenomenon, stigma may lead to rejection and marginalization, and it extends to all aspects of a woman's life. Culture and context will influence how stigmatization affects women differently than men.[43] Male ex-combatants may face stigmatization related to the perception that they may be criminals and murderers, and thus may feel a disadvantage in searching for employment and in returning to their former communities. Female ex-combatants, on the other hand, find their very womanhood questioned. Researchers refer to the double stigma that women face: first, for having been associated with armed opposition groups, and second, for having transgressed social norms of female behavior, which extend to questions about their roles as "good" wives and mothers.[44]

Stigmatization is expressed differently from context to context, and women confronted with stigma devise equally diverse coping strategies. Women's backgrounds, capacities, resources, and networks also shape the effect and type of stigmatization. It is important to point out that in spite of regional variations of DDR processes, the majority of women — across all ranks, irrespective of military/political or urban/rural divides — are affected by a double stigma, regardless of whether they joined the armed struggle willingly or were forcefully recruited or abducted, or whether they registered formally in DDR or self-demobilized. DDR programs do not usually engage with the effects of gendered stigmatization. In fact, DDR programs are more likely to contribute to the stigmatization of female ex-combatants through some of the gendered practices described above.

The consequences of stigma have serious and life-altering consequences for women ex-combatants. In some contexts, women ex-combatants are seen as sexually impure, which may hinder their marriage prospects. This stigma can, in turn, affect their access to different resources and social networks needed to obtain shelter, land, property, food, labor exchange, family, and child support, and more sustainable livelihood opportunities.[45] Furthermore, stigmatization can result in partners divorcing or abandoning female fighters to replace them with more feminine and "obedient" civilian women who do not have the "scars" left by war.[46] In Eritrea, women heroes in the nationalist struggle are finding that the very qualities that made them good soldiers and comrades stigmatize them as wives and potential wives.[47] In Sierra Leone, female ex-combatants found that "their husbands have given up on them," while a former fighter from DRC has said, "We cannot find husbands, no one wants to marry us."[48] Moreover, being too visibly associated with fighting forces, especially in contexts where ex-combatants are seen as perpetrators of atrocities, may result in threats to women's physical security. Given these many factors, women are often extremely guarded in their interactions with authorities, and they try to avoid being identified as combatants or collaborators — a fact that has implications for their participation in truth commissions and other transitional justice initiatives.

By ignoring the gender implications of how they categorize women in the reintegration process, DDR programs can further the marginalization of women. Megan MacKenzie has drawn attention to the reticence of official DDR programs to call women "combatants," instead using such labels as "females associated with the war," "dependents," or "camp followers," hence effectively eliminating them from the category of "soldier," reducing their importance as a security priority, and removing them from significant policy discourses.[49] She notes that, when it comes to reintegrating women and girls, DDR policy is often framed around the notion of "returning to normal"—something that would either happen naturally with time or through a sensitization process in which communities and families are urged to "take women and girls back."[50] By encouraging women and girl soldiers to return to their "normal places" in the community, DDR programs strip them of any new roles or positions of authority they may have held during the conflict, and any opportunities to rethink and reshape gender stereotypes and hierarchies are destroyed.[51]

This section on the experiences of women ex-combatants in DDR has highlighted the gendered implications of excluding women ex-combatants from the negotiation and planning processes for DDR, as well as the obstacles that inhibit the ability of female ex-combatants to take full advantage of DDR program benefits and services. Many of these issues are also significant factors in the participation of female ex-combatants in truth commissions.

## TRUTH COMMISSIONS AND FEMALE EX-COMBATANTS

By the time transitional justice measures, such as prosecutions, reparations programs, security sector reform, and TCs, initiate their operations, female ex-combatants have usually gone through a series of empowering and disempowering processes, including DDR. An analysis of the relationship between women and TCs must be based on the acknowledgment that accountability measures like truth commissions are not neutral players in a general context in which gender dynamics are being renegotiated. TCs may play an important role in perpetuating or dismantling specific gender stereotypes, prioritizing certain categories of women over others, and highlighting specific gendered patterns of violence over others.

TCs, as nonjudicial transitional justice mechanisms, represent both an alternative and a complementary approach to judicial accountability. While prosecutions processes focus primarily on investigating specific violations committed by individual perpetrators,[52] TCs are characterized by their capacity to provide space for victims, and have tended to operate on narrowly defined and mutually exclusive categories of victims and perpetrators.[53] A comparative analysis of international experiences suggests considerable power asymmetries between ex-combatants and victims in post-hostility contexts, and is evidenced by victims' comparative lack of access to money, skills training and education, judicial advice, and health services, among other benefits.[54] In stark contrast with victims, ex-combatants receive state attention, are often well organized, and are sometimes cared for by their former organizations.[55] There is also a symbolic imbalance, in the sense that perpetrators of human rights abuses often do not acknowledge their wrongdoings, or worse, demand to be recognized as heroes. Even in postconflict contexts, they may maintain structures of power based on fear in the communities.[56]

Still, perceiving former fighters as a homogenous, threatening group blurs the diverse motivations behind combatants' enlistment and participation in armed groups, and may also hide varied motivations for their engagement with transitional justice. The challenge for accountability institutions is how to accommodate the multiple roles of ex-combatants, as well as their dual conditions as perpetrators and victims, while at the same time safeguarding, respecting, and addressing victims' claims. A significant development in recent TC experiences has been the shift of focus from the state as the main perpetrator of atrocities, as was the case in Argentina, Chile, and apartheid-era South Africa, toward an increased recognition of the responsibility of nonstate armed actors. In this sense, the situation confronting the Peruvian Truth and Reconciliation Commission (TRC) changed the pattern of TCs in Latin America, which prior to that point had been established to address conflicts in which insurgent groups had a comparatively limited level of responsibility for human rights violations. For example, in Guatemala the UN-sponsored Commission for Historical Clarification found that nonstate armed groups were responsible for less than 10 percent of the atrocities committed. The truth commission in El Salvador found that the FMLN was responsible for 5 percent of violations committed in that country.[57] In contrast, the Peruvian TRC established that the Shining Path was responsible for 54 percent of the atrocities committed during the course of the country's internal armed conflict.

TCs have significantly broadened their scope of engagement and activities in the past twenty years. They have evolved from what was essentially research and report-writing functions to the present-day models that seek direct engagement with actors of the conflict—for example, through amnesties, reconciliation activities, victim-perpetrator encounters, truth-telling exercises, and cleansing ceremonies. In addition, some TCs have been significant in creating and implementing public policy, such as reparations programs for victims. This expansion has occurred through broadened mandates, the creation of new institutional arrangements, and longer periods of operation, as evidenced by the experiences of the amnesty commission of the South African TRC,[58] the community reconciliation processes in the Commission for Reception, Truth and Reconciliation in Timor-Leste,[59] and the DDR component in Colombia's National Commission for Reparation and Reconciliation (CNRR), which also has as part of its mandate the pursuit of historical memory.[60]

Advances in international law and policy, along with increased levels of women's activism, have had an impact on the design and work of TCs in regard to women. The Rome Statute of the International Criminal Court—which identifies "rape, sexual slavery, enforced prostitution, forced pregnancy, enforced sterilization, or any other form of sexual violence of comparable gravity" as crimes against humanity[61]—is one such advance, as is the adoption of UNSCR 1325 and 1820. Further, the adoption of methodologies that highlight crosscutting themes has meant that many recent truth commissions have paid particular attention to the experiences of women, children, and indigenous populations (where relevant). TCs in Sierra Leone, Haiti, and Timor-Leste included gender equity explicitly into their mandates, had a greater number of female commissioners,[62] and have created gender units, gender focal points, or brought in outside experts from such sources as the United Nations Development Fund for Women (UNIFEM) in order to mainstream a women-centered approach into TCs' operations.[63] There is also an increasing trend to reference gender in TC mandates, particularly with respect to sexual and gender-based violence, as evidenced by the mandates and work of the TCs in Peru, Sierra Leone, and Liberia.

In spite of these important developments, the gender perspective adopted in recent TCs promotes a particular aspect of women's experiences of conflict: their victimization. Scholars have noted that accountability institutions implicitly encourage women to assume a victim identity in order to be acknowledged, feeding into stereotypes of women as perpetual victims—powerless and acted upon.[64] Fiona Ross has traced how the South African TRC shaped public perceptions of women, first, through women's initial appearance in front of the TRC as mothers reporting on the deaths of predominantly male family members, and thus as "secondary witnesses." Later, the focus shifted to women victims in their own right, but to women as victims of sexual and gender-based violence—regardless of their diverse experiences, even as victims.[65]

This particular focus of TCs on women as victims has broader implications for postconflict dynamics, including the movement toward inclusive democracy. It perpetuates unequal and gendered power relations, and it has direct consequences for female ex-combatants. The classification of women only as victims of sexual and gender-based violence obscures the patterns of multiple violations perpetrated against women in conflict contexts and perpetuates the stereotypical notion of women as peaceful by nature. It also obscures any responsibility women may have had in the perpetration of atrocities and violent acts, their diverse engagements in perpetuating the conflict, and their roles in instigating others to commit violence. Finally, it oversimplifies the complex and contradictory experiences of women in armed conflict and undermines their agency as well as their capacity for resistance and coping strategies. In some situations, female ex-combatants might use their experiences in mass organizing in order to engage communities across religious and ethnic divides and build networks to address the practical needs of their families and communities.[66] The narrow focus on women as victims rather than as agents, however, can effectively inhibit any recognition of female ex-combatants as potential leaders in community reintegration and reconciliation processes.

There are very limited examples of TCs engaging directly with female ex-combatants. These engagements have centered around two purposes. First, women's input has been important to report writing, in order to establish a complete account on the conflict, the patterns of violations committed, and the motivations, operations, and daily functioning of armed groups. Second, women have been engaged in specific TC activities, including truth-telling, thematic hearings, and reconciliation activities, such as cleansing ceremonies and other community-oriented interventions, that seek to dignify victims and create the conditions for national reconciliation.

Female ex-combatants have engaged with TCs for a range of reasons. Among them are the desire to report on a particular act of violence perpetrated against themselves or other members of their armed groups by their former adversaries; to provide alternative accounts of specific situations as a political statement that will be part of national narratives; to provide evidence on systematic patterns of violations; to seize the opportunity to be listened to, either as individuals or as members of a collective; to assert themselves as victims; to air frustration and disappointment with their former commanders; to affirm their disposition to participate in reconciliation processes; and to influence pending judicial processes.[67] From this list it is evident that female ex-combatants have a variety of reasons to seek engagement with TCs, even if not always for the same reasons that TCs seek their engagement.

## MANDATE AND INSTITUTIONAL DESIGN

Several factors shape a TC's mandate: the country context, the type of conflict the commission is meant to address, and particulars of the transition from war to peace. The mandate lays out the objectives and general guidelines for a TC's work, which may include addressing injustices suffered by victims, writing a detailed history of the conflict, recommending measures for social healing, and initiating activities related to reconciliation.

A TC's victim-centered focus shapes the mandate and affects the nature of the engagement with armed groups and male and female ex-combatants. If the main perpetrator of violence and mass atrocity is the state, then the relations between ex-combatants and the TC may be more cooperative, as was the case in Guatemala and El Salvador. In other cases, where the members of armed groups are seen as the prime perpetrators, the TC may position itself against the group. The background and agendas of the TC commissioners may play a role in this positioning. The inclusion of representatives of Peru's armed forces within the Peruvian TRC shaped the overall position of the commission vis-à-vis the Shining Path and ex-combatants—for example, by referring to armed opposition groups as "terrorist violence and terrorist organizations."[68] The TCs in South Africa and Sierra Leone may be described as operating with a more conciliatory approach. The South African TRC used more moderated language when referring to individual perpetrators, who may or may not have been ex-combatants, as "persons responsible for the commission of the violations." The Sierra Leone TRC explicitly recognized both victims and perpetrators as its main constituency, establishing up front an objective to create a climate favoring constructive interchange between them.[69]

Early TCs, such as the Commission on the Truth for El Salvador, which produced its report in 1993, lacked any specific gender perspective. The El Salvador commission's report, *From Madness to Hope: The 12 year War in El Salvador*, considered sexual and gender-based violence a private and domestic issue, and did not address it.[70] While some commissions include a gender perspective explicitly in their mandates, other TCs, such as Peru's and South Africa's, have addressed gender-equality concerns through the interpretation of the mandate and creation of relevant institutional design. These TCs have used a variety of mechanisms to include a gender perspective in their work: the creation of internal gender units, the designation of gender focal points, and the use of external gender expertise.

Gender units have played key roles in coordinating a gender-mainstreaming process in at least two TCs: those of Peru and Timor-Leste. These units aimed to build the commissions' internal capacity on gender issues, undertook outreach and research activities, and supported work on the TCs' final reports. Similar to other mainstreaming efforts, these gender units were underfunded, understaffed, and held little decision-making power. As a result, the approach to gender was ad hoc, and there was limited collaboration with other areas of the commissions.

Strategies to tap into external gender expertise have involved partnerships with UN bodies, such as UNIFEM in Sierra Leone, to take advantage of their technical expertise, provide comprehensive gender training, arrange closed hearings for women, and develop a strategy for thematic consultancies related to gender. This kind of expertise can come in various forms. The South African TRC, for example, received substantial input from women's networks and a written submission by women activists and academics.[71]

Although TCs increasingly address gender equality within their mandates and institutional design, these efforts rarely include female ex-combatants. Gender units prioritize female victims of armed conflicts and are often overcharged with mainstreaming gender with the TCs' operations and implementation.

## STATEMENT TAKING

Different forms of voluntary statement taking have been part of the work of many TCs. The rationale behind this activity is to establish accurate accounts of past events, provide personal and institutional insights into the motivations and political strategy behind the violence, and give victims an opportunity to speak on their own behalf or on the behalf of their loved ones. Victims are still the primary statement givers; ex-combatants, however, have also increasingly provided statements to TCs.

Statement taking is not a neutral undertaking, and gender considerations require that attention be given to the ratio of female and male statement givers, including when statements are received from ex-combatants, as well as what kind of information is solicited from male and female combatants and what the gendered motivations are (if any) of the statement givers.

In the Peruvian context, roughly 1,200 (7 percent) of a total of 17,000 statements were taken from ex-combatants held in twenty-one prison facilities across the country. Of those, 208 (18 percent) were taken in women's prisons. An important number of statements were collected from inmates without stated political affiliations, or from ex-combatants who had renounced active membership in their former groups. Given the low percentage of ex-combatant statements and the number of statements taken from informants without group allegiance, it can be inferred that the ideologically motivated ex-combatants constituted a minority of statement givers.

In South Africa, of the 7,112 petitions for amnesty that the TRC registered, those coming from ex-combatants were quite low. Out of a total of 998 African National Congress (ANC) members or supporters who applied for amnesty, only 26 (3 percent) were female, while out of 180 petitioners belonging to Umkhonto we Sizwe (the military wing of the ANC), only 8 were women.[72] Those few women who sought amnesty did so for such acts as sabotage, theft of dynamite, escape from custody, hiding weapons, and arms transport. The highest level of responsibility claimed by a woman in the amnesty petitions was intelligence—that is, spying. It can be inferred that women who engaged in higher levels of responsibility did not come forward, especially a considerable number of women within the liberation forces passed on to high-level positions in the new government, or in the military or police forces. According to one former combatant, those women were focused on challenges of the future, rather than the past.

Apart from the question of who provides statements to commissions, it is important to establish how the statement givers identify themselves—for example, as victims, witnesses, or ex-combatants. In Sierra Leone, 7,706 statements were taken by the TRC, out of which 2,748 (36 percent) came from women. The statistical annex of the TRC's final report establishes that 78 percent of women's statements identified them as victims, 16 percent as relatives of witnesses, and 3 percent as hearsay witnesses, while the rest is divided between other witnesses and unspecified categories. The figure presented under the category of female perpetrators is 0.0 percent, which suggests that female ex-combatants participated as victims or witnesses, were labeled as such by the TRC, or did not participate. There is, however, anecdotal evidence that female ex-combatants did participate.[73] In another example, Therese Abrahamsen and Hugo van der Merwe in their work exploring the ways in which applicants experienced their passage through the South African TRC's Amnesty Commission describe the discomfort that ex-combatants felt about being labeled as perpetrators and not as liberation fighters.[74] Former fighters resented that they "had to apply before the TRC as perpetrators as most of the respondents identified themselves as liberation fighters who had fought for a just cause," while they perceived the TRC to "equalize the defenders of apartheid with the destroyers of apartheid."[75] Quoting an ex-combatant, "In the hearing it wasn't like I expected: We were told that we will merely be asked about motivation, why we did what we did, but to my surprise people were cross-questioned to an extent that some became scared and could not justify that their cases were politically motivated."[76]

This brief overview of information provided in TC final reports provides a basis for claiming that TCs do not necessarily engage with politically motivated or high-ranking female ex-combatants, and that those providing statements may not identify themselves as ex-combatants for different reasons.

## WOMEN-SPECIFIC AND THEMATIC HEARINGS

Women-specific hearings have been important entry points for making the voices of women heard in the TC process. Statements or testimonies from female combatants can add new information related to patterns of violations perpetuated by different actors along gendered lines, including the torture, sexual violence, and inhumane and degrading treatment inflicted on female ex-combatants—issues that also should be included in the final report.[77]

In 1996 and 1997, the South African TRC held thematic women's hearings. While some analysts argued that these hearings provided an appropriate space for women to testify about crimes—including gender-based violence—others questioned whether the emphasis on women as victims would overshadow or effectively sideline other expressions of women's roles in conflict.[78] On those few occasions in which female ex-combatants participated in women's hearings in South Africa, it became evident that their experiences of victimization were prioritized over their political activities. While observing and accompanying one female ANC activist's passage through the testimonial process, Fiona Ross established that the many facets of violence and multiple experiences of harm and suffering that the ex-combatant reported were subsumed into the category of sexual violence in the final report. Furthermore, an ex-combatant's identity as a mother would be emphasized over her identity as a political activist and combatant, effectively reversing her own presentation of herself and her role in the armed conflict.[79]

In examining the way women's experiences are addressed or not by other types of thematic hearings, such as hearings on armed opposition groups, it becomes evident that women-specific issues are rarely included. In Sierra Leone, during a 2003 TRC hearing focused on institutions, the National Committee for Disarmament, Demobilization, and Reintegration was invited to two hearings, one on militias and armed groups and another on promoting reconciliation and national reintegration. Women-specific issues were not mentioned in either hearing. Moreover, female ex-combatants rarely participate in thematic hearings. The Peruvian TRC, for example, held special audiences with individual commanders of both insurgent groups—all men. The effect was to render invisible an important number of female mid- and high-ranking commanders in Peruvian insurgent groups.

Women-specific and other thematic hearings are a clear example of how TCs disregard female ex-combatants in practice. Female-centered activities focus predominantly on women who identify themselves only as victims of armed conflict and rarely allow for an alternative portrayal of women's experiences or agency during armed conflict. Even when female ex-combatants can provide valuable information—for example, by testifying in women-specific or thematic hearings on patterns of violence or the structure and motivations of armed groups—they are seldom invited to provide statements.

## SUBMISSIONS TO COMMISSIONS

In the past, civil society organizations, religious and faith-based groups, and academic institutions have submitted written submissions to TCs, which have become an important means for drawing attention to the differential effects of conflict on women. The submission made to the South African TRC—"Gender and the Truth and Reconciliation Commission"—included a detailed analysis of women's experience of repression under the apartheid regime over thirty-three years, and it also referred to women as perpetrators of violence. The submission had an important impact, as it led to the approval of special hearings on women and the appointment of two gender experts to advise the South African TRC on how to respond to the submission. In Sierra Leone, the Coalition for Women's Human Rights in Conflict Situations provided a submission to the TRC on sexual and gender-based violence and on abuses experienced by women and girls abducted by armed groups.[80]

In at least one case, female ex-combatants have publicly struggled for recognition in the truth-seeking process. The Peruvian TRC received written statements and letters from imprisoned militants, including female ex-combatants, critical of what they perceived as the TRC's bias. They stressed the need for objectivity—demanding that the TRC's focus include the responsibility for violations of human rights of armed groups on both sides of the conflict, and calling for the voices of members of the armed opposition movements to be included in the TRC hearings. A letter from Chorillo women's prison in Peru was annexed to a chapter on prisons in the commission's final report, providing an opportunity to raise awareness of female ex-combatants' demands for a public hearing.[81]

## RECONCILIATION

Reconciliation activities can be the most direct form of engagement between TCs and the ex-combatant population, yet the value of these experiences may be contested. Reconciliation, as well as reintegration, cannot be imposed by decree or top-down policies. There are mixed evaluations of direct victim-perpetrator encounters, such as those conducted in South Africa and Timor-Leste, and there is little documentation on the participation of female ex-combatants in reconciliation activities.

In Sierra Leone, where the TRC organized community reconciliation and cleansing ceremonies with the objective of facilitating the reintegration of former combatants into receiving communities, no female ex-combatants gave testimony, and there is no evidence of them engaging in reconciliation activities. In Peru, the TRC limited itself to a conceptual discussion of reconciliation during a series of reconciliation workshops, which included the participation of different groups of female prisoners imprisoned for acts undertaken as members of former armed opposition groups. In this case, there were no direct encounters between victims and perpetrators. A series of videotaped reconciliation workshops, conducted at prison institutions, added a different perspective to the dialogue. Although some militants acknowledged that there were mass atrocities and human rights violations, they largely did not assume responsibility for acts of violence in the way the TRC expected and demanded. The TRC's rule that ex-combatants must disengage from their armed groups as a precondition to participation in dialogue about national reconciliation also encountered fierce opposition among the highly ideological militants.[82]

## FINAL REPORTS

The final report is the most visible outcome of a TC, and it can have a major influence on national narratives of the armed conflict.[83] The Peruvian TRC included two chapters in its final report that refer specifically to women and sexual violence, which constituted a significant advance vis-à-vis other TC reports in mainstreaming gender-equity issues as well as women's specific experiences. The TRC identified as torture a number of violations against female combatants, including withholding medical services and ignoring basic health needs, such as pre- and postnatal attention, and it recommended redressing the injustices women experienced.[84] Furthermore, the TRC recommended that indiscriminate transfers of male and female prisoners (who were primarily ex-combatants) be halted, and that the militants be concentrated in a few prisons close to their zones of origin or close to their families. In addition, the TRC recommended the consolidation of groups of ex-combatant prisoners according to their political group.[85]

The Sierra Leone report addressed the difficulties encountered in engaging female ex-combatants. Among these were absence during the information-gathering process and the interview phase, gender-unresponsive DDR programs, and stigmatization resulting in women and girls concealing their wartime experiences.[86] Further, the TRC highlighted particularities of women's experiences with armed groups, highlighting victims of abduction and the fate of bush wives. In this sense, the TRC pointed toward institutional shortcomings of national and international DDR implementing bodies with regard to female ex-combatants.

Sierra Leone mainstreamed gender throughout its final report. It included a chapter on women capturing the experiences of both women and girls with respect to sexual violence, as well as their gendered experiences with political, legal, health, and social welfare institutions. It also included a formal acknowledgment of female fighters' experiences and their double role as victims and perpetrators. The final report points to the commonality of men's and women's motivations for enlisting and engaging in human rights violations.[87] Many women combatants simply yearned to belong to the group, wishing not to be perceived as weak or to exhibit signs of femininity. These yearnings often led women to perpetrate even more cruel and violent acts than men in their efforts to qualify for inclusion and recognition.[88]

More recently, there are a few examples of final reports, specifically in Sierra Leone and Peru, that refer to female ex-combatants. They either include reference to them in women-specific chapters or in analysis of armed groups' operations and internal structures. Female ex-combatants are also mentioned as statement givers. The final report of the Sierra Leone TRC also includes a discussion of the lack of information on female ex-combatants.

## DDR, TCS, AND OPPORTUNITIES FOR ENGAGING FEMALE EX-COMBATANTS

The increasing tendency of DDR and transitional justice to overlap in time, particularly during the reintegration process, is likely to lead to situations where these processes become increasingly intertwined. There is, hence, an opportunity to challenge a series of assumptions about women in both types of initiatives.

There have been different kinds of formal and informal engagement between DDR and transitional justice measures. In Colombia, the national reintegration program and the CNRR share research and exchange information on engaging with ex-combatants. Information exchange is one useful point of cooperation since DDR programs are likely to have systematized information based on sex-disaggregated data, including specific analysis of the special needs of female ex-combatants and other women participating in DDR, information that may be important for TCs. Additionally, DDR implementing agencies may be in the best position to identify educational programs, health clinics, productive projects, skills training, business management courses, and microcredit schemes in which women tend to enroll, and which may be targeted by a TC's outreach efforts in order to bring more women into the process.

On a more formal level, working groups, donor roundtables, and academic events have been organized between DDR and transitional justice practitioners, which is useful for coordination and information-sharing purposes. Another example in Colombia is the interagency working group on Women, DDR, and Transitional Justice, in which the national DDR agency sits together with representatives of the CNRR's gender unit and DDR unit. International organizations working in Colombia also share information, resources, and lessons learned related to female ex-combatants and other women associated with armed groups.

Outright cooperation has taken place when both DDR and TCs operate in the same time frame. Particularly relevant is the participation of DDR representatives in TC hearings, as occurred during the Sierra Leone TRC's institutional hearings on militias and armed groups, as well as its hearing on reconciliation and national reintegration. Also in Sierra Leone, the public information unit of the DDR program collaborated with the public outreach program of the Special Court for Sierra Leone and the TRC on joint outreach and sensitization campaigns. An example of potential cooperation between DDR and transitional justice institutions is the inclusion of a DDR unit in the CNRR, which also has a mandate to create a report on historical memory related to the armed conflict. In October 2008, the CNRR and the High Commissioner for Social and Economic Reintegration, who directs Colombia's national DDR program, signed a memorandum of understanding acknowledging the links between these initiatives and recognizing their shared objective of peace.[89]

Given that overlap between DDR programs and TCs is likely to continue, there will also be more opportunities to engage with female and male ex-combatants. Analyzing the relationship between DDR and TCs through a gender lens provides some initial evidence for the assertion that both public policies operate on traditional gendered assumptions and stereotypes. It is not

unreasonable to argue that if these stereotypes are not adequately acknowledged and addressed they are likely to result in the further exclusion of female
ex-combatants. Additionally, the perpetuation of such stereotypes through
DDR programs and TCs sustains traditional categorizations of women in
a context where gendered power relations are being negotiated. TCs have
the opportunity to address the marginalization of female ex-combatants by
acknowledging women's wide range of experiences during armed conflict. TCs
may also reach out actively to female ex-combatants, whether formally demobilized in DDR programs or self-demobilized, as well as (released) political
prisoners. Finally, TCs may address the stigma associated with fighting forces.

Gender mainstreaming in both initiatives should be seen not only as a technical process in which a gender unit or the hiring of gender experts ensures a
positive impact on female ex-combatants, but also as a process that requires
political will and commitment at the policy, management, and implementation levels. Unlike actors in other peacebuilding scenarios, female ex-combatants are rarely organized to lobby TCs on their own behalf. In accordance with
UNSCR 1325, TCs should proactively seek opportunities to engage with female
ex-combatants.

One final issue to consider is that, in a few cases, female ex-combatants
have engaged with TCs voluntarily — for example, by providing statements,
information, or testimonies, as well as via TC-organized reconciliation activities. These examples suggest that ex-combatant participation is not dependent
upon such incentives as judicial and amnesty-granting powers, but rather is
shaped by personal motives. Although information is scarce, the available
documentation indicates that women who were forced into armed struggle are
motivated to engage in the TC process because of a myriad of reasons related
to frustration with the DDR process, disappointment with their former commanders, general feelings of injustice, and the desire to claim their status as
victims as well as ex-combatants. Those women who entered the armed struggle out of their own volition describe their motivations as the desire to explain
their reasons for joining the armed struggle, to explain the motives and strategies of the armed group (including by justifying the actions of the group), and
to acknowledge mass atrocities and human rights violations.

## BEYOND THE MARGINALIZATION OF FEMALE EX-COMBATANTS?

In conclusion, TCs' engagement with female ex-combatants has been limited,
as has been their impact on women ex-combatants. Although TCs increasingly

address gender equality in their mandates and institutional design, this rarely includes consideration of or outreach to female ex-combatants. Rather, TCs have by and large contributed to the further marginalization of female ex-combatants. This chapter argues that this marginalization sustains the unequal, gendered power relations of DDR programs. By effectively failing to seize the opportunity to challenge gender relations in the postconflict context, TCs undermine the empowerment, positive experiences, or skills female ex-combatants may have acquired through their participation in armed groups.

Women who have been involved with armed groups challenge stereotypes about women and women's socially accepted behavior. Their transgression of gendered norms leads to different forms of rejection—by themselves, their families, their partners, and the community at large. Public policies operating in a postconflict context, such as DDR programs and TCs, have tended not to include female ex-combatants, since they fall outside the available postconflict categories—because they are not "real" women, "real" combatants, or "real" victims.

There are two challenges for those working on DDR and transitional justice in postconflict settings, as well as for further research on female ex-combatants. First is the question of how to approach female ex-combatants and their gendered needs and capacities appropriately. This task may include acknowledging their diversity as well as accommodating their double role as victims and perpetrators, while ensuring respect for victims' claims. Second is the challenge of how to assess critically the gendered assumptions of both DDR programs and TCs. Those working in peacebuilding contexts should consider the broader implications of the gendered power relations that these measures sustain for all war-affected populations, including female ex-combatants, in the postconflict period and beyond.

## NOTES

1    I am deeply indebted to Marie Manrique, Sofia Macher, Julissa Mantilla, Ruth Borja, Rosario Narvaez, Thandi Modise, Norma Guevara, Yasmin Sooka, Vanessa Farr, Gunhild Schwitalla, Ana Sonia Medina, Gladis Melara, Maria Chichilco, and those who shared their experiences without wanting to be named. I thank Alexander Segovia, Ana Patel, and Maya Ollek for helpful comments on a draft version of this paper.

2   United Nations Security Council Resolution (UNSCR) 1325, "Women, Peace and Secu-
    rity," S/RES/1325 (October 31, 2000).

3   Ibid., para. 13.

4   Sanam Naraghi Anderlini, "Reclaiming Human Dignity" (unpublished draft, Interna-
    tional Center for Transitional Justice, 2009).

5   Vasuki Nesiah et al., *Truth Commissions and Gender: Principles, Policies, and Procedures* (New
    York: International Center for Transitional Justice, 2006).

6   Tsjeard Bouta, "Gender and Disarmament, Demobilization and Reintegration—Build-
    ing Blocs for Dutch Policy" (The Hague: Netherlands Institute of International Relations
    "Clingendael," 2005), 5; and Emily Schroeder, "A Window of Opportunity in the Demo-
    cratic Republic of the Congo: Incorporating a Gender Perspective in the Disarmament,
    Demobilization and Reintegration Process," *Peace, Conflict and Development* 5 (2004).

7   Caroline O. N. Moser and Cathy McIlwaine, "Gender and Social Capital in Contexts of
    Political Violence: Community Perspectives from Colombia and Guatemala," in *Victims,
    Perpetrators or Actors?: Gender, Armed Conflict and Political Violence*, ed. Caroline O. N.
    Moser and Fiona Clark (London: Zed Books, 2001).

8   Tina Sideris, "Problems of Identity, Solidarity and Reconciliation," in *The Aftermath:
    Women in Post-Conflict Transformation*, ed. Sheila Meintjes, Meredeth Turshen, and Anu
    Pillay (London: Zed Books, 2001); Nahla Valji, "Gender Justice and Reconciliation," in
    *Building a Future on Peace and Justice: Studies on Transitional Justice, Peace and Development*,
    ed. Kai Ambos, Judith Large, and Marieke Wierda (Berlin: Springer, 2009); and Victoria
    Gonzalez and Karen Kampwirth, eds., *Radical Women in Latin America: Left and Right*
    (University Park, PA: Pennsylvania State University Press, 2001).

9   Vanessa Farr, "Gendering Demilitarization as a Peacebuilding Tool," Paper 20 (Bonn:
    Bonn International Center for Conversion, 2002).

10  Ibid.

11  Luisa Maria Dietrich Ortega, "Accountability Institutions and Female Ex-Combatants:
    Lessons Learned from International Experience" (unpublished draft, International Cen-
    ter for Transitional Justice, 2008).

12  See, e.g., Mohamed Gibril Sesay and Mohamed Suma, "Transitional Justice and DDR in
    Sierra Leone," Country Cases (New York: International Center for Transitional Justice,
    April 2009), www.ictj.org/en/research/projects/ddr/country-cases/2383.html.

13  Laura Sjoberg and Caron E. Gentry, *Mothers, Monsters, Whores: Women's Violence in Global
    Politics* (London: Zed Books, 2007).

14  The United Nations International Research and Training Institute for the Advancement
    of Women (UN-INSTRAW), "Gender and Security Sector Reform: An Introduction,"
    Gender, Peace and Security Working Paper Series, www.un-instraw.org/en/gps/general/
    gender-and-security-sector-reform.html.

15  Donna Pankhurst, "The Sex War and Other Wars: Toward a Feminist Approach to

Peacebuilding," in *Development, Women and War: Feminist Perspectives*, ed. Haleh Afshar and Deborah Eade (UK: Oxfam, 2004), 19.

16   Dietrich Ortega, "Accountability Institutions and Female Ex-Combatants."

17   Bouta, "Gender and Disarmament." It is relevant to note that there are inconsistencies between the numbers of combatants reported during armed struggle and (proxy) data collected in later phases of the conflict-to-postconflict continuum.

18   Alba Nubia Rodriguez Pizarro, "Entre el compromiso y la huida—Mujeres militantes en los grupos insurgentes colombianos," *Revue de Civilisation Contemporaine de l'Université de Bretagne Occidentale Europes/Amériques* 8 (2008).

19   This also holds true for ideologically motivated and socialist-inspired movements. These included formal commitments to gender equality that, in practice, were not respected. Timothy P. Wickham-Crowley, *Guerrillas and Revolution in Latin America: Comparative Study of insurgents and regimes since 1956* (Princeton: Princeton University Press1993) In El Salvador, women held twelve high-ranking political and military leadership positions, although there were more women in mid-command structures. (Vazquez, 1996) Norma Vazquez, Cristina Ibanez, Clara Murguialday, *Mujeres-Montaña: Vivencias de guerrilleras y colaboradoras del FMLN* (Madrid: horas y HORAS Publicaciones: 1996) One explanation for this is that many women joined the armed struggle after the guerrillas were created, and thus were not present when the groups' organizational and management structures were developed. In Peru's MRTA (Tupac Amaru Revolutionary Movement), e.g., six women were reported on a police list among the forty most prominent command cadres. Benedicto Jiménez Bacca, *Inicio, desarrollo y ocaso del terrorismo en el Perú: el ABC de Sendero Luminoso y el MRTA ampliado y comentado* (Lima: Imprenta Sanki, 2000)

20   Afshar argues that "whether real or symbolic, the presence of women in the formal and informal armed forces has not fundamentally changed their social position," in *Development, Women, and War*.

21   Codou Bop argues that the sense of power entailed in belonging to a dominant group has led women fighters to transform the way they perceive themselves. It has contributed to changing their traditional identity as wives and mothers to that of fighters and liberators of their countries. See Codou Bop, "Women in Conflicts: Their Gains and Their Losses," in *The Aftermath*.

22   Julia D. Shayne, *The Revolution Question: Feminisms in El Salvador, Chile and Cuba* (Piscataway, NJ: Rutgers University Press, 2004).

23   Elise Fredrikke Barth, "Peace as Disappointment: The Reintegration of Female Soldiers in Post-Conflict Societies: A Comparative Study from Africa," Report 3 (Oslo: Peace Research Institute, August 2002).

24   Gunhild Schwitalla and Luisa Maria Dietrich Ortega, "La desmovilización de las mujeres ex-combatientes en Colombia, en Violencia sexual: Arma de guerra, obstaculo para la paz," *Forced Migration Review* 27 (January 2007): 58.

25    Ibid.

26    A study in Colombia reviewed approximately thirty official peace negotiation docu-
      ments signed in the various attempts to bring an end to decades of armed conflict. It
      found 280 signatures from men and 15 from women, among whom only 1 was a female
      combatant. See Luz Maria Londoño and Yoana Fernanda Nieto, *Mujeres no Contadas.
      Proceso de desmovilización y retorno a la vida civil de mujeres excombatientes en Colombia 1990-
      2003* (Colombia: La Carreta Editores, 2006).

27    Meredeth Turshen, "Engendering Relations of State to Society," in *The Aftermath.*

28    Camille Pampell Conaway and Salome Martinez, "Adding Value: Women's Contri-
      butions to Reintegration and Reconstruction in El Salvador," Case Studies (Women
      Waging Peace and The Policy Commission, January 2004), www.huntalternatives.org/
      pages/7614_case_studies.cfm.

29    Londoño and Nieto, *Mujeres no Contadas*; Norma Vazquez, Cristina Ibañez, and Clara
      Murguialday, eds., *Mujeres-Montaña: Vivencias de guerrilleras y colaboradoras del FMLN*
      (Madrid: Horas y horas, 1996); and Bouta, "Gender and Disarmament."

30    Dyan Mazurana, "Women in Armed Opposition Groups in Africa and the Promotion of
      International Humanitarian Law and Human Rights" (report of a workshop organized
      in Addis Ababa by Geneva Call and the Program for the Study of International Organi-
      zations, November 23–26, 2005).

31    Chris Coulter, Mariam Persson, and Mats Utas, *Young Female Fighters in African
      Wars — Conflict and Its Consequences* (Uppsala, Sweden: Nordiska Afrikainstitutet, 2008);
      and Megan MacKenzie, "Securitization and De-Securitization: Female Soldiers and the
      Reconstructions of Women in Post-conflict Sierra Leone," *Security Studies* (forthcoming,
      2009).

32    Coulter, Persson, and Utas, *Young Female Fighters*; and Susan McKay and Dyan
      Mazurana, *Where Are the Girls? Girls in Fighting Forces in Northern Uganda, Sierra Leone and
      Mozambique: Their Lives During and After War* (Canada: International Center for Human
      Rights and Democratic Development, 2004). As a comment from Liberia shows, "such
      women are hard to find — you can't find them, it is like they never existed." Elise Fre-
      drikke Barth, *Peace as Disappointment: The Reintegration of Female Soldiers in Post-conflict
      Societies : a Comparative Study from Africa : a Report for the Norwegian Ministry of Foreign
      Affairs* (Norway: International Peace Research Institute, 2002)

33    Coulter, Persson, and Utas, *Young Female Fighters*; and Irma Specht and Larry Attree, "The
      Reintegration of Teenage Girls and Young Women," *Intervention* 4, no. 3 (2006): 219–28.

34    Sanam Naraghi Anderlini, *Women Building Peace: What They Do, Why It Matters* (Boulder
      and London: Lynne Rienner Publishers, 2007), chap. 4.

35    MacKenzie, "Securitization and De-Securitization."

36    Dyan Mazurana and Khristopher Carlson, "From Combat to Community: Women and
      Girls of Sierra Leone," Case Study (Women Waging Peace and The Policy Commission,

January 2004), www.huntalternatives.org/pages/7614_case_studies.cfm.

37   See, e.g., Diana Pearce, "The Feminization of Poverty: Women, Work, and Welfare,"
     *Urban and Social Change Review* (February 1978): 30; and United Nations, "Review and
     Appraisal of the Implementation of the Beijing Platform for Action: Report of the Secre-
     tary-General," E/CN.6/2000/PC/2 (May 2000).

38   Megan Mackenzie, "Securitization and De-securitization: Female Soldiers and the
     Reconstruction of the Family," Security Studies (forthcoming 2009).

39   Ilja A. Luciak, *After the Revolution: Gender and Democracy in El Salvador, Nicaragua and
     Guatemala* (Baltimore: The Johns Hopkins University Press, 2001).

40   Wenche Hauge, "The Demobilization and Political Participation of Female Fighters
     in Guatemala: A Report to the Norwegian Ministry of Foreign Affairs" (Oslo: Peace
     Research Institute, 2007); Wenche Hauge, "Group Identity — A Neglected Asset: Deter-
     minants of Social and Political Participation among Female Ex-fighters in the Guate-
     mala Conflict," *Conflict, Security & Development* 8, no. 3 (October 2008): 295–316; and
     Mazurana, "Women in Armed Opposition Groups."

41   Irma Specht, *Red Shoes: Experiences of Girl Combatants in Liberia* (Geneva: ILO, 2006).

42   Hauge, "The Demobilization and Political Participation of Female Fighters in
     Guatemala."

43   For men, on the other hand, joining an armed opposition group entails an opportunity
     to enhance their manhood, fulfill their expected roles as warriors and protectors, and
     gain a source of recognition from others: "War does not challenge women to prove that
     they are women, whereas wars have been historically symbolized as the touchstone of
     manliness." Jacklyn Cock, *Colonels & Cadres: War and Gender in South Africa* (Cape Town:
     Oxford University Press, 1991)

44   Londoño and Nieto, *Mujeres no Contadas*; and Sjoberg and Gentry, *Mothers, Monsters, and
     Whores.*

45   Mazurana, "Women in Armed Opposition Groups."

46   Coulter, Persson, and Utas, *Young Female Fighters*; and Chris Coulter, "The Post War
     Moment: Female Fighters in Sierra Leone," Migration Studies Working Paper 22 (Forced
     Migration Studies Programme, University of Witwatersrand, 2005).

47   Victoria Bernal, "Equality to Die For? Women Guerrilla Fighters and Eritrea's Cultural
     Revolution," *Political and Legal Anthropology Review* 23, no. 2 (2000): 61–76.

48   MacKenzie, "Securitization and De-Securitization"; Vivi Stavrou, "Breaking the Silence:
     Girls Forcibly Involved in the Armed Struggle in Angola" (Christian Children's Fund,
     2006); and Megan MacKenzie, "From Soldiers to Citizens, or Soldiers to Seamstresses:
     Reintegrating Girls and Women in Sierra Leone" (paper presented at the International
     Studies Association 48th Annual Convention, Chicago, February 28 – March 3, 2007).

49   MacKenzie, "Securitization and De-Securitization."

50   Ibid.

51  Ibid.

52  Priscilla Hayner, *Unspeakable Truths: Confronting State Terror and Atrocity* (New York: Routledge, 2002).

53  Mats Utas, "Victimcy, Girlfriending, Soldiering: Tactic Agency in a Young Woman's Social Navigation of the Liberian War Zone," *Anthropological Quarterly* 78, no. 2 (Spring 2005): 403–30.

54  See Pablo de Greiff, "Establishing Links Between DDR and Reparations," in this volume.

55  Alexander Segovia, Luisa Maria Dietrich Ortega, and Yoana Nieto, *Reconciliation Between Victims, Communities and Ex-Combatants in Colombia: Lessons for Public Policies in Reconciliation* (Colombia: USAID/IOM Mission, forthcoming, 2009). In 2006, of the twenty-two countries implementing DDR programs, involving an estimated 1.25 million beneficiaries, not one had implemented a reparations initiative for victims. Escola de Cultura de Pau, *Analysis of the Disarmament, Demobilization, and Reintegration Program Existing in the World During 2006.* (Barcelona: ECP, 2007)

56  Ibid.

57  Alexander Segovia, "DDR and Transitional Justice: The Case of El Salvador," Country Cases (New York: International Center for Transitional Justice, April 2009), www.ictj.org/en/research/projects/ddr/country-cases/2380.html.

58  Hugo van der Merwe and Guy Lamb, "DDR and Transitional Justice in South Africa: Lessons Learned," Country Cases (New York: International Center for Transitional Justice, April 2009), www.ictj.org/en/research/projects/ddr/country-cases/2384.html.

59  Lars Waldorf, "Ex-Combatants and Truth Commissions," in this volume.

60  The duration of the TC was six months in El Salvador, eighteen months in Sierra Leone, and two years in Peru. More recently, the Colombian National Commission was given a mandate of eight years.

61  The Rome Statute of the International Criminal Court, "Crimes Against Humanity" (1999), pt. 2, art. 7.

62  There were three male commissioners in El Salvador, two female commissioners out of twelve in Peru, three women out of seven commissioners in Sierra Leone, and seven out of seventeen in South Africa. Although gender balance within a commission alone is an insufficient indicator of whether a commission will adequately address the human rights abuses women have suffered, the internal power dynamics among commissioners can be critical in determining which issues get prioritized. See Nesiah et al., *Truth Commissions and Gender.*

63  Nesiah et al., *Truth Commissions and Gender.*

64  Valji, "Gender Justice and Reconciliation."

65  Fiona C. Ross, "Women and the Politics of Identity: Voices in the South African Truth and Reconciliation Commission," in *Violence and Belonging: The Quest for Identity in Post-Colonial Africa*, ed. Vigdis Broch-Due (New York: Routledge, 2005).

66 Shayne, *The Revolution Question.*

67 Dietrich Ortega, "Accountability Institutions and Female Ex-Combatants."

68 *Final Report of the Truth and Reconciliation Commission in Peru.*

69 Sierra Leone Truth and Reconciliation Commission, *Sierra Leone Truth and Reconciliation Commission Final Report,* trcsierraleone.org/drwebsite/publish/index.shtml.

70 The Commission for the Truth in El Salvador, *From Madness to Hope: The 12 Year War in El Salvador* (March 15, 1993), www.usip.org/library/tc/doc/reports/el_salvador/tc_es_03151993_toc.html.

71 Beth Goldblatt and Sheila Meintjes, "Gender and the Truth and Reconciliation Commission: A Submission to the Truth and Reconciliation Commission" (May 1996), www.doj.gov.za/trc/submit/gender.htm.

72 The TRC final report indicates that 65 percent of the applications to the amnesty committee were submitted by people who were in custody, that 5,392 out of 7,112 petitioners were refused amnesty, and that 849 were granted amnesty.

73 See Roger Duthie and Irma Specht, "DDR, Transitional Justice, and the Reintegration of Former Child Combatants," in this volume.

74 Therese Abrahamsen and Hugo van der Merwe, "Reconciliation through Amnesty? Amnesty Applicants' Views of the South African Truth and Reconciliation Commission" (Cape Town: Centre for the Study of Violence and Reconciliation, 2005). pp 7–12

75 Ibid., p.8

76 Ibid., p.12

77 Abuses of women combatants along gendered lines have included (in the Peruvian case) forced nudity, sexual violence, rape and the threat of sexual violence as forms of torture, as well as withholding medical services for pregnant women in order to humiliate and degrade women, often targeting specifically their conditions as mothers.

78 Pumla Gobodo-Madikizela, "Women's Contributions to South Africa's Truth and Reconciliation Commission," Women Waging Peace Policy Commission Case Studies (2005); and Fiona Ross, "Women and the Politics of Identity." and Ross, Fiona, Bearing Witness: Women and The Truth and Reconciliation Commission in South Africa, (London, Pluto Press, 2003)

79 Ross, "Women and the Politics of Identity."

80 Coalition for Women's Human Rights in Conflict Situations, "Submission to the Truth and Reconciliation Commission," Sierra Leone, May 2003, www.womensrightscoalition.org/site/advocacyDossiers/sierraleoneTR/submissiontotr.php.

81 The Peruvian Truth and Reconciliation Commission, "Carta desde penal de Chorillos: Las carceles" (August 2003), Annex chap. 2.22, http://www.cverdad.org.pe/ifinal/pdf/TOMO%20V/SECCION%20TERCERA-Los%20Escenarios%20de%20la%20violencia%20(continuacion)/2.%20HISTORIAS%20REPRESENTATIVAS%20DE%20LA%20VIOLENCIA/2.22%20LAS%20CARCELES.pdf (accessed April 14, 2009).

82 Ibid., Tomo IX, "Fundamentos de la reconciliation," 34–35, www.cverdad.org.pe/ifinal/index.php (accessed April 14, 2009).

83 Before the Peruvian Truth and Reconciliation Commission issued its final report, which established the number of victims at close to 70,000 dead, specialists had estimated the death toll at only 25,000.

84 Peruvian TRC, "Recommendaciones," Tomo IX, "Reformas Institutionales," chap. 2.1, 130–34, www.cverdad.org.pe/ifinal/index.php (accessed April 14, 2009).

85 Ibid. Further, the different categories of ex-combatants are the following: militants of Shining Path and MRTA; detached members of their former armed groups who renounced armed struggle; those who accepted the repentance laws; and those who maintained that they were innocent.

86 Truth and Reconciliation Commission of Sierra Leone, "Women and the Armed Conflict in Sierra Leone" (2007), chap. 3, art. 22.

87 Ibid.

88 Ibid.

89 Comisión Nacional de Reparación y Reconciliación (CNRR), "CNRR y ACR se unen para trabajar por la reintegración y la reconciliación," Bogota, October 29, 2008, www.cnrr.visiondirecta.com/09e/spip.php?article547&var_recherche=ACR.

# CHAPTER 6

# DDR, Transitional Justice, and the Reintegration of Former Child Combatants

*Roger Duthie and Irma Specht*[1]

## INTRODUCTION

Children and armed conflict and, more narrowly, children and disarmament, demobilization, and reintegration (DDR) programs have become the subject of substantive discussion among advocates, practitioners, and scholars. More recently, some attention has been paid to children and transitional justice measures, such as criminal prosecutions, truth commissions, reparations programs, and institutional reform. There was, for example, significant debate around the issue of whether child perpetrators should be prosecuted at the Special Court for Sierra Leone. Little, however, has been written about how transitional justice measures affect the goals of DDR programs with respect to former child combatants[2] and how, in turn, DDR programs affect the goals of transitional justice measures with respect to children. As the leading international coalition against child combatants stated at a 2006 international forum, there is a "necessity of deepening the understanding of the impact of justice processes, international or national, on other initiatives, including the demobilization and reintegration of children and peace processes."[3]

This chapter takes a step toward filling this gap, drawing heavily on the input of child rights and child combatant experts, as well as interviews with former child combatants themselves. The chapter also seeks to situate the topic within the broader literature and debates regarding children, conflict, and reintegration. The aim is not to relabel DDR concerns as justice concerns, or vice versa, but to try to sort out precisely where DDR and transitional justice for children overlap, reinforce, and conflict with each other. Our main argument is that the primary avenue through which transitional justice measures may positively affect the reintegration of former child combatants is likely to be their potential impact on receiving communities—that is, minimizing social exclusion through the reduction of community members' and victims' feelings of injustice. Potential negative effects, however, are important and should not be overlooked.

It should first be noted that for children the relationship between DDR and transitional justice will likely play out in many of the same ways that it does for adult ex-combatants, as examined throughout this volume. Truth commissions, for example, can provide societies with an evenhanded account of the causes, nature, and consequences of a conflict, thereby possibly sensitizing both victims and perpetrators and diminishing the general stigmatization of former child combatants; but truth-telling may also be detrimental to the reintegration of individual former child combatants by drawing attention within the community to their past crimes. Reparations programs may reduce the resentment that can be created within communities and among victims by the provision of DDR benefits to former child combatants (and the perpetrators among them). Criminal prosecutions may help put an end to a general culture of impunity, individualize guilt, and break down perceptions within communities of collective responsibility; but prosecutions may also foster resentment and fear, particularly among child ex-combatants, creating a disincentive for them to come forward and participate in DDR programs.

The first section of this chapter discusses the concept of reintegration as it relates to DDR programs and transitional justice in the sense of both short-term programs and long-term process. We use a fairly broad understanding of the term "reintegration" here, one that incorporates both *program* and *process* — program in the sense of the official reintegration stage of organized DDR programs, and process in the sense of the longer-term, holistic notion of fully reintegrating former child combatants into civilian life. The section argues that while there is already much that is done successfully to reintegrate former child combatants into civilian life through DDR programs and a variety of other initiatives, and while empirical studies suggest that former child combatants actually tend to reintegrate into society fairly well, there is evidence to suggest that some former child combatants experience a great deal of difficulty adjusting to normal life and being accepted by their communities, at least in part because of the past crimes they or other child combatants committed. It seems reasonable, then, to suggest that there may be room for transitional justice measures to play a positive role in facilitating this long-term process of reintegration, with an eye to avoiding the disruption of short-term DDR programs.

The next four sections look at the relationships between DDR and specific transitional justice measures — truth commissions, reparations, local justice, and prosecutions (discussed last, as we want to emphasize its nature as a measure of "last resort" for children). In each case, both the positive and problematic elements of the relationship will be discussed. In general, we focus more on process than program, and so much of the interaction discussed is in terms of reinforcement or hindrance rather than on specific programmatic links, although the latter are highlighted wherever possible. We conclude by highlighting a number of key issues that repeatedly surface throughout the chapter, such as the overlap of the concepts of perpetrator and victim with regard to child combatants; the existence of both complementarity and tensions between the best interests of the child and the interests of victims; and the need for more empirical research to shed light on how this relationship plays out in practice rather than in theory.

## REINTEGRATION OF FORMER CHILD COMBATANTS: ROLES FOR BOTH DDR AND TRANSITIONAL JUSTICE?

The reintegration of former child combatants is a primary goal of many DDR programs, as well as for transitional justice measures (to the extent that they involve former child combatants) and other child-focused peacebuilding initiatives. According to the UN's *Integrated Disarmament, Demobilization and Reintegration Standards (IDDRS)*, reintegration is "the process by which ex-combatants acquire civilian status and gain sustainable employment and income," and "is essentially a social and economic process with an open time-frame, primarily taking place in communities at the local level."[4] Child-specific reintegration

> shall allow a child to access education, a livelihood, life skills and a meaningful role in society. The socio-economic and psychosocial aspects of reintegration for children are central to global DDR programming and budgeting. Successful reintegration requires long-term funding of child protection agencies and programmes to ensure continuous support for education and training for children, and essential follow-up/monitoring once they return to civilian life.[5]

Furthermore, in order to be sustainable, child-specific reintegration "must be based on broader community development processes."[6]

The UN considers reintegration as the third stage of DDR programming, but acknowledges the need for a longer-term, multidimensional, community-oriented process aimed at facilitating the (re)creation of a meaningful role for children in society. Similarly, the recent strategic review of Graça Machel's 1996 study, "Impact of Armed Conflict on Children," by the Office of the Special Representative of the Secretary-General for Children and Armed Conflict and

UNICEF, describes reintegration for children as a process requiring programming beyond DDR programs, one with "wide-ranging aims, different for each boy and girl involved, including building emotional trust and reconciling with family and community, providing access to education and developing a means of livelihood."[7] This understanding is shared by the practitioner and scholar Michael Wessells, who sees reintegration as "less about reinserting former soldiers back into communities or jobs than about helping children become functional in their society—helping them find meaningful and respected social roles and create civilian identities."[8] Ultimately, the objective of reintegration programs and processes is to create "human security" at the local level, not just for the former adult and child combatants, but for their communities as well. The process can take decades, however. It also involves extremely complex challenges, and positive results depend on a multitude of factors.[9]

Reintegration of children in this broad sense is also a concern of transitional justice. The *IDDRS*, for example, suggests that because children recruited into armed groups are the victims of an international crime, reintegration itself can be considered as a form of justice: "measures that aim to prevent their [children's] recruitment, or that attempt to reintegrate them into their communities, should not be viewed as a routine component of peacemaking, but as an attempt to prevent or redress a violation of children's human rights."[10] Under international law, specifically the Convention on the Rights of the Child (CRC), states have an obligation to "take all appropriate measures to promote physical and psychological recovery and social reintegration of a child victim of: any form of neglect, exploitation, or abuse; torture or any other form of cruel, inhuman or degrading treatment or punishment; or armed conflicts. Such recovery and reintegration shall take place in an environment which fosters the health, self-respect and dignity of the child."[11] In terms of children as perpetrators of crimes, the CRC also requires that state responses (which would include transitional justice) must take into account the "desirability of promoting the child's reintegration and the child's assuming a constructive role in society."[12]

There are many DDR and justice efforts that may overlap and/or reinforce each other. The U.S. Agency for International Development (USAID), for example, identified nine forms of intervention that contributed to the successful reintegration of child combatants in Sierra Leone with their families and communities. These were: "community sensitization; formal disarmament and demobilization; a period of transition in an ICC [interim care center]; family tracing, mediation, and reunification; traditional cleansing and healing ceremonies, and religious support; school or skills training of adequate quality and duration; ongoing access to health care, particularly for war-related conditions, for those in school or training; individual supportive counselling, encouragement, and facilitation; and an effective collaborative approach." With the help of such a range of interventions, the agency reports, 98 percent of demobilized children were reunited with their parents or relatives.[13] Effective reintegration efforts should, in general, also be complemented with income-generating support to families who receive young child soldiers, and assistance should be provided to the youth themselves to improve their employability through skills training, business start up, and other kinds of assistance. Again, some of these interventions can be considered to incorporate elements of justice, if only at an individual level. While not one of its primary aims, psychosocial counseling by NGOs can "provide a framework and safe context for the children to admit to things they have done. In part, returning to the theme of impunity, this can represent a form of confrontation with guilt."[14]

These kinds of intervention can contribute to some extent to successful reintegration processes. Recent empirical studies suggest that former child combatants for the most part actually do better than expected. For example, a study by Christopher Blattman and Jeannie Annan in Uganda found that the main impacts on child combatants of participating in armed groups were human capital losses (education and employment) and moderate psychological distress concentrated in a minority who experienced violence the most.[15] In Mozambique, a longitudinal study conducted between 1988 and 2004 of the life outcomes of thirty-nine male former child combatants found that "the majority of this group of former child soldiers that we have followed for the past 16 years have become productive, capable and caring adults": they had "emerged from violent childhoods to become trusted and productive adult members of their communities and nation."[16] These children were doing as well as or better than the national averages for socioeconomic and child welfare indicators.[17] The study suggests that the combination of rehabilitation programs, community sensitization campaigns, community projects, and traditional ceremonies facilitated the subject children's recovery.[18] Another study of a sample of ex-combatants in Sierra Leone, which suggests that the "vast majority" of the 79,000 demobilized fighters have experienced "high levels of acceptance" and "reintegration success," found no evidence that age affected the outcomes (that is, children reintegrated just as successfully as adults did).[19]

The record of these processes in facilitating the reintegration of girls is not as well documented. Girls participate in formal DDR processes in far fewer numbers than boys, and thus frequently do not benefit from reintegration support. In the Democratic Republic of the Congo (DRC), for example, only 3,000 girls were officially demobilized by the end of 2005 — only about 15 percent of the total number of estimated girls involved in the conflict.[20] Girls also face greater social barriers and exclusion, as their association with armed groups may break with cultural stereotypes for girls' behavior, or they may be seen to have "lost value through involvement in sexual activity."[21]

What are the implications of such research for DDR, transitional justice, and other types of reintegration-related interventions for children? First, it is unclear how much credit DDR programs can actually take for success in the reintegration of former child combatants. According to Wessells, "the postconflict landscape is littered with questionable DDR processes offering inadequate assistance to children," and many child combatants avoid formal programs and self-demobilize.[22] Similarly, Lucia Withers of the Coalition to Stop the Use of Child Soldiers speaks of the "harsh reality that in many situations the focus is on the disarmament and demobilization, while provisions for reintegration of child soldiers are inadequate (e.g., Sierra Leone) or non-existent (Aceh), or indeed that many child soldiers, both boys and girls, will not go through any DDR process at all."[23] Furthermore, the Sierra Leone study referenced above found only weak evidence that participation in DDR programs improved the reintegration of individuals.[24] Improvement in such interventions could be valuable, for one reason because for those who are affected negatively by their experiences as combatants — in terms of loss of education and skills, for example — the impact can be serious and long lasting. "It is my very unfortunate fate that I was drawn into wars," reflected one former boy combatant in Afghanistan.

> If instead of war skills, I knew other skills and knowledge, now I could use my knowledge and expertise. Then today I would be an engineer or doctor or something else useful for my society and myself. If I knew some skills I could contribute to solve our problems and I could help others. For instance, now many Afghani children are illiterate and if I was able to teach I could teach some of them.[25]

Second, there does seem to be potential for transitional justice to contribute to reintegration (both positively and negatively). According to the Sierra Leone study cited above, the most important determinant of successful reintegration was whether an individual combatant's unit had participated in widespread human rights abuses during the war (there is no indication that this did not hold true for children).[26] In addition, there is a great deal of anecdotal evidence that some former child combatants, even if a minority, do in fact have great difficulty returning to or reintegrating into their communities, and part of the reason for this is precisely the mutual fear created by the perception that they are perpetrators of abuses. It can be argued that social ostracism may be an appropriate form of punishment for those who have committed crimes, but there is a danger that former child combatants as a group are treated this way. "Those children who are able to find their homes or families may hesitate, fearing reprisals or ostracism by community members who blame the children for complicity in atrocities," writes P. W. Singer. "Their home communities often consider them beyond redemption. It is very difficult to convince family members who witnessed the children taking part in the destruction of their towns and villages that they must now be forgiven." He points to one survey in Africa in which 80 percent of parents did not want their children to mix with former child combatants.[27]

Such children are often initially both feared and in fear of retaliation, as they, in Wessells's words, "enter a difficult terrain awash in unhealed grievances, vigilante justice, and contested privileges. In some cases, *villagers' strong feelings of injustice block child soldiers' attempts to reenter the community*."[28] In Liberia, for example, many youth who were former combatants together squatted in Monrovia because they feared the way they would be received in their places of origin as a result of their crimes and atrocities.[29] One former child combatant in Sierra Leone described killing his own brother (whom he was told was a rebel collaborator), and subsequently being treated as a hero by his squad. "Now," however, "my family does not want to see me, and my father has sworn that he is going to kill me if he ever sets his eyes on me again."[30] Sometimes there are actual "revenge attacks," such as in October 2001, when a camp of former child fighters in Sri Lanka was overrun and twenty-six children were beaten to death by local citizens, the type of event that "risks deterring other child soldiers from demobilizing, possibly unraveling the peace."[31]

It is argued here that transitional justice's main (positive or negative) contribution to the reintegration of former child combatants is likely to be the potential effect of such measures on the receiving community. This is not to say that justice measures will not also affect reintegration directly through their impact on the former child combatants themselves; but, across the range of transitional justice interventions, it seems more plausible to think that transitional justice's impact can come from minimizing social exclusion through the reduction of community members' and victims' feelings of injustice. "Ultimately," as Singer puts it, "a successful reintegration is as much about whether the families and communities are prepared for acceptance as about whether the children have been properly rehabilitated."[32]

An effective DDR program for children will and should maintain as its core constituency the former child combatants themselves. DDR efforts may include the community as part of the equation, but transitional justice can make it an even greater part. DDR and other interventions, such as psychosocial treatment, may simply not be enough for victims and communities. "Confronting atrocities through a process of counseling, especially one that draws in the wider community," writes Andrew Mawson, "could be seen as a step toward addressing impunity" and could "contribute to the social acceptance of a low-key, individualized, nonpunishment-orientated approach to confronting atrocities. It may not, however, be an approach that in the long term enables the direct victims of violence to feel that justice has been particularly well served."[33] This is where the space exists for transitional justice to make a difference in the reintegration process. In the next sections, we look more closely at how various transitional justice measures may fill this space.

It is important to note here that reintegration interventions—both DDR and transitional justice—are affected by other contextual factors and the different types of interventions that are aimed at addressing those factors. Two examples would be conditions of poverty and the continuation of violence, particularly violence involving former child combatants. The success of reintegration efforts will depend in part on development and poverty-reduction strategies, as well as security sector reform (SSR) that helps to curb the violence committed by children after demobilization. Reintegration efforts, for example, need to be complemented by community development programs; otherwise, child and adult combatants often return to an "impoverished countryside struggling with basic survival needs and without schools, hospitals, vocational training or job opportunities which would allow them to envisage any prospects of a better future."[34] They also need to be complemented by functioning police and judicial institutions that can help to change the behavior of those former child combatants who continue to perpetrate violence after the war is over, as well as to make those children who would otherwise be the victims of this ongoing violence—particularly girls—feel safer. Children who follow the law and feel safe are more likely to reintegrate successfully. In Liberia, for example, community members were becoming more at ease with the returned child combatants because they were starting to behave well, no longer using abusive language, and readapting to the authority of parents and local elders.[35] In Sierra Leone, on the other hand, community members complained that those who went through the truth commission continued to loot and misbehave.[36] Successful reintegration is dependent on more than just effective and coordinated DDR and transitional justice efforts.

## TRUTH-TELLING AND THE REINTEGRATION OF CHILDREN

Truth-telling is often considered an important element of a holistic approach to transitional justice, although its use in some contexts may be problematic.[37] Depending on how they are designed and implemented, truth-telling efforts may both facilitate and hinder children's reintegration. Truth commissions may sensitize victims and perpetrators and diminish the general stigmatization of former child combatants, but they may also draw attention within the community to children's past crimes or scare the children away from participating in disarmament and demobilization.

To begin with, truth-telling can provide an evenhanded account of the conflict and the role of children in it, including children associated with armed groups. Truth-telling may have a positive impact on the reintegration of children through its effects on both the children themselves and the rest of society, including the communities to which they are returning. As is now widely recognized, child combatants who commit human rights abuses should be considered both perpetrators and victims, because their presence within an armed group is itself often a crime and because they are often forced to commit atrocities. Many consider truth commissions to be more appropriate than prosecutions to deal with children and their various roles in the conflict because they recognize that the distinction between perpetrator and victim is not always clear.[38]

There are reasons to think that truth commissions may make communities more receptive to returning child combatants by revealing the extent to which, even if they have committed crimes, they are also victims of crime. Truth-telling, for example, could provide opportunities for children to tell their stories, for creating or raising public awareness of children's experiences, and for helping victims to understand the context in which abuses took place.[39] "The participation of children in truth commissions or informal, community-based truth-seeking processes can help communities appreciate children's experiences."[40] Truth commissions in Peru, Argentina, El Salvador, and Guatemala all had chapters in their final reports dedicated to children, while South Africa's TRC held children's hearings, and in Sierra Leone's TRC children themselves could give statements and participate in hearings. An examination of how children were illegally recruited into armed groups can be an explicit part of this focus. Singer contends that efforts should be made "to reinforce the acknowledgment by society that the children were also victims in the process. Truth and reconciliation programs have been run to some good effect in places like South Africa, but programs more specific to child soldiers are needed."[41] Indeed, the Sierra Leone commission devoted a section of its final report to the issue of children as "victim-perpetrators," in an attempt to "understand how children came to carry out violations as part of an important learning curve in preventing future conflicts."[42] In Liberia, a child protection officer observed that currently "there are surprisingly a good number of children in Liberia who are more than willing to tell their 'stories both good and bad' to the TRC."[43]

Truth commissions may also facilitate the reintegration of former child combatants through their educational and rehabilitative effects on the children themselves. "A truth-seeking process can help children and young people understand what has happened to them during the war," say An Michels and Saudamini Siegrist, "and thus can contribute to their understanding of right and wrong."[44] Once they return to their communities, these children may be less likely to behave in ways that would make the community reject them. By "drawing on lessons from the fields of juvenile and restorative justice," truth commissions "can be particularly appropriate for children's rehabilitation and recovery on the one hand, while also providing a form of accountability."[45] Truth commissions can also contribute to children's rehabilitation by linking up with or coordinating with DDR and other types of interventions. Sequencing can also be important: truth-telling efforts that follow disarmament and demobilization efforts, rather than occurring simultaneously, are less likely to create any sort of disincentive for children to give up their arms and demobilize.

In the other direction, DDR programs themselves can also take on a truth-telling role, or at least an information-gathering role—information that could then potentially be shared with a truth commission. For example, while some children are forced to join armed groups against their will, the majority of children associated with armed groups around the world today were not physically forced to join (although the notion of "voluntarism" has been seriously challenged in the context of children[46]). In order to ensure effective reintegration and the design of preventive measures against recruitment, it is crucial to understand why these children opted to join in the first place:

> Particularly in situations when the young people were not abducted or physically forced to join in the first place, the demobilization and

reintegration are unlikely to be successful or sustained unless the reasons why they became involved are addressed. . . . It is essential, therefore, to understand the reasons that they themselves identify for joining armed forces or armed groups, whether by individual choice or as the result of other factors. In turn, understanding why they joined indicates what needs to be done if others are not to follow in their footsteps.[47]

While early DDR programs never asked this question, today answers can partly be found by listening to the children themselves as part of DDR planning processes.[48] While not a public form of truth-telling, this kind of procedure may serve some of the same purposes from the perspective of the child combatants, and it can be done in a protected environment with social workers and sometimes family members.

The impact of truth-telling measures on the reintegration of children associated with armed conflict, however, may be negative, and will depend on how the process itself is designed and implemented. According to Rosalind Shaw, in Sierra Leone "whole communities agreed not to give statements or to give statements that withheld information that they thought might be damaging to the ex-combatant children of their neighbors."[49] "The Paris Principles: Principles and Guidelines on Children Associated with Armed Forces or Armed Groups" set the following standards in this regard: "Where truth-seeking and reconciliation mechanisms are established, children's involvement should be promoted and supported and their rights protected throughout the process. Their participation must be voluntary and by informed consent by both the child and her or his parent or guardian where appropriate and possible. Special procedures should be permitted to minimize greater susceptibility to distress."[50] Using the CRC and the "best interests of the child" as guidance as well, others have articulated that truth commission procedures should always keep the reintegration of the children who participate in mind. According to No Peace Without Justice (NPWJ) and UNICEF, for example, truth commission "proceedings should, as a primary concern, consider the best interest of the child and, where appropriate, ensure the integration of measures that are aimed at the rehabilitation and reintegration of the child, including measures designed to foster the child's respect for the rights of others."[51]

In reality, how does the participation of children formerly associated with armed forces in truth-telling processes affect their reintegration, either in the short run or the long run? Research and interviews conducted for this chapter with former children associated with armed groups who did—and did not—participate in Sierra Leone's TRC provide anecdotal evidence of both positive and negative effects on the reintegration of individuals. "My life became better because I faced the TRC," said one boy. "I still carry the guilt of the things I did. I still feel very sad that I got involved in evil things. Since I left the TRC, my family has been assuring me every day that they have forgiven me and they love me so much." When asked if children who have committed crimes in other countries should be encouraged to face a truth commission, he said:

> There is nothing as powerful as the truth, nothing sets you free except the truth. Even if one goes to jail after saying the truth, you feel stronger and courageous. My life became better when I went through the TRC. I believe that theirs would become much better after they face a truth commission. Depriving them from one if they choose to face it will only make matters worse for them.[52]

Another boy heard about the truth commission when he was in a DDR camp. "I asked two UN peacekeepers from Bangladesh who spent some time explaining to me about it," he recalls.

> I decided then that nothing was going to stop me from facing the TRC. My friends said that from the TRC I will go to prison, but I was desperate to let the world know what I did wrong, the people I killed and how their families could forgive me.... The TRC did me good, people now understand that I am sorry for what I did and I will never do it again.[53]

For other children, however, participating in the truth commission made life more difficult. One girl had the following to say, based on her experience:

> If the person wants to live in peace with few people knowing what he or she did, then I will advise the person not to go [to the TRC], but if the person wants to make publicity and endanger his or her life, then I will advise the person to go. Children should not be made to face the TRC.... The TRC brings stigma and stigma brings neglect and abandonment; people run away from you. Parents keep their children from you and you are almost like the HIV/AIDS kids. I do not think it should continue in any part of the world.

Asked if she regretted facing the TRC, she responded:

> Yes, now I can no longer hide. Everybody is running away from me. Even boys do not come close to me. And I have friends who were former RUF [Revolutionary United Front] but who never faced the TRC

and only few people know about them. They are having boyfriends and living normal lives. I think it was a mistake on my part and I am only sad that I cannot turn back the hands of time.... People point at me as I walk on the street and when I go to local cinemas, people move off the seat I am seated [in] and I feel so bad. Never has someone come to me and tried to encourage me to go on with life, never has someone come up and said he/she wants to help me.[54]

According to another boy,

I honestly regret facing the TRC. I had to change my name and the place I was staying because I became very popular after the testimony and lots of people came to know me.... If I had not faced the TRC I would have been safer and only few people would have known what I did. The TRC leaves children vulnerable and once people know what some did they become afraid of them and they get left out in society. I have also heard that children have been used to testify at the Special Court. I think it is wrong, information always goes out to the wrong people and there are people who never forgive or forget.[55]

Beyond such anecdotal evidence, we do not really know much yet about the long-term effects of truth-telling on the reintegration of children. As Lucia Withers explains, there exists "little research that provides evidence as to the impact truth commissions have, positive or negative, on former child soldiers and their prospects for reintegration."[56] More empirical and comparative studies are needed of how former child combatants who have engaged with truth commissions in different ways have fared in terms of their long-term reintegration (compared with those who did not engage with truth commissions).

## REPARATIONS AND THE REINTEGRATION OF CHILDREN

As with adult ex-combatants, there are many good reasons to provide DDR benefits to children, including security- and development-related ones. Former child combatants can act as spoilers in a peace process; they can become involved in rising levels of postconflict crime; they may have missed many years of education or work experience in which they would have developed employable skills; and they may require psychosocial assistance because of the trauma they experienced. They are not, however, the only group of children to have suffered during war. As David Nosworthy emphasizes in a contribution to the ten-year review of the Machel study, child combatants "represent only a small percentage of the overall number of children whose lives have been impacted by armed conflict and who are striving with their families and communities to recover from war's grave effects."[57] Wessells claims that one of the "great fallacies" that exists concerning the issue of child soldiers is that they are worse off than other children during war. "In fact," he points out, "child soldiers often have better access to food and protection than do other children, who are subject to scourges such as attack, displacement, and HIV/AIDS, and who have no means to defend themselves. Child soldiers may also be better off because their groups meet their basic needs by looting and robbing villages." He concludes that "former child soldiers are neither uniquely vulnerable nor definable in terms of vulnerability."[58]

The point here is not that children should go without DDR benefits, but that in the absence of addressing the needs of other vulnerable groups, including the justice claims of victims of serious human rights abuses, reintegration may be resisted. According to Trish Hiddleston, a child protection officer at the time in the DRC, "Most of these children are going back to very vulnerable communities. If these children receive benefits that are not available to other children in the community, there is a possibility that they will be resented, which will not facilitate their reintegration."[59] Similarly, in Liberia, where children received cash initially (although this was stopped after child protection agencies were critical), "Local communities tended to see the cash payments as rewards ('blood money') given to the children who had attacked them; this raised tensions and placed children at risk."[60]

With this in mind, recent DDR programs have enlarged their scope to address the needs of other war-affected groups, not just ex-combatants; this has been found "to lessen distrust and increase tolerance between the different conflict-affected groups and thus to support the reconciliation and reintegration process."[61] Reparations to victims, as Pablo de Greiff argues, may contribute to reintegration in much the same way.[62] Of particular importance for the reintegration of former child combatants may be reparations provided to other child victims.

What do we know about such reparations to children? The UN has set forth several general recommendations in its *Guidelines on Justice in Matters Involving Child Victims and Witnesses of Crime*, which state that child victims should "receive reparation in order to achieve full redress, reintegration and recovery." The "procedures for obtaining and enforcing reparation should be readily accessibly and child-sensitive," and combined with criminal proceedings and informal and community justice procedures. Reparation, according to the *Guidelines*, "may include restitution from the offender ordered in the criminal court, aid from victim compensation programs administered by the State and damages ordered to be paid in civil proceedings." Furthermore, "costs of social and educational reintegration, medical treatment, mental health care and legal services should be addressed."[63] In practice, Dyan Mazurana and Khristopher Carlson identify the common forms of individual reparations for child victims of armed conflict as educational benefits, access to health care, and financial reparation. The challenges faced in providing such reparations include recognizing and acknowledging crimes against children, defining child beneficiaries, and ensuring children's access to and participation in reparations.[64]

As with adults, reparations programs that go some way toward achieving the goals of bringing justice to child victims and restoring trust among citizens may contribute to reducing community resistance to the reintegration of former child combatants. The key issue is one of balance between DDR and reparations benefits. Past DDR programs, however, have had even more difficulty with children than with adults in reaching and providing benefits to all those who deserve them. It has been documented that children tend to be associated with armed groups in many different ways—for example, as combatants, informers, cooks, and porters. As a result, they are "not always considered to be full members of an armed force or group," which can limit their access to DDR programs. DDR staff cannot always identify these children or address their specific needs, and they themselves often do not want to be identified as being part of an armed group or are unaware of their right to benefits.[65]

An important issue from the perspective of this chapter is that for children the categories of ex-combatant and victim overlap much more than they do for adults. All of the children associated with armed groups are victims, not only of the human rights abuses they suffer while members of those groups, such as rape, forced marriage, and torture, but of being recruited in the first place. They therefore have a legitimate claim (often more than one) on reparations benefits as well as on DDR benefits. And in a number of countries— Guatemala, Peru, and Sierra Leone—the crime of illegal recruitment into fighting forces has been recognized as qualifying children for individual reparations as primary victims (in the proposed but unimplemented reparations programs).[66] This does not mean that DDR benefits should be cut, nor, as Mazurana and Carlson argue, "does [it] mean that such children should be excluded from reparations." Instead, they propose using "creative strategies" to ensure that individual reparations are provided "within larger community-based reparations programs that seek to benefit broader categories of 'war-affected children' and help ease the stigmatizing affects of the abuse on the individual beneficiary." This could include extending individual reparations benefits to more war-affected children or providing collective reparations, which target communities, groups, or areas particularly damaged in the conflict, and could include such things as girls' and boys' centers and clubs, which could provide children with safe spaces.[67] This may have the same affect as enlarged DDR programs.

The effect that more comprehensive individual reparations or the provision of collective reparations would have on the reintegration of former child combatants, however, is unclear for two reasons. First, in both cases, there is the potential for governments to use reparations programs to provide benefits or services to child victims that are already owed to them as citizens, regardless of whether their rights were violated. Reparations programs that simply double as, say, development initiatives may be less likely to reduce resentment among victims. Second, as Mazurana and Carlson put it, collective reparations have been criticized because, in distributing "mostly public or non-excludable goods, both victims and perpetrators can access them and hence they lose their recognition potential and reparative value for victims."[68] If the reparative value of reparations is reduced, the role that they might play in facilitating reintegration, as identified by de Greiff, may also be reduced. Again, however, there may be no simple or unproblematic resolution to this dilemma, in part because of the difficulty in distinguishing between child victims and perpetrators. Because "the line between victim and perpetrator is unclear," argue Mazurana and Carlson, "collective reparations for children should not look to define and exclude so-called child perpetrators from accessing important services for their health and well-being."[69]

It may be the case that, with children, reparations will to varying degrees have both positive and negative effects on the reintegration of former child combatants. The challenge, then, is to maximize the former and minimize the latter. In this sense, balance and coordination become a concern both *between* DDR and reparations benefits, but also *within* reparations programs. If reparations are provided to children who were illegally recruited into armed forces, for example, they should also be provided to other groups of child victims, but without being broadened to the point where they become a substitute for basic social services. Furthermore, reparations programs in some countries have prioritized the most vulnerable victims and those with the most urgent needs; if this approach is applied in a situation in which child combatants have been adequately provided for by a DDR program, then those children may not be among the most vulnerable or the most in need. As part of the proposed reparations program in Sierra Leone, children are eligible to receive free education up to the senior secondary level if they are victims of, among other harms, abduction or forced conscription; but they are excluded as beneficiaries if they have gone through the DDR program and are receiving schooling or other training as part of that program.[70] They are excluded from reparations, not because they are not victims or because they are perpetrators, but because they have already received benefits as ex-combatants. The outcome is that perpetrators are not doubly rewarded, which may seem fairer to communities and other victims. Finally, it could be considered that some children would forfeit their right to reparations if they were convicted of committing serious violations by a court of law or tribunal. While it may be inappropriate for convicted child perpetrators to be imprisoned, it may be equally inappropriate for them to receive reparations, even if they are victims of a crime. All of these considerations will depend on context-specific factors, of course, such as the scarcity of resources and the legitimacy of the criminal justice system.

## LOCAL JUSTICE AND THE REINTEGRATION OF CHILDREN

As discussed elsewhere in this volume, local justice processes in such countries as Rwanda, Timor-Leste, Sierra Leone, Peru, Mozambique, and Uganda contain elements of the main transitional justice approaches to various extents. Local justice may therefore facilitate reintegration by fostering trust between ex-combatants and their receiving communities, as well as by serving as a civic education tool and demonstrating acceptance of local norms, rules, and authority. It is reasonable to think that this positive impact on reintegration holds for children as well as adults. The *IDDRS* acknowledges the potential of such processes:

> Cultural, religious and traditional rituals can play an important role in the protection and reintegration of girls and boys into their communities, such as traditional healing, cleansing and forgiveness rituals; the development of solidarity mechanisms based on tradition; and the use of proverbs and sayings in sensitization and mediation activities.... Reconciliation ceremonies can offer forgiveness for acts committed, allow children to be "cleansed" of the violence they have suffered, restore cultural links and demonstrate children's involvement in civilian

life. Such ceremonies increase the commitment of communities to the children's reintegration process.[71]

In Sierra Leone, for example, research showed that children who had been "compelled to commit atrocities during the conflict reported that they had gained acceptance in their communities through dialogue based on traditional healing mechanisms."[72] Similarly, one observer in Uganda found a "very high" level of acceptance by family and community members of children who had escaped from the Lord's Resistance Army (LRA) after they went though cleansing ceremonies in Gulu.[73] Additionally, in interviews in 2003–2004, former child combatants in Mozambique stated that participating in traditional ceremonies upon returning home had "helped them return to civilian life."[74] The traditional ceremonies attended to many issues these children faced during their initial reintegration and thus

> helped repair social ills, cleansing those that came home "contaminated" from the atrocities of war, and resolving social conflict in cases where normal social roles had been perverted. Not only were these ceremonies important for these former child soldier as individuals, but they were also reported to be vital for rebuilding trust and cohesion.[75]

A balanced assessment of local justice processes should examine such issues as practicality, local legitimacy, respect for international standards, subject matter, and limitations.[76] Here we want to highlight the issues of particular relevance to children. Local justice processes generally, though not always, involve lesser forms of punishment and fewer applications of direct individual accountability; many observers categorize them as restorative more than retributive. In Northern Uganda, for example, reconciliation ceremonies "serve as a cultural strategy" for dealing with "abducted children both as victims and perpetrators of violence."[77] The cleansing and reintegration ceremonies in Mozambique and Angola, which Alcinda Honwana has examined in detail, emphasize transformation more than punishment.[78] In Sierra Leone, Wessells describes the methods used by a local chief to promote justice in the case of former boy combatants, which involve elements of truth-telling, reparation, and punishment through community service—"the greater the wrongdoing, the greater will be the community services the chief requires." The local process, he writes, represents a

> sophisticated system of diagnosis and action that collects evidence from multiple sources. This evidence is used to make decisions regarding

remorse and the likelihood of rehabilitation, and to assign mentoring and community service. The boy's prostration before the chief signals his complete submission to local authority, and, by implication, his willingness to obey local rules. This gesture is also a ritualized means through which the boy breaks with his past as a soldier and reformulates himself as part of the civilian community. The boy's remorse and willingness to make reparation with the village finds expression in his community service, which is a widely used means of developing community spirit and positive relations between youth and community.[79]

We should remember, though, that local processes include a wide range of practices and there will be, of course, communities and victims for whom the punishment distributed by some local processes is not enough. "In Liberia, Sierra Leone, and the DRC," relates one child rights practitioner, "I saw many forgiveness ceremonies. These were useful in terms of the child being able to go home but not always in the long term for a healthy community life." In addition to these ceremonies, she argues,

> some sort of local traditional justice which can measure motive and severity of action and which means the child feels the impact of his/her behavior in a formal way may be helpful, rather than the child living in fear of silent retribution or not having boundaries for his/her behavior. I know at least two children in Liberia who were poisoned by their communities. Having accepted them back after forgiveness ceremonies, the community (or members of the community) could not live with the presence of the people who offended them and took justice into their own hands.[80]

As discussed above, the absence of retribution for child perpetrators may hinder the reintegrative function of other transitional justice measures, including local processes.

The second issue of particular relevance to children's reintegration is that among young people, local justice processes may lack legitimacy or may reinforce the sense of grievance that played a role in the conflict to begin with. In general, the community-based nature of local justice can make it more accessible and legitimate than other measures through its location, the participation of the local population, and its incorporation of existing local practices, structures, customs, norms, and values. This legitimacy, however, can be diminished for children in particular by the fact that the local leaders who administer local justice processes may have discredited themselves by becoming implicated in human rights abuses, specifically in the recruitment of child combatants.[81] Furthermore, the use of local justice processes may reinforce gender or other biases that are embedded in local practices and structures, thus being discriminatory and harmful to girls and boys. According to Amnesty International, for example, "those who need the protection of a formal court system—especially vulnerable women and children—are those most likely to be coerced into a 'traditional' resolution in the absence of clearly recognized procedures."[82] As Lucia Withers puts it, "it is important not to romanticize [local processes] and to be aware of the many dangers involved. From my own experience in East Timor and subsequently in Afghanistan, where such mechanisms are used extensively for ordinary crimes both in preference to and in the absence of a functioning criminal justice system, there were clearly many dangers. Not least, discrimination against women and girls."[83] Local processes that lack legitimacy or reinforce the grievances of children may be less likely to facilitate their reintegration.

## PROSECUTIONS AND THE REINTEGRATION OF CHILDREN

Three main issues relate to criminal prosecutions that are relevant to the discussion of children and DDR: first, whether children under the age of eighteen should be prosecuted at all; second, how children should be treated if they are prosecuted or if they participate as witnesses; and, third, the potential effects of prosecuting those responsible for illegally recruiting children into armed forces.

### CHILD COMBATANTS AND CRIMINAL PROSECUTION

We begin with the question of whether children should be prosecuted for committing human rights abuses during war. While international law does allow for children accused of breaking the law to be prosecuted in a court of law, it calls upon states to look for alternatives. Article 40 of the CRC requires states to ensure, "Whenever appropriate and desirable, measures for dealing with such children without resorting to judicial proceedings, providing that human rights and legal safeguards are fully respected." States must also respect a number of minimum guarantees and take into account "the desirability of promoting the child's reintegration."[84] Article 37 prohibits capital punishment or life imprisonment for those children tried and found guilty.[85] Part of the argument is that children below the age of eighteen have not reached a level of maturity and thus cannot be held legally responsible for their actions. This is backed up by other international legal instruments, including the "Beijing Rules," the "Paris Principles and Guidelines," and the Rome Statute of the International Criminal Court (ICC), which all use eighteen as the minimum age for legal responsibility. The "Beijing Rules" state that one ought to "consider whether a child can live up to the moral and psychological components of criminal responsibility; that is, whether a child, by virtue of her or his individual discernment and understanding, can be held responsible for essentially anti-social behavior."[86] It is also commonly argued that, because children illegally recruited into armed forces are victims and may have been forced to commit atrocities, they should not be held criminally responsible.

The issue was intensely debated during the creation of the Special Court for Sierra Leone. In the end, the Special Court was given jurisdiction over children under eighteen who committed atrocities during the conflict, but Special Prosecutor David Crane stated clearly that he would not prosecute them because he did not consider children to be among "those most responsible" for the abuses, which was the Court's mandate.[87] With this precedent set for hybrid courts and with the ICC having no jurisdiction over children under eighteen, it is unlikely that children will be prosecuted in international proceedings in the near future. The "Paris Principles" state quite clearly that "[c]hildren should not be prosecuted by an international court or tribunal."[88]

How was the issue debated in Sierra Leone? As Ilene Cohn explains it, one side argued that

> some children and young adults would benefit from participation in a process that ensures accountability for one's actions, respects the procedural guarantees appropriate in the administration of juvenile justice, and takes into account the desirability of promoting the child's reintegration and capacity to assume a constructive role in society. The Special Court might help to ensure that the most recalcitrant and feared young offenders, those perhaps least likely to seek programmatic and therapeutic support, would be brought into a credible system of justice that would result in guided, supervised access to rehabilitation and ensure opportunities for reinsertion into productive civilian life.[89]

On the other hand, it was claimed that "the threat of prosecution would undermine [UNICEF and NGO] efforts at child soldier rehabilitation, stigmatize the child, reduce the likelihood of community reintegration, and place the child at increased risk of re-recruitment."[90] Both are reasonable arguments, and both, as Cohn points out, draw on the same basic principles of the CRC (although in support of opposing approaches).[91]

Some practitioners agree that, depending on the nature of the crimes committed, judicial accountability may facilitate reintegration by rehabilitating children and changing their behavior. This argument is especially made with regard to older children. As one specialist puts it,

> Older children are well aware of what they have done and why and, therefore, they need systems that will address their offences—but, of course, these systems need to be ones that focus on changing behavior and not long sentences.[92]

According to her:

> I have known very violent children who joined armed forces in order to take revenge or to loot and there needs to be systems to say to them that a simple forgiveness ceremony or local compensation systems are not enough. Children, especially older ones, need to be held accountable. It is a vitally important part of growing up.[93]

But, as argued above, it may also make the child's community more receptive by addressing their legitimate desire for retribution: "I don't think communities in places like Liberia, Sierra Leone, and the DRC can always accept that kids who have killed and raped just simply need to adjust to civilian norms and standards."[94] In the words of one victim,

> I believe that they should not only be tried but also killed for what they did. They were so wicked. When I hear them saying they are sorry for what they did I do not believe them. If they have an opportunity of doing it again, they will. I feel sad that children were not made to face the Special Court. I really thought the court was going to also try them.[95]

In Sierra Leone, it was argued that the Special Court was necessary "to prevent the Sierra Leonean population from administering its own vigilante justice on juvenile offenders."[96] In the absence of judicial accountability, communities may in fact resort to vigilante justice or former child combatants may live in fear of it.

Others believe that bringing children before any judicial proceedings, regardless of the potential punishment, will hinder rehabilitation and reintegration. As a report by the Save the Children Fund argues, there is worldwide evidence that detention and custodial sentences do not serve children's best interests or, in the longer term, those of society. As far as ex-combatant children are concerned, trial by court is considered incompatible with their reintegration, and is likely to undermine it. Trial by court further stigmatises ex-combatant children by drawing attention to their past; there is also a possibility that they could be singled out for retribution. Children still in fighting forces may be reluctant to demobilise because they fear prosecution, or those who have already left may drop out of reintegration programmes.[97]

Fear generated by the threat of prosecution and punishment along with the stigmatization that trials might foster, as with adult ex-combatants, would seem to be one of the main obstacles to reintegration.[98] And child combatants may be particularly susceptible to exaggerated fears of punishment. In Sierra Leone, for example, some of them were told by their commanders to expect to "be drowned in the sea" or "mob justice, hard labour and rejection by their family."[99]

In some cases, prosecution or the threat of it could hinder DDR and feasibly feed into further conflict. As Wessells contends, "retribution can fuel ongoing cycles of violence. When children who were forcibly recruited are treated as criminals, this can rouse in them anger and defiance that can lead them to commit more violence." It may also prolong ongoing conflict. He quotes a former RUF child combatant in Sierra Leone saying: "I am sorry for what I did during the war, but if people treat me as a criminal, I will go back to the bush."[100] Some former child combatants in Sierra Leone interviewed for this chapter had similar views. One girl said the following: "I would have preferred dying while fighting than giving myself up to be tried. The war would never have ended if the amnesty was not given. Even though we were tired of fighting, there was no way we were going to give up without an amnesty granted."[101] And one boy said: "[Only] a mad man will agree to give up arms knowing that he will be tried."[102] In Liberia, among the many reasons that girl ex-combatants gave for not participating in the DDR process was the fear of prosecution: "Some girl ex-combatants did not want to reveal their past as ex-combatants because they were afraid of repercussions. They did not want to be registered and photographed (a precondition at the DDR camps), as they feared they might later be prosecuted in a criminal court for their involvement in the war."[103] What is a difficult undertaking already—reaching girl ex-combatants through DDR programs—may become even more difficult with the threat of prosecutions out there.

Confusion on the ground about exactly what transitional justice measures children may face may also hinder both justice and DDR processes.[104] It is crucial, then, that DDR programs have clarity at least about what transitional justice measures are currently being applied in the country before the public campaign on DDR starts, so that they can quell unfounded rumors as much as possible. As is well known to DDR practitioners, it is the rumors about what might happen to ex-combatants that can have disastrous consequences on reaching and convincing them to participate. Outreach efforts must be clear from the start. If child combatants do not trust these institutions, it is unlikely they will engage either the DDR or the justice process. Trust or the lack of it — and this can be created by perceptions alone — is critical to having combatants come forward.

### CHILDREN'S TREATMENT IN DOMESTIC PROSECUTIONS

It is unlikely that international or hybrid courts will prosecute children under eighteen for human rights abuses in the near future. The issue is currently more relevant for national judicial and juvenile justice systems, which are often seriously damaged by the recent armed conflict and in which the minimum age of criminal responsibility varies or does not exist.[105] As Withers explains, "if one is talking specifically about prosecutions, in most cases the only real option will be domestic courts." Thus, it is important, from the standpoint of both justice and reintegration, to consider how such efforts are actually implemented in practice, which is not necessarily in accordance with international standards. According to Withers, prosecuting children in domestic courts

> raises all sorts of issues around capacity, independence, impartiality, fairness, and provisions for juvenile justice. Those promoting justice in post-conflict situations have to contend with the reality of institutions, including the judiciary, which are often severely degraded, meaning that fair trials are not possible without extensive support and far-reaching judicial reform.[106]

Juvenile justice plans, for their part, often "run aground on the lack of separate facilities for children and a paucity of trained personnel to staff and manage prisons in ways that protect children's rights."[107]

Weak or corrupt judicial systems, sometimes without functioning courts, observe Michels and Siegrist, can have "major repercussions on children who are alleged to have committed crimes under international law," who might end up in custody for lengthy periods of time:

When deprived of their liberty, either awaiting trial or as a sentence, certain groups of children are at specific risk in juvenile justice systems in post-conflict situations, in particular former child soldiers. They may face greater risks for ill treatment, abuse, torture and extended periods of detention. They might suffer from discriminatory application of criminal procedures and penalties or be at risk of violence perpetrated by other detainees and detention personnel. There are also specific risks for girls and women, including sexual violence and abuse by detainees or detention centre personnel.[108]

In practice, then, the threat of prosecution by a corrupt and unfair judicial system, with inadequate juvenile justice plans, may deter child combatants from participating in DDR programs at all. Furthermore, the actual experience of being charged in such a system or being incarcerated for extended periods may hinder the reintegration process of some former child combatants.

Children, including former child combatants, may appear in court not just as accused perpetrators but also as victims and witnesses. Some of the same concerns that apply to the accused may apply to witnesses, such as possible stigmatization and traumatization, so the issue should be of concern to reintegration efforts. In Sierra Leone, for example, former child combatants

reported that stigmatisation as a "rebel" by the community is often an obstacle to developing normal social contacts and to reintegrating into the society. Some of them fear rejection and threat by the community if it becomes public that they are testifying for the Special Court and/or if the content of their testimony becomes known. They are often worried that their newly re-established relationships with family and the community and their education could be disrupted by this knowledge or as a result of being forced to leave for security reasons.[109]

There are ways to address these concerns, however. In Sierra Leone, these included specific support strategies, such as psychosocial assistance, follow-up monitoring, medical care, housing and educational support, and protective measures, such as the use of closed-circuit television and voice distortion during testimony.[110] According to two UNICEF child protection officers, "It does appear that no children have been unduly exposed to danger as a result of being involved with the Special Court. Neither has there been a negative impact on the social reintegration process of children formerly associated with the fighting forces."[111]

## PROSECUTING THOSE RESPONSIBLE FOR ILLEGALLY RECRUITING CHILDREN

Former child combatants may appear as witnesses in trials of those accused of illegally recruiting children into armed groups. Those trials raise two issues from the perspective of the interaction between DDR and transitional justice. First, along with the child ex-combatants themselves, DDR practitioners may also serve as important witnesses. The former Chief of Prosecutions of the Special Court in Sierra Leone explained: "Evidence of the use of child soldiers from other sources, notably an expert witness who was involved in the demobilization of child soldiers, corroborated important parts of the children's accounts of events and may well add more weight to their testimonies." Such evidence, he claims, was "available, reliable and compelling."[112] This points to the larger issue of information sharing between DDR programs and transitional justice measures, as well as other types of agencies, which is discussed elsewhere in this volume,[113] and which could involve information of a less sensitive nature than individual testimony. Keith Wright and Donald Robertshaw point to the Security Council's Resolution 1612 (2005), which mandates that the UN monitor violations of children's rights in armed conflict (particularly relating to illegal recruitment), as a development that could be beneficial for both DDR and justice efforts. Such long-term collection of information, they suggest, "enables a much more accurate analysis of the use and pattern of distribution of children in the armed groups that will guide the design of a DDR programme and that of a Special Court."[114]

Second, the prosecution of those accused of illegally recruiting children should also be considered in terms of potential short- and long-term effects on DDR for children. Recent prosecution efforts include the ICC trial of Thomas Lubanga Dyilo for conscripting and enlisting children under fifteen and using them in active hostilities in the DRC, as well as the prosecution and sentencing of a commander for recruiting children by a local tribunal in the DRC; the ICC's issuance of arrest warrants for LRA senior members, including leader Joseph Kony, for crimes including the forcible enlistment of children under fifteen in Uganda; and the Special Court for Sierra Leone's conviction of members of the Armed Forces Revolutionary Council and the Civil Defence Forces for crimes including the recruitment of child combatants, as well as its trial of Charles Taylor, the former president of Liberia, for crimes including conscripting and enlisting children under fifteen and using them in active hostilities.

In the short run, such prosecutions may deter armed groups from admitting to having children in their ranks and releasing them into demobilization programs, for fear of repercussions:

the vulnerability of children associated with armed forces may in some situations be heightened when prosecutions are threatened. In particular, armed groups might conceal children or refuse to negotiate while the threat remains. There are no easy answers to such dilemmas.[115]

This has been called the "Lubanga syndrome," and there are reports of it happening in the DRC.[116] Ensuring the participation of children has often been an obstacle in past DDR programs[117] and it might become an even greater one now. Furthermore, it is also possible that those adults who recruited child combatants will be more reluctant to demobilize, again out of fear that they will be prosecuted. Remaining armed and not reintegrated into civilian society, these adults are more likely to recruit children again in the future.

On the other hand, one of the motivations behind such prosecutions is the possibility that criminal accountability could lead to deterrence in the longer run. "They know it's a war crime, but they seem to believe they'll never be brought to justice. There is a sense of rampant impunity," says one expert.[118] "What is needed is the full measure of international law be applied to those leaders who adopt the child soldier doctrine," urges P. W. Singer, in order "to affect the decision calculus behind the use of child soldiers."[119] According to two members of Human Rights Watch, while the Lubanga syndrome "may have created problems for child protection workers and their efforts to demobilize children in the short term, there is general agreement that increased awareness about the seriousness of this crime is positive."[120]

## CONCLUSION

This chapter has examined the relationship between transitional justice, DDR, and the reintegration of children associated with armed forces and armed groups. It has focused more on the process of reintegration than the program of DDR, and therefore much of the interaction discussed is in terms of how the two different types of initiatives can reinforce or hinder each other rather than on specific programmatic links between them, although the latter are highlighted wherever possible.

After arguing that there is a potential role for transitional justice to play in the reintegration process for children, the chapter looked at how this might play out in relation to different transitional justice measures—truth-telling, reparations, local justice and reconciliation processes, and prosecutions. In each case, it was argued that transitional justice may reinforce the reintegration of children, primarily through fostering trust, but also that it may hinder such reintegration, primarily through fostering stigmatization and fear. This point needs to be stressed: as with adult combatants, the impact that transitional justice and DDR have on the reintegration of children can be both positive and negative. Designing appropriate responses to instances of armed violence and abuse in which children have been seriously involved is an extremely complicated and sensitive endeavor. Both DDR and justice efforts seek to build trust, and yet both can be undermined by the absence of trust. The relationship can therefore be mutually reinforcing or mutually undermining, or, most likely, somewhere in between. It is critical for these programs to consider how they might impact each other.

We conclude by drawing attention to three issues that repeatedly surface throughout the chapter. First, a central theme of the chapter is that child combatants who commit atrocities can be regarded as both perpetrators and victims. This is not a new observation (though there are those who feel that such children should be considered more as victims than perpetrators, as well as those who feel the opposite, but generalizing in either direction is problematic). Its importance, however, cannot be overstated. What this chapter has tried to do, in this regard, is look at some of the specific ways in which this victim/perpetrator overlap can affect how transitional justice measures interact with the reintegration process. It suggests, for example, that imprisonment for former child combatants who committed crimes is inappropriate, but that some form of punishment may be called for in certain circumstances; that truth commissions should fulfill the dual function of drawing attention to the plight of child combatants as victims, but also to the horrible acts that some of them carried out; that achieving some sort of balance between reparations and DDR benefits might have to address the fact that child perpetrators may have claims to both types of benefits; and that local justice processes may represent a particularly appropriate method of reintegrating child ex-combatants.

Second, while we have argued that both DDR and transitional justice can facilitate the reintegration of children formerly associated with armed groups, and while we agree that both types of interventions should be guided by the best interests of the child, it has to be remembered that justice measures should also be guided by the best interests of victims, which means that in some cases there will be tensions between the interests of the child and those of the victims. Some of these tensions may be unavoidable. For example, despite the existence of consensus in the international community that children should not serve prison sentences, there will always be those who feel that any form of punishment short of imprisonment for the commission of atrocities does not adequately respect the interests or rights of victims. Similarly, a child-friendly truth-telling process, whether conducted through a national truth commission or a local ceremony, that withholds the identities of children or offers the forgiveness of the community may, again, leave victims feeling slighted. Furthermore, providing any kind of benefit, whether through a DDR or a reparations program (or both), to child perpetrators may fuel the resentment of victims, regardless of whether those victims also receive reparations. While it is argued here that accounting for the interests of victims will often be in the interests of child perpetrators, this will not necessarily always be the case.

Finally, while this chapter has tried to think through some of the ways in which transitional justice and DDR may interact for children, we do not yet know how this relationship unfolds. There is a real need for further empirical research in this area. This may be true of the field of child rights and armed conflict in general, which Ilene Cohn argues tends to "avoid assessing the long-term qualitative impact of the many and varied interventions that have been mounted on behalf of war-affected children—so we don't know much about what works."[121] It certainly is the case for justice and reintegration. As acknowledged by a recent international forum, "little is known about how these [justice and reconciliation] processes are perceived by armed groups and local communities, their actual impact on child soldier use and whether they facilitate the complex long-term process of reintegration."[122] And as Cohn specifically asks, "Will young adults in Sierra Leone be better served without resort to judicial proceedings? Have those children and young adults who participated in the TRC proceedings benefited in some way? We do not know."[123]

What we do know, however, is that DDR and transitional justice represent but two types of initiative among a range of interventions that are (at least partly) aimed at reintegrating former child combatants. In practice, then, the nature of the relationship between justice and reintegration will depend on a number of context-specific factors, including the types and effectiveness of other interventions, the experience and profile of former child combatants, the nature and extent of the crimes committed by child combatants, the needs of other war-affected children, available resources and capacity, and local attitudes toward fighting groups and armed forces. In parts of Southeast Asia, for example, such as the Philippines, Myanmar, and Aceh, armed groups containing children have deep community roots and support and have better human rights records than the RUF in Sierra Leone, so in those cases the issue of accountability might be of less relevance to reintegration.[124] In countries with fewer resources and less institutional capacity, making sure that judicial and juvenile justice systems conform to international standards and that reparations reach some kind of balance with DDR benefits may be more difficult than in more well-off and developed countries. As the child protection officer Saudamini Siegrist puts it, "the best answer we can give is to say there is no 'one' answer. The appropriate process for accountability and/or the best approach to amnesty is case-by-case, depending on local context."[125]

## NOTES

1   The authors would like to thank Ana Patel, Lars Waldorf, Pablo de Greiff, Samar Al-Bulushi, and Debbie Sharnak for comments on earlier versions of this chapter, as well as the participants in the project's May 2007 authors meeting for their feedback on a draft. Special thanks to Ibrahim Bangura, who conducted the interviews with former child combatants cited throughout the chapter. The chapter benefited from the input of a wide range of experts and practitioners, including Eldridge Adolfo, Ibrahim Bangura, Gloriosa Bazigaga, Fatuma Hamidali Ibrahim, Una McCauley, Katharina Montens, David Ntambara, Caroline Ort, Saudamini Siegrist, Renata Tardioli, John Williamson, and Lucia Withers.

2   We use the term "child combatants" throughout the chapter, although the generally agreed upon term is "children associated with armed forces and groups" (CAAFG), as used in "The Paris Principles: Principles and Guidelines on Children Associated with Armed Forces or Armed Groups," UNICEF, February 2007 (hereafter "The Paris Principles"). We fully recognize that children are associated with armed groups in various ways and that many do not actually bear arms during conflict.

3   Coalition to Stop the Use of Child Soldiers, "International Forum on Armed Groups and the Involvement of Children in Armed Conflict: Summary of Themes and Discussions," Switzerland, July 4–7, 2006, 7.

4   United Nations Department of Peacekeeping Operations (DPKO), *Integrated Disarmament, Demobilization and Reintegration Standards (IDDRS)* (New York: DPKO, 2006), sec. 2.10, 5.

5   Ibid., sec. 5.30, 2.

6   Ibid.

7   United Nations, *Report of the Special Representative of the Secretary-General for Children and Armed Conflict*, A/62/228, August 13, 2007, 31.

8    Michael Wessells, *Child Soldiers: From Violence to Protection* (Cambridge, MA: Harvard University Press, 2006), 182.

9    Irma Specht, "Jobs for Rebels and Soldiers," in *Jobs After War: A Critical Challenge in the Peace and Reconstruction Puzzle*, ed. Eugenia Date-Bah (Geneva: International Labor Organization, 2003), 77, 95, 103. On "human security," see *Human Security Centre, Human Security Report 2005: War and Peace in the 21st Century* (New York: Oxford University Press, 2005).

10   DPKO, *IDDRS*, sec. 5.30, 1.

11   "Convention on the Rights of the Child. Adopted and opened for signature, ratification and accession by General Assembly resolution 44/25, of 20 November 1989. Entry into force 2 September 1990, in accordance with article 49" (CRC), art. 39.

12   CRC, art. 40.

13   John Williamson, "The Disarmament, Demobilization and Reintegration of Child Soldiers: Social and Psychological Transformation in Sierra Leone," *Intervention: The International Journal of Mental Health, Psychosocial Work and Counselling in Areas of Armed Conflict* 4, no. 4 (2006): 185–205.

14   Andrew Mawson, "Children, Impunity and Justice: Some Dilemmas from Northern Uganda," in *Children and Youth on the Front Line: Ethnography, Armed Conflict and Displacement*, ed. Jo Boyden and Joanna de Berry (New York: Berghahn Books, 2004), 137.

15   Christopher Blattman and Jeannie Annan, "The Consequences of Child Soldiering," Households in Conflict Network (HICN) Working Paper 22, August 2007.

16   Neil Boothby, Jennifer Crawford, and Jason Halperin, "Mozambique Child Soldier Life Outcome Study: Lessons Learned in Rehabilitation and Reintegration Efforts," *Global Public Health* (February 2006): 88, 104.

17   Ibid.

18   Ibid.

19   Jeremy Weinstein and Macartan Humphries, "Disentangling the Determinants of Successful Demobilization, and Reintegration," Center for Global Development, Working Paper No. 69, September 2005, 13. On Liberia, see Irma Specht and Hirut Tefferi, "Impact Evaluation of the Reintegration Programme of Children Associated with Fighting Forces (CAFF) in Liberia," UNICEF, April 2007.

20   Coalition to Stop the Use of Child Soldiers, *Child Soldiers Global Report 2008* (UK: Coalition to Stop the Use of Child Soldiers, 2008), 29.

21   Ibid.

22   Wessells, *Child Soldiers*, 155.

23   Lucia Withers, Coalition to Stop the Use of Child Soldiers, communication with Irma Specht, May 1, 2007.

24   Humphries and Weinstein, "Disentangling the Determinants of Successful Disarmament, Demobilization, and Reintegration."

25    Rachel Brett and Irma Specht, *Young Soldiers: Why They Choose to Fight* (Boulder: ILO / Lynne Rienner Publishers, 2004), 121.

26    Humphries and Weinstein, "Disentangling the Determinants of Successful Disarmament, Demobilization, and Reintegration."

27    P. W. Singer, *Children at War* (New York: Pantheon Books, 2005), 91, 114, 201.

28    Wessells, *Child Soldiers*, 218 (emphasis added). See also Mawson, "Children, Impunity and Justice," 135.

29    Mats Utas, "Fluid Research Fields: Studying Excombatant Youth in the Aftermath of the Liberian Civil War," in *Children and Youth on the Front Line*, 220.

30    Interview by Ibrahim Bangura, Transition International consultant, 2007 (location withheld for protection-related reasons).

31    Singer, *Children at War*, 180.

32    Ibid.

33    Mawson, "Children, Impunity and Justice," 138.

34    Specht, "Jobs for Rebels and Soldiers," 93.

35    Specht and Tefferi, "Impact Evaluation of the Reintegration Programme of Children Associated with Fighting Forces (CAFF) in Liberia," 34.

36    Unpublished research conducted by Ibrahim Bangura, Transition International, 2007.

37    See, generally, Priscilla B. Hayner, *Unspeakable Truths: Facing the Challenge of Truth Commissions* (New York and London: Routledge, 2002); and UN Office of the High Commissioner for Human Rights (OHCHR), *Rule-of-Law Tools for Post-Conflict States: Truth Commissions* (New York and Geneva: United Nations, 2006). For a critique of the use of truth-telling in Sierra Leone, as an approach that had little popular support and was at odds with local strategies of "forgive and forget," see Rosalind Shaw, "Rethinking Truth and Reconciliation Commissions: Lessons from Sierra Leone," United States Institute of Peace, Special Report No. 130, February 2005.

38    Miriam J. Auckerman, "Extraordinary Evil, Ordinary Crime: A Framework for Understanding Transitional Justice," *Harvard Human Rights Journal* 15 (2002): 83.

39    Withers, communication with Irma Specht.

40    International Center for Transitional Justice, "Children and Transitional Justice: Background Document," unpublished.

41    Singer, *Children at War*, 201.

42    Sierra Leone Truth and Reconciliation Commission, *Witness to Truth: Report of the Sierra Leone Truth and Reconciliation Commission* (Freetown: Graphic Packaging Limited, 2004), vol. 3b, chap. 4, para. 228.

43    Fatuma Ibrahim, Project Officer, Protection, UNICEF Liberia, communication with Irma Specht, April 12, 2007.

44    An Michels and Saudamini Siegrist, "Transitional Justice and Children: Concept Paper" (prepared for the Expert Discussion on Transitional Justice and Children, November

10–12, 2005), 12.

45   ICTJ, "Children and Transitional Justice."

46   Brett and Specht, *Young Soldiers*, 105–120.

47   Ibid., 5.

48   For examples, see ibid; Irma Specht, *Red Shoes: Experiences of Girl-Combatants in Liberia* (Geneva: ILO, 2006); and Susan McKay and Dyan Mazurana, *Where Are the Girls? Girls in Fighting Forces in Northern Uganda, Sierra Leone and Mozambique: Their Lives During and After War* (Montreal: Rights and Democracy, 2004).

49   Shaw, "Rethinking Truth and Reconciliation Commissions," 8.

50   "The Paris Principles," 42.

51   No Peace Without Justice (NPWJ) and UNICEF Innocenti Research Centre, *International Criminal Justice and Children* (NPWJ/UNICEF, 2002), 130.

52   Interview by Ibrahim Bangura, 2007 (location withheld for protection-related reasons).

53   Ibid.

54   Interview by Ibrahim Bangura, Magburaka, Northern Sierra Leone, April 25, 2006.

55   Interview by Ibrahim Bangura, Bo, Southern Sierra Leone, April 22, 2007.

56   Withers, communication with Irma Specht.

57   David Nosworthy, "Children's Security in Post-Conflict Peacebuilding: Discussion Paper," A Contribution to the 10-Year Strategic Review of the Machel Study, Geneva Centre for the Democratic Control of Armed Forces (DCAF), June 2007, 1.

58   Wessells, *Child Soldiers*, 23.

59   Trish Hiddleston, "Reform of Juvenile Justice in DRC" (paper prepared for the Expert Discussion on Transitional Justice and Children, November 10–12, 2005), 119.

60   Wessells, *Child Soldiers*, 169, citing Guillaume Landry, *Child Soldiers and Disarmament, Demobilization, Rehabilitation and Reintegration in West Africa* (Dakar: Coalition to Stop the Use of Child Soldiers, 2005).

61   Specht, "Jobs for Rebels and Soldiers," 96.

62   Pablo de Greiff, "Establishing Links Between DDR and Reparations," in this volume.

63   United Nations Economic and Social Council, *Guidelines on Justice in Matters Involving Child Victims and Witnesses of Crime*, Resolution 2005/20, sec. 8, "The Right to Reparation," July 22, 2005.

64   Dyan Mazurana and Khristopher Carlson, "Reparations as a Means for Recognizing and Addressing Crimes and Grave Rights Violations against Girls and Boys during Situations of Armed Conflict and under Authoritarian and Dictatorial Regimes," in *The Gender of Reparations*, ed. Ruth Rubio-Marín (Cambridge: Cambridge University Press, 2009). For specific examples of reparations programs that have provided reparations to children, see the case studies on Guatemala, Peru, Rwanda, Sierra Leone, South Africa, and Timor-Leste, which make up the first volume on this project, in Ruth Rubio-Marín, ed., *What Happened to the Women? Gender and Reparations for Human Rights Violations*

(New York: Social Science Research Council, 2006); see also the case studies on Argentina and Chile in Pablo de Greiff, ed., *The Handbook of Reparations* (New York: Oxford University Press, 2006). See also Ilene Cohn, "The Protection of Children in Peacemaking and Peacekeeping Processes," *Harvard Human Rights Journal* 12 (Spring 1999): 129–96.

65  DPKO, *IDDRS*, sec. 5.30, 3, 8.

66  Mazurana and Carlson, "Reparations as a Means for Recognizing and Addressing Crimes and Grave Rights Violations against Girls and Boys."

67  Ibid.

68  Ibid.

69  Ibid.

70  Jamesina King, "Gender and Reparations in Sierra Leone: The Wounds of War Remain Open," in *What Happened to the Women?*, 268.

71  DPKO, *IDDRS*, sec. 5.30, 26.

72  United Nations, *Report of the Special Representative of the Secretary-General for Children and Armed Conflict*, 31.

73  Fatuma Ibrahim, communication with Irma Specht, April 12, 2007.

74  Boothby, Crawford, and Halperin, "Mozambique Child Soldier Life Outcome Study," 96.

75  Ibid.

76  See Roger Duthie, "Local Justice and Reintegration Processes as Complements to Transitional Justice and DDR," in this volume.

77  Angela Veale and Aki Stavrou, *Violence, Reconciliation and Identity: The Reintegration of Lord's Resistance Army Child Abductees in Northern Uganda* (Pretoria: Institute for Security Studies), Monograph No. 92, November 2003, 47.

78  Alcinda Honwana, "Children of War: Understanding War and War Cleansing in Mozambique and Angola," in *Civilians in War*, ed. Simon Chesterman (Boulder: Lynne Rienner Publishers, 2001).

79  Wessells, *Child Soldiers*, 222–23, citing Constance Flanagan and Beth Van Horn, "Youth Civic Development," in *Community Youth Development*, ed. Francisco A. Villarrual et al. (Thousand Oaks, CA: Sage, 2003) and David A. Hamburg and Beatrix A. Hamburg, *Learning to Live Together* (Oxford: Oxford University Press, 2004).

80  Una McCauley, Representative UNICEF Togo, communication with Irma Specht, 2007.

81  See Sierra Leone Truth and Reconciliation Commission, *Final Report*, sec. 25; and Honwana, "Children of War," 135.

82  Amnesty International, "East Timor: Justice Past, Present and Future," Amnesty International, July 2001, 39–42, also quoted in Chris Dolan, "Reconciliation with Justice? The East Timor Experiment in Transitional Justice and Reconciliation," Report for International IDEA, March 2004, 23.

83  Withers, communication with Irma Specht.

84   CRC, art. 40.

85   Ibid., art. 37.

86   "United Nations Standard Minimum Rules for the Administration of Juvenile Justice ('The Beijing Rules'). Adopted by General Assembly resolution 40/33 of 29 November 1985."

87   See David Crane, "Strike Terror No More — Prosecuting the Use of Children in Sierra Leone," in *International Criminal Accountability and the Rights of Children*, ed. Karin Arts and Vesselin Popovski (Cambridge: Cambridge University Press, 2006).

88   "The Paris Principles," sec. 8.6, February 2007.

89   Ilene Cohn, "Symposium: Peacekeeping and Security in Countries Utilizing Child Soldiers: Panel 2: International Law Barring Child Soldiers in Combat: Problems in Enforcement and Accountability: Progress and Hurdles on the Road to Preventing the Use of Children as Soldiers and Ensuring Their Rehabilitation and Reintegration," *Cornell International Law Journal* 37 (2004): 538–39.

90   Ibid. See also Wessells, *Child Soldiers*, 221.

91   Cohn, "Symposium," 538. That the prosecution of children by the Special Court would have been aimed at reintegration is made clear by the sanctions that the Court is authorized to employ: "care guidance and supervision orders, community service orders, counselling, foster care, correctional, educational and vocational training programmes, approved schools and, as appropriate, any programmes of disarmament, demobilization and reintegration or programmes of child protection agencies." Statute of the Special Court for Sierra Leone, art. 7 (2). Note that participation in DDR is included on the list. In this way, the Special Court would share with other child-friendly juvenile justice systems the key elements of "the establishment of alternatives to deprivation of liberty and a successful reintegration of the child into society." NPWJ and UNICEF, *International Criminal Justice and Children*, 120. As Michael Custer has pointed out, in a comparison of the Special Court with the juvenile justice system in the United States, "one of the chief motivations of the founders" of the latter was "the rehabilitation of juvenile offenders and their reentry into society as productive citizens." "The focus," he continues, "was less on punishment and more on rehabilitation and socialization." While sharing the goal of reintegration with other interventions, Custer argues, "only a tribunal such as the Special Court can mandate that a child soldier enter into one of these." Michael Custer, "Punishing Child Soldiers: The Special Court for Sierra Leone and the Lessons to Be Learned from the United States' Juvenile Justice System," *Temple International and Comparative Law Journal* 19, no. 2 (Fall 2005): 462, 471.

92   Una McCauley, communication with Irma Specht.

93   Ibid.

94   Ibid.

95   Interview by Ibrahim Bangura, Magburaka, Northern Sierra Leone, April 25, 2006.

96  Custer, "Punishing Child Soldiers," 460, citing Mark Iacono, "Child Soldiers of Sierra Leone: Are They Accountable for Their Actions in War?" *Suffolk Transitional Law Review* 26 (2003): 445–67.

97  Isobel McConnan and Sarah Uppard, *Children — Not Soldiers: Guidelines for Working with Child Soldiers Associated with Fighting Forces*, The Save the Children Fund, December, 2002, 199.

98  See also Wessells, *Child Soldiers*, 219: "The trial of child soldiers as criminals also risks stigmatizing them, reducing their chances of successful reintegration."

99  Ibid., 126.

100  Ibid., 220.

101  Interview by Ibrahim Bangura, Magburaka, Northern Sierra Leone, April 25, 2006.

102  Interview by Ibrahim Bangura, Bo, Southern Sierra Leone, April 22, 2007.

103  Specht, *Red Shoes*, 87.

104  In Sierra Leone, e.g., many people had difficulties distinguishing between the truth commission and the Special Court, having no particular familiarity with either. "In addition, assurances that information was not being shared [between the two institutions] were undermined by popular perceptions in terms of social contact between staff of the institutions, and in terms of the close geographic proximity of the institutions. The public confusion that resulted may have meant that fewer persons participated in the TRC process." Una McCauley, communication with Irma Specht. At the same time, however, when the prosecutor clarified that no children would be prosecuted, "this helped encourage children to come forward" to the truth commission process. UNICEF, *Adolescent Programming in Conflict and Post-Conflict Situations* (UNICEF, 2004), 59.

105  Michels and Siegrist, "Transitional Justice and Children," 14.

106  Withers, communication with Irma Specht.

107  Wessells, *Child Soldiers*, 220. See also, generally, UN Committee on the Rights of the Child, *Children's Rights in Juvenile Justice*, General Comment No. 10, CRC/C/GC/10, April 25, 2007.

108  Michels and Siegrist, "Transitional Justice and Children," 14. In Rwanda, where the age of adult responsibility is fourteen, more than 4,000 minors between the ages of fourteen and eighteen at the time of the 1994 genocide remained in prison in 2001. While these now young adults were not necessarily child combatants, the example is instructive for our purpose because the extended custody of these young people affected their prospects of reintegration. "Only in rare instances have any of these minors had legal representation," Constance Morrill observes, "and they have been detained in conditions that have severely compromised not only their physical health, but their potential for intellectual growth, and their potential for successful reintegration into society." Those provisionally released were unable to find employment or to afford going to school. Constance Morrill, "Perpetrators Only: The 'Role' of Accused Youth in Rwanda's 'Modern'

Gacaca" (paper prepared for the Expert Discussion on Transitional Justice and Children, November 10–12, 2005), 106, 114.

109 An Michels, "Protecting and Supporting Children as Witnesses: Lessons Learned from the Special Court for Sierra Leone" (paper prepared for the Expert Discussion on Transitional Justice and Children, November 10–12, 2005), 34.

110 Ibid., 35.

111 Keith Wright and Donald Robertshaw, "The Role of Child Protection Agencies in Supporting Children's Involvement in Transitional Justice Mechanisms, in Particular the Special Court for Sierra Leone" (paper prepared for the Expert Discussion on Transitional Justice and Children, November 10–12, 2005), 42.

112 Luc Côté, "Prosecuting Child Related Crimes at the Special Court for Sierra Leone: A Mid Term Assessment" (paper prepared for the Expert Discussion on Transitional Justice and Children, November 10–12, 2005), 28, 29.

113 See Eric A. Witte, "Beyond 'Peace vs. Justice': Understanding the Relationship between DDR Programs and the Prosecution of International Crimes," in this volume.

114 Wright and Robertshaw, "The Role of Child Protection Agencies," 48.

115 Coalition to Stop the Use of Child Soldiers, "International Forum," 7.

116 Géraldine Mattioli and Anneke van Woudenberg, "Global Catalyst for National Prosecutions? The ICC in the Democratic Republic of Congo," in *Courting Conflict? Justice, Peace and the ICC in Africa*, ed. Nicholas Waddell and Phil Clark (London: The Royal African Society, 2008), 56.

117 In Liberia in 2003–2004, reports Wessells, "Commanders denied repeatedly that children were or had been part of their forces," and the "DDR process encountered enormous obstacles." Wessells, *Child Soldiers*, 168, citing Human Rights Watch, *How to Fight, How to Kill* (New York: Human Rights Watch, 2004).

118 Quoted in Singer, *Children at War*, 149.

119 Singer, *Children at War*, 150, 153.

120 Mattioli and van Woudenberg, "Global Catalyst for National Prosecutions?" 56.

121 Cohn, "Symposium," 535.

122 Coalition to Stop the Use of Child Soldiers, "International Forum," 8.

123 Cohn, "Symposium," 539.

124 Withers, communication with Irma Specht.

125 Communication with Saudamini Siegrist.

# CHAPTER 7

# Local Justice and Reintegration Processes as Complements to Transitional Justice and DDR

*Roger Duthie*[1]

## INTRODUCTION

Justice measures that occur at the local or community level in postconflict societies have attracted a growing amount of attention within the field of transitional justice in recent years. In part, this has resulted from the operation of the high-profile gacaca trials in post-genocide Rwanda and the controversial arrest warrants issued by the International Criminal Court (ICC) for leaders of the Lord's Resistance Army (LRA) in northern Uganda, where local Acholi leaders have proposed the use of traditional ceremonies to deal with perpetrators of human rights violations. The attention also stems from several lines of thinking among practitioners and scholars of transitional justice, including the acknowledgment of the limitations of state or international responses to massive human rights violations in postconflict situations; the need to take into account the cultural context in which justice is pursued; and initial work to assess the impact of past transitional justice efforts, which involves comparison with places, such as Mozambique, where no formal transitional justice measures were implemented and yet a return to armed conflict has been avoided.

In his August 2004 report on transitional justice and the rule of law, the UN secretary-general wrote that "due regard must be given to indigenous and informal traditions for administering justice or settling disputes, to help them to continue their often vital role and to do so in conformity with both international standards and local tradition."[2] The UN Security Council in October of the same year underlined the "importance of assessing the particular justice and rule of law needs in each host country, taking into consideration the nature of the country's legal system, traditions and institutions, and of avoiding a 'one size fits all' approach."[3] Donors too are interested in localized justice, providing extensive support for gacaca in Rwanda in particular.[4] The information available and the literature on these local processes is also expanding, but remains small relative to transitional justice as a larger field of study.[5]

This chapter examines local justice processes from the perspective of both transitional justice and the reintegration (or integration) of ex-combatants into communities following their demobilization from armed groups.[6] Local justice is sometimes presented as an alternative to or substitute for other measures of transitional justice, often due to political, cultural, or practical considerations. Some have claimed, for example, that in general local processes should be implemented instead of other measures because they are less likely to disrupt peace negotiations and lead to instability, or because they are more culturally appropriate, or because they are simply more effective or affordable. And, indeed, it is always important to take account of politics, culture, and available resources, and acknowledge the ways in which these considerations will affect the policy choices that are and can be made in particular situations. The main argument of this chapter is that local justice addresses the (comparatively neglected) reintegration aspect of disarmament, demobilization, and reintegration (DDR) programs more directly, quickly, and efficiently than other transitional justice measures.[7] The chapter therefore examines how local justice processes can best *complement* DDR efforts without foreclosing other transitional justice measures. In postconflict societies in which state institutions are often weak and economies are damaged and/or underdeveloped, communities will likely continue to use local justice processes to reintegrate returning ex-combatants and perpetrators of abuses and to restore trust and rebuild social relationships.

The first section of this chapter discusses the concept of local justice. The types of processes that may fall under this category are labeled and described in many different ways in the literature, and so it is worth clarifying how they are understood for the purposes of this chapter—as both justice and reintegration mechanisms. The next section looks at some of the concrete links that exist between local justice processes and both DDR programs and other, more formal transitional justice measures (although many of these processes in fact operate in the absence of, or alongside but without any connections to, transitional justice and DDR efforts). The following section then examines some of the salient issues related to the use of local justice in a transitional justice and DDR context. Local justice is often discussed in terms of its positive features (for example, its accessibility, economy, efficiency, or local or cultural relevance) and negative features (for example, its violation of international standards, its inappropriateness for addressing serious human rights violations, its gender bias, its lack of accountability).[8] This section addresses these issues, but from the understanding that each issue is contested, rather than a straightforward benefit or problem. The aim is to highlight both the potential benefits of local processes and the reasons why they should be thought of as comple-ments to both transitional justice and DDR.

## LOCAL PROCESSES AS JUSTICE AND REINTEGRATION

Local processes aimed at reintegrating ex-combatants and perpetrators of human rights violations into communities in the aftermath of armed conflict are or have been used in such countries as Rwanda, Timor-Leste, Sierra Leone, Liberia, Peru, Mozambique, and northern Uganda. These processes encom-pass a range of different activities, and, as a result, there is a range of termi-nology used to describe them.[9] Many commentators have given highly posi-tive assessments of such processes.[10] Luc Huyse described the discussion of "traditional justice" in recent years as initially containing a "great deal of myth making," leading to a "knowledge gap" and "decision making that was based on weak data, *ex ante* evaluation and speculation." This has begun to change, however, he observes, as "normative approaches" based on this knowledge gap are "gradually giving way to more realistic, empirically based assessments of the potential role of traditional mechanisms within the broader reconciliation and transitional justice policy framework." And while it is still too early to fully assess their achievements, Huyse contends, "tradition-based practices have the potential to produce a dividend in terms of the much-needed post-conflict accountability, truth telling and reconciliation that is not negligible."[11]

Local justice processes are often grouped together or compared with each other, and, as different as they can be, there is good reason for this: there are common elements within these processes and their application in differ-ent contexts can provide useful lessons. The extent to which each process is actually local, however, varies. Local processes may straddle the line between informal and formal, state and nonstate, as illustrated by the gacaca system in particular. In other cases, such as Mozambique, practices fall completely out-side the formal, state legal system. While all involve public participation to some extent, the initiatives discussed here differ in their "localness" in three main ways: the extent to which they are actually under local or state con-trol;[12] whether they are essentially top-down or bottom-up initiatives; and the linkages between these local processes and other, more formal transitional justice measures. These are discussed below, but the focus is on the more bottom-up initiatives.

Even in such cases as Mozambique, the measures discussed here draw on or incorporate established or existing practices.[13] I say that these processes draw on "established" practices, rather than describing them in themselves as "traditional," "customary," or "indigenous" practices, because of their dynamic nature. The term "traditional" may imply that something is unchanging, whereas these practices may have changed significantly during the conflict or in the process of applying them to crimes committed during the conflict. As Rosalind Shaw emphasizes, "established" "means neither traditional nor homogenous. It is important to examine...the range of practices of conflict resolution and reconciliation that people and communities are adapting and retooling *now*. But in doing so, we need to be aware of introducing compromised practices of 'customary law,' or of authorizing a static and unitary 'tradition.'"[14] Lars Waldorf uses the term "local justice" "because it is more neutral than the alternatives. The terms 'customary law' and 'traditional justice' are inherently essentialist, historicizing, and mythopoeic, while the term 'popular justice' connotes popularity, which is sometimes lacking."[15] International IDEA's study focusing on Africa retains the word "traditional," as Huyse writes, "for want of a more accurate alternative," but fully acknowledges the hybrid nature and "dynamic processes that drive the form and content of our subject."[16]

The processes being discussed are also usually referred to as either justice measures or reconciliation measures, and, more often than not, both. One observer writes, for example, that "Gacaca's overarching goal is to promote reconciliation and healing,"[17] while others have described the system as "a promising alternative to achieve not only justice, but reconciliation."[18] In Timor-Leste, Fausto Belo Ximenes argues that "the process was not only a Community-based Reconciliation Process, but it was indeed a Community-based *Justice* and Reconciliation Process"[19] (emphasis in original). The local ceremonies and rituals in Sierra Leone, Mozambique, and Uganda are also all referred to in the literature as reconciliation and justice efforts.

Local justice processes are often referred to in terms of "restorative justice," a form of justice that has been defined as an approach to wrongdoing that attempts to address and balance the needs of the victim, the needs of the offender, and the need to restore the community,[20] and that treats crime "only secondarily as a violation against the state."[21] Overall, local processes do tend to be generally less punitive than most criminal prosecutions, but this is not necessarily the case.[22] Nor does the element of punishment necessarily make a justice measure retributive rather than restorative. Kimberly Theidon finds, for example, in her research on what she calls "the micropolitics of reconciliation" in Peru, that "retributive emotions are very common and not intrinsically

'Western' and that some form of punishment may be conducive both to the reincorporation of the perpetrator as well as to restoring social relations among transgressors and those they have wronged."[23]

Local processes in Rwanda, Timor-Leste, Peru, Sierra Leone, Liberia, Burundi, Mozambique, and Uganda to various extents contain elements of other transitional justice measures—prosecuting or punishing perpetrators, making reparations to victims, truth-telling, and institutional reform. Gacaca, for example, includes punishment, such as imprisonment and community service, reparations directly from the perpetrator to the victim, truth-telling in its encouragement of confessions and victim and witness participation, and institutional reform, in a form of vetting, by barring perpetrators from participating in public institutions. The CRP in Timor-Leste involved punishment (community service, possible prison sentence or fine), reparation (again, directly from the perpetrator to the victim), and truth-telling (perpetrators were required to publicly disclose their participation in the crime, and "the victims and the community members...played the key role in seeking truth from the perpetrators"[24]). In Mozambique, observes a U.S. Agency for International Development (USAID) report, there was much variation among cleansing ceremonies that ex-combatants often underwent upon returning to communities, but elements of transitional justice, such as truth-telling and reparation, do appear: "In some, repayment dominates over cleansing, in others the focus is confession and absolution, and some involve spirits while others do not."[25] In northern Uganda, the traditional ceremony of "*mato oput* encompasses the same principles of truth, accountability, compensation and restoration of relationships as other justice processes."[26] And in Liberia, Ezekiel Pajibo suggests that one local dispute resolution mechanism, the palava hut process—in part because of its "universality...in the Liberian context"—could be used in the postconflict period "as a reconciliation ritual or as a process of addressing some of the violations the TRC [truth and reconciliation commission] might uncover," including rape and land disputes. "As a transitional justice tool," Pajibo writes, "the palava hut process does embody the key dimensions of truth telling, accountability, reconciliation and reparation."[27]

Local justice processes are often described, as illustrated above, in terms of reconciliation or their ability to improve social relations within communities. The CRP in Timor aimed "to provide a space for perpetrators, victims and communities to seek solutions for reconciliation and reacceptance of those who have committed 'harmful acts' to the community."[28] Acholi ceremonies involve "reconciliation through symbolic acts and spiritual appeasement";[29]

they are "aimed at ultimately furthering both the act and the process of forgiveness through the remaking of relations of trust and the restoration of social cohesion."[30] In the view of Brynna Connolly, "Perhaps most fundamentally, NSJSs [nonstate justice systems] typically aim to restore the social harmony that has been unbalanced by the conflict."[31]

The element of reconciliation may rely heavily on ritual. As Craig Etcheson has observed, "The use of rituals in seeking reconciliation appears to have been relatively little-discussed to date in the literature. Yet, in many countries, ritual appears to play a central role in facilitating reconciliation in the aftermath of violent social upheavals."[32] One report on the role of *magamba* spirits in post-war Mozambique, for example, speaks of "socio-cultural practices that take the form of restorative justice and reconciliation in the aftermath of civil war." Rituals involving *magamba*, the authors argue, relate closely to transitional justice, and "engage with the grisly past in a profound way—that is, discursively, bodily and by means of performance—to create post-war healing of war-related wounds." Specifically, such rituals seek to reveal the underlying causes of current social conflicts "through the re-enactment of the violent past," leading to healing, justice, reconciliation, and stability.[33]

It should also be noted that the justice and reconciliation components of such local processes often include a religious or spiritual element, something that is less central, although not necessarily absent, from more national and formal transitional justice and reconciliation measures.[34] In the villages of the region of Ayacucho in Peru, for example, Theidon describes returning ex-combatants engaging in public apologies informed by biblical narratives and an administration of justice partially based on sacramental principles. "In these communities," she writes, "villagers combine the religious tradition of confession—the curing of souls and the reaffirmation of community—with legal confession and the need for a process of judgment and punishment. In these juridico-religious practices... [t]here is a place for both Christian charity as well as righteous wrath and an emphasis on settling accounts between perpetrators and those they have injured."[35]

Even with a minimal definition of reconciliation based on civic trust,[36] it may be difficult to show empirically the extent to which any transitional justice measure contributes to reconciliation, and particularly so with such an emerging and under-researched category as local processes. However, it can be concluded that these local processes are developed at least in part with the intention of reconciling individual perpetrators with victims. To the extent that they do lead to some degree of reconciliation, local justice processes may function as a means of reintegration. The UN conceives of reintegration as "the process by which ex-combatants acquire civilian status and gain sustainable employment and income," and says it "is essentially a social and economic process with an open time-frame, primarily taking place in communities at the local level."[37] And, according to a paper prepared by the World Bank's Multi-Country Demobilization and Reintegration Program (MDRP), "Acceptance or reacceptance of an ex-combatant as a member of the community may require ex-combatants to take part in some form of local reconciliation process." It points to a survey carried out by Rwanda's Demobilization and Reintegration Commission, in which 96 percent of local administration officials said that participating in such activities as gacaca helped to build mutual trust and acceptance between ex-combatants and their communities.[38] Mark Drumbl argues that even gacaca sentences are "geared to reintegrating the offender."[39] And with northern Uganda's local processes, writes James Ojera Latigo, "the objective is to reintegrate the perpetrators into their communities and reconcile them with the victims."[40]

Local justice can also function as a mechanism of social reintegration in different ways, however. It can serve as an important civic educational tool and demonstrate acceptance of local norms, rules, and authority. In Mozambique, for instance, people believed that the reintegration ceremonies provided a form of civic education for the ex-combatants, teaching them how to function in civilian society again. According to one observer, the cleansing ceremony served "to calm down the heart, [help the individual] continue as a person, to help someone to know how to live: how to live at home, how to respect his mother, how to greet his father, how to greet people when they come to visit."[41] Local processes can also demonstrate an ex-combatant's acceptance of society's rules. In some communities in Sierra Leone, public apologies were followed by blessings from community authorities, "thereby dramatizing the reassertion of civilian gender, age, and status hierarchies." One local elder emphasized "the acceptance of civilian authority" by ex-combatants.[42] The processes discussed in this chapter, then, can be considered measures of both justice and reintegration.

## LINKING LOCAL JUSTICE WITH DDR PROGRAMS AND OTHER TRANSITIONAL JUSTICE MEASURES

The previous section presented local justice as incorporating a range of processes and activities that can be applied in transitional contexts in order to facilitate the pursuit of justice and the reintegration of ex-combatants. In this section, I briefly review how such local processes may be linked in concrete ways with DDR programs and other, more formal transitional justice measures.

## LINKS WITH DDR PROGRAMS

Since they generally contain to some extent one or more of the elements of transitional justice — prosecutions, truth-telling, reparation, institutional reform — local justice processes may interact with DDR programs, and particularly the process of reintegration, in some of the same ways as these other justice measures, as explored throughout this volume. Local justice that involves punishment may provide a disincentive for combatants to demobilize and disarm, but might at the same time reduce resentment among victims and other community members or allow ex-combatants to contribute to the economy through community service. The truth-telling aspects of local justice may provide ex-combatants with the opportunity to tell their side of the story and apologize for wrongful acts. Reparations or restitution as well might reduce the resentment of victims, but, if ex-combatants are themselves required to pay the compensation, it may also provide a disincentive to return.[43]

These types of interactions will vary and depend on contextual factors, and we should not assume that they will occur a certain way. Lars Waldorf's case study on DDR and transitional justice in Rwanda, for example, demonstrates that, contrary to his expectations, the operation of gacaca did not seem to disrupt the demobilization and reintegration of ex-combatants, despite their vulnerability to accusations and potentially serious punishment.[44] As discussed at more length above, most local justice processes are intended to, at least in part, function as mechanisms of reintegration.

As with other transitional justice measures as well, however, there may also be much potential for operationally linking local justice processes with DDR programs. As suggested by one report on DDR in Africa, "Local reconciliation customs and practices should be supported and incorporated into the overall structure of DDR programmes."[45] Similarly, drawing on her research in Colombia, Kimberly Theidon argues for "incorporating local-level transitional justice initiatives into DDR programs" and "expanding our unit of analysis and intervention beyond the individual combatant to include the neighborhoods and communities to which these warriors return," by which she believes "we can reintegrate demobilized fighters into civilian life in a way which respects both the needs of these former combatants as well as those of the broader community."[46] And, according to the UN, "Reintegration programmes for ex-combatants should work together with other reintegration programmes to support the establishment of local conflict-resolution mechanisms that can work towards finding equitable and sustainable solutions to potential conflict about access to land and other resources. Such mechanisms can transform potential conflict into reconciliation opportunities."[47]

In Sierra Leone, the National Committee for Disarmament, Demobilisation and Reintegration (NCDDR) used local processes to facilitate the reintegration of ex-combatants into communities. The NCDDR's work involved bringing ex-combatants to ad hoc community reconciliation meetings throughout the country, and facilitating the return of some ex-combatants alleged to have committed war crimes.[48] In Mozambique, DDR designers were reluctant to directly involve themselves in local reintegration processes, but noted that reintegration payments were used for these purposes, for ceremonies, and other events. A USAID report asks, "In what ways could this support be extended?"[49]

It is crucial, however, if DDR programs seek to promote, facilitate, or make connections with local justice processes, that they do not do so uncritically. In a recent paper on the World Bank's MDRP in the Great Lakes Region of Africa, for example, Johanna Herman argues that the lack of theoretical linkages between the fields of social integration and transitional justice has consequences for the MDRP's approach to local justice: superficial treatment of local processes; a focus on reintegration activities that are unlikely to contribute to reconciliation in practice; and, critically, "an acceptance of traditional reconciliation processes without consideration of the problems or impacts they have, the diversity and evolution of such practices (and the communities that practice them)" without attention given to "the need for evaluation for use in a post-conflict context or of the impact on transitional justice." This could lead, she writes, to problems with reintegration "at the national and field level by either linking to activities that are unsuitable in a certain form or missing out on initiatives that could perhaps be useful." In Uganda, overlooked problems included ex-combatants' fear of discovery, arguments over the meaning of "tradition," and the difficulty of applying such practices in postconflict contexts (discussed more below). The use of local justice processes (and other transitional justice measures, it could be said) by DDR programs should, Herman argues, be determined only after a "full examination of both the DDR and transitional justice strategy (if any) so that one does not undermine the other."[50]

## LINKS WITH OTHER TRANSITIONAL JUSTICE MEASURES

Local justice processes in transitional contexts can vary greatly in the extent to which they are linked to more formal, state-run transitional justice measures.

Cleansing and reintegration ceremonies, such as those used in Mozambique, can operate in the absence of or without any inducement from or connection to criminal prosecutions, truth commissions, reparations programs, or processes of institutional reform.[51] The healing and cleansing ceremonies in postconflict Mozambique were a national phenomenon,[52] but they functioned outside of the government's control and represented a completely bottom-up initiative. Local courts, such as those in South Africa, may even be considered by some to be at odds with the institutions and goals of formal transitional justice measures if they are seen to be overly punitive and to undermine the rule of law.[53] At the other end of the spectrum, however, both the CRP in Timor-Leste and gacaca in Rwanda are linked closely with state prosecution efforts. In between, transitional justice processes may promote, facilitate, or reinforce the functioning of local justice process.

In Timor-Leste, the CRP operated within local communities and drew on local practices, and began in response to a bottom-up process initiated more by local communities than central authorities, but still functioned under UN or state control. Serious criminal offenses, such as genocide, war crimes, crimes against humanity, murder, sexual offenses, and torture, were referred to the General Prosecutor for Serious Crimes, and the process remained very much under the authority of that office. Many participants believed that the connection between the CRP and the prosecutor's office and the courts was "extremely important."[54] The "CRP represents the first concrete example," writes one observer, "of implementing a process that spans aspects of both traditional and formal justice practices, in a new format that accords with constitutional and human rights imperatives, and incorporates a written record of the process and content."[55]

In Rwanda, the gacaca system is very much a state-controlled and state-initiated process. Lars Waldorf goes as far as to say that the gacaca courts being used in Rwanda now "bear no resemblance to 'traditional' gacaca. Genocide gacaca is a state institution intimately linked to the state apparatus of prosecutions and incarceration, and applying codified, rather than 'customary,' law."[56] Waldorf takes a negative view of the Rwandan government's control of the system. "Once gacaca is seen as state-imposed 'informalism' designed to expand the state's reach into local communities," he writes,

> its difficulties start to resemble those encountered in other such state efforts: increased formalism, decreased popular participation, and increased state coercion. The overarching lessons for transitional justice are that successor regimes should resist the temptation to co-opt

or control local justice and to expand local justice's jurisdiction to reach genocide, crimes against humanity, and war crimes.[57]

His conclusion is that "if successor regimes want local justice to retain legitimacy and popularity, they need to adopt a largely hands-off approach."[58]

In Sierra Leone and Liberia, the acts establishing the truth and reconciliation commissions (TRCs) contained provisions that, using identical language, allowed those bodies to "seek assistance from traditional and religious leaders to facilitate its public sessions and in resolving local conflicts arising from past violations or abuses or in support of healing and reconciliation."[59] According to the Sierra Leone TRC's *Final Report*, "Community based reconciliation is one of the main focuses of [its] activities on reconciliation." The TRC frequently organized local reconciliation ceremonies at the end of its hearings, one of which is described in some detail by an observer, Tim Kelsall, as having a "remarkable impact on the hearings, transforming the atmosphere from one of virtual crisis and farce, to one of emotional release and reconciliation." He suggests that greater integration of such local practices—very much based on performance and ritual, and with clear religious elements to them—into the truth commission's hearings may have strengthened their truth-telling component (although he also acknowledges that certain TRC staff members may have resisted such a move).[60] The Sierra Leone TRC also started a nationwide program on community-based reconciliation that continued after its own mandate ended, beginning in October 2003 and lasting for nine months. The program "allows all chiefdoms in the country to organize reconciliation activities according to the wishes and the needs of the people." It consisted of training, district workshops, and District Support Committees, whose work included traditional activities, such as traditional secret society rituals and dances, cleansing ceremonies, and the pouring of libation.[61]

Liberia's TRC established a Traditional Advisory Council (TAC), although in the view of one observer, the lack of published criteria for membership in the TAC suggests that it is "simply intended to placate the public and give the appearance of involvement by traditional leaders."[62] In Uganda, the June 2007 Accountability Agreement and its February 2008 annex both promoted local justice mechanisms as central to the overall accountability and reconciliation framework. They also included provisions for the establishment of a truth-telling body, the functions of which include, the annex states, "to promote truth-telling in communities and in this respect to liaise with any traditional or other community reconciliation interlocutors."[63] In Burundi, one report suggests that the traditional justice institution, *bashingantahe*, could be an objective source of evidence for a truth commission or other transitional justice measures, in that it may hold reliable information about the 1993 crisis, as well as play a role in preparing and sensitizing communities, collecting testimonies, and advising on a reparations program.[64] And the National Council of Bashingantahe has suggested that this traditional mechanism should contribute to the proposed special tribunal for the country.[65]

## LOCAL JUSTICE AND REINTEGRATION AS COMPLEMENTS TO TRANSITIONAL JUSTICE AND DDR

Having looked at how local justice processes in themselves can function as both justice and reintegration measures, and at how these processes may be linked with DDR efforts and more formal, state-led transitional justice, I now turn to a brief discussion of a number of important issues surrounding local justice and its application in transitional justice and DDR settings. Taken together, these issues suggest that local justice processes in themselves can make an important contribution to justice and reintegration, but that they are also flawed, which reinforces the argument that they should be considered as complements to rather than alternatives to more formal measures.

### PRACTICALITY: STATE CAPACITY AND DEVELOPMENT

Some of the arguments in support of using local justice processes in a post-conflict and transitional justice context, and among the reasons why they in fact are applied, have to do with the capacity of state institutions and development. Local justice processes are common in some underdeveloped countries to begin with. As the UK's Department for International Development (DFID) points out, "It is estimated that, in many developing countries, NSJS systems deal with the vast majority of disputes. They are widely used in rural and poor urban areas, where there is often minimal access to formal state justice."[66] Access to the state justice system may already be limited by its general incapacity, as well as issues of distance, costs, language, and corruption.[67] In a postconflict situation, when a society is struggling to recover from serious damage to its public institutions and the devastating socioeconomic effects of civil war, local processes may take on even greater importance. "The formal state system may be entirely incapacitated," writes Connolly, "either in terms of infrastructure or lack of personnel, or both," and unable to reach most of the population.[68]

Local processes can help to fill this gap. They can be cheaper and faster than formal measures, and deal more efficiently with large numbers of perpetrators. In many postconflict societies, there is a need to deal with massive numbers of perpetrators with few resources and a damaged or even crippled national legal system and state structure. In Rwanda, Timor-Leste, and Sierra Leone, local processes have been encouraged by the government in large part for these pragmatic reasons: state or international transitional justice measures simply cannot handle the numbers of suspected perpetrators. In Rwanda, estimates are that when gacaca was launched in 2002, more than 100,000 people were in prison awaiting trials. At that time, the national court system was judging around 1,000 cases per year, a rate that would have required more than a century for the court system to complete its task.[69] Peter Uvin and Charles Mironko argued at the time that "the strongest element in favor of gacaca is the lack of an alternative. Neither the ICTR nor the formal justice system seems capable of providing the basis for justice or reconciliation in Rwanda."[70] According to Bert Ingelaere, the establishment of and support for gacaca was "clearly motivated by the fact that the ordinary justice system was virtually non-existent after the genocide"; the gacaca trials, he says, are "breaking all records in quantitative terms."[71] (It is important to note, however, that this does not explain why other transitional justice measures, such as a truth commission, were rejected by the government.)

In Timor-Leste, without massive increases in investment and capacity, there was "widespread consensus that the formal justice system will have only limited reach" in addressing both past and current human rights violations.[72] One author spoke of a "void created by the judicial trials as a result of their weakness and incompetence, to which the CRP can make a potential contribution."[73] According to Connolly,

> the NSJS can be instrumental in dealing with the urgent problems caused by the violence in an efficient and legitimate manner. Because NSJSs are often already in existence and require less administration and less expense, they will in many cases be the only alternative to months or years of delay that will result from the slow process of rebuilding the formal justice system.[74]

Not only may local justice processes fill this gap inexpensively, but they may also have a certain positive developmental impact through the use of community service as a primary form of sanction, tapping the "enormous potential resource of perpetrators toward rebuilding the country."[75]

It should be noted, however, that while local justice processes may be less expensive than more formal justice measures, they are not free. The issue of cost does not disappear, and in fact can still present formidable obstacles in poor communities. In northern Uganda, for example, the "inability of persons to access the necessary materials for rituals prevents the restoration of Acholi social and spiritual worlds," explains a report by the Justice and Reconciliation Project. "Reconciliation in Acholi-land," it concludes, "cannot occur in the face of absolute poverty."[76] Without the assistance of state resources or donor funding, then, local justice may also be beyond reach for many.

## LOCAL LEGITIMACY

Local justice processes can contribute to transitional justice because their community-based nature may make them more accessible and legitimate than other justice measures. First, they are usually located either in local communities themselves or close by; second, the processes themselves often encourage the participation of the local population; and, third, they draw on existing local practices, structures, customs, norms, and values. This legitimacy is particularly strong in cases, such as Timor-Leste, where the process is more bottom-up than top-down, in that the initiative emerges at the local level itself. As Chris Lundry explains, in Timor-Leste "local elites felt as though they were best-equipped to determine the culpability and fates of returning militia members, through traditional means of justice."[77] Diane Orentlicher agrees. "In principle," she writes, concerning the ICC and northern Uganda, "an approach toward the LRA that is rooted in local culture is inherently more likely to be meaningful to victims — and in other important respects to 'work' — than prosecutions that seem alien to Acholi culture."[78]

Local legitimacy, however, should not be assumed. Lars Waldorf argues that participation in gacaca has been poor for a number of reasons, including that the process is being imposed from the top down, that people fear being the subject of accusations, and that many Rwandans are involved in subsistence agriculture and need to work.[79] A number of additional factors may detract from the legitimacy of local processes. First, local practices may not be appropriate for dealing with cases of mass violence because they have been damaged in some way by many years of conflict. In Timor-Leste, for example, traditional systems of justice had been weakened by the Indonesian occupation.[80] In Sierra Leone, traditional leaders and the social institutions previously "critical to the effective functioning of these mechanisms" were targeted and "methodically destroyed" during the war.[81] Local leaders may have also been implicated in human rights abuses, such as the recruitment of child soldiers, and therefore been discredited in the eyes of the community.[82] More significantly, the massive internal displacement that accompanies many conflicts can destroy the physical and cultural structures that previously made local practices possible. In northern Uganda, for example, the impact of "large-scale displacement caused by the war is a strong belief that traditional mechanisms can no longer be applied in any meaningful way in a context of displacement: ceremonies have little meaning when there is no place to perform them."[83] Alcinda Honwana explains the limits of local ceremonies in Mozambique after years and years of brutal armed conflict:

> In communities where people were killed by their neighbours, where families were divided for long periods of time, where people can no longer muster the resources necessary to carry out ceremonies properly, and where the reputation of traditional leaders was compromised during the war, the effectiveness of customary remedies has come into question.[84]

Second, it should not be assumed that local justice processes operate outside the realm of politics and are necessarily representative of their communities. As Waldorf puts it, "Local justice is political justice."[85] Mark Drumbl explains that

> in many places local dispute resolution entities may be viewed cynically insofar as they may serve as instruments of social control and institutionalize the power of unaccountable local elites. This makes it necessary to differentiate between manipulated constructions of the local, on the one hand, and the truly representative or indigenous, on the other... the content of the local often is determined through profoundly undemocratic means.[86]

Similarly, Lisa Schirch argues that "traditional trauma healing rituals" can be problematic because they "are subject to political motives of forgetting about the past at the expense of justice or human rights."[87]

## INTERNATIONAL HUMAN RIGHTS STANDARDS

One of the most common concerns about local justice processes is that, due to the fact that they operate outside formal legal systems and sometimes outside any kind of state control, they do not always respect national or international legal or human rights standards — in particular, that they do not always afford due process. In Rwanda, for example, while the system is under state control, this does not mean that the tribunals, with judges who have little training[88] and which prohibit legal assistance for the accused,[89] respect the rights of the suspected perpetrators.[90] Furthermore, punishments may also not conform to human rights standards. Local practices in Sierra Leone can involve humiliating and beating the guilty. Such practices "are in conflict with a culture of human rights and perpetuate a culture of violence."[91] In one township in postapartheid South Africa, explains Richard Wilson, the local courts, *imbizo*, which occupy "an ambiguous position with regard to state legality," frequently require "a public beating in the football stadium with whips, *sjamboks* (quirts, or mule whips), and golf clubs with the heads removed."[92] One recent report contends that "any mechanisms that may be used need to be accepted not only as legitimate on the ground, but they also need to be seen as acceptable within the wider paradigms of international law."[93] Others contend, though, that a fair assessment of local processes should keep a balanced view of international standards and local reality and goals.[94]

The use of local justice processes may in particular reinforce gender or other biases that are embedded in local practices and structures. In northern Uganda, women are generally not part of the decision-making, arbitration, or negotiations of mato oput.[95] In Timor-Leste, notes an International Rescue Committee report about traditional justice, "Women have minimal and often superficial participation in justice hearings and find that the rulings which are passed are often based on the administrators of justice own biases and cultural beliefs regarding women's status in society."[96] According to Amnesty International, "those who need the protection of a formal court system—especially vulnerable women and children—are those most likely to be coerced into a 'traditional' resolution in the absence of clearly recognized procedures"; "informal non-judicial mechanisms do not afford women in East Timor adequate legal protection against abuses such as rape."[97] Similarly, in many communities in Sierra Leone, notes one report, "men have the last word on governance and dispute resolution over all conflicts."[98] And in Mozambique, the *magamba* rituals do not involve justice for women killed in the war, only men, and so "structurally the justice they offer helps to reinforce patriarchal power in a country that is struggling for gender equality."[99]

At the same time, however, the modification of local processes as they are applied in transitional contexts may provide an opportunity to change such practices and improve the situation of women. In both Rwanda and Timor, for example, efforts were made to ensure women's proportional representation in the new structures. The panels overseeing the CRP hearings were required to have "appropriate gender and cultural representation,"[100] and gacaca elections "encourage selection of women, who have been traditionally excluded from gacaca, and adults of all ages, rather than simply the most senior men of the community."[101] In Burundi, Assumpta Naniwe-Kaburahe argues that the status of women "can be improved in the context of ongoing efforts to rehabilitate the institution of *bashingantahe*," which traditionally excluded women.[102]

## SUBJECT MATTER

It can reasonably be argued that local processes are simply not appropriate for dealing with serious human rights violations, such as abductions, amputations, rape, and murder, particularly when these represent war crimes, crimes against humanity, or genocide. Most of the processes discussed here are or draw on local practices that were originally intended to deal with civil conflicts between family and community members, not violent crimes. And while the processes discussed in this chapter are mostly, and sometimes significantly, modified versions of the original practices, they are still not necessarily appropriate for serious human rights abuses. As one author writes about Sierra Leone, "traditional forms of dispute resolutions do not seem well-fitted to deal with war crimes types of cases and other related abuses."[103] According to Alcinda Honwana, while local ceremonies across Mozambique need to be recognized and accommodated, they have their limits: "It is also evident that the horrors experienced by many Mozambicans cannot simply be erased from the collective memory as customary practices sometimes require. If drawing a line under the past fosters denial and impunity, there is also the risk of facilitating further human rights abuses."[104] Similarly, the traditional justice system used by the Acholi "in its original form was not conceptualized as a method for adjudicating over war crimes and crimes against humanity...it is not well suited to being applied as the sole reconciliation measure to the LRA architects of terror."[105]

Furthermore, local ceremonies that are based on perpetrators or their clans providing compensation to victims or their clans may simply not be feasible in the wake of mass violence. The unprecedented scale of killings and damage may make such practices impossible: perpetrators will often not be known, nor will adequate compensation be affordable. As one resident of an internally-displaced-person camp in northern Uganda observed, "a general cleansing ceremony can be done, but only when the man comes back, he admits that he has done that, he asks for forgiveness, and then the ceremony is performed....

But then it is hard, because 220 lives cannot really be compensated by his clan."[106] And, even if they were only to deal with the nonserious violations as intended, some may object to such crimes as arson being considered "nonserious" crimes.

At the same time, however, it can also be argued that local processes may be particularly useful in postconflict situations where, due to the nature of past abuses, establishing legal guilt for most perpetrators is difficult or impossible. Mass violence during conflicts often involves not just huge numbers of perpetrators but perpetrators with varying, uncertain, and complicated levels of guilt and complicity. Even if a country's court system was capable of handling such large numbers of trials, the nature of the violence would often lead to moral and evidentiary problems that a court of law may not be able to resolve. Local processes, in such cases, are useful not because they are able to make distinctions between such degrees of guilt and resolve such dilemmas, but precisely because they often avoid them to some degree or even altogether. Local justice processes generally, though not always, involve lesser forms of punishment and fewer applications of direct individual accountability.

This can be seen particularly clearly in the case of child ex-combatants, who can very often be considered as both perpetrators and victims.[107] While conflicts often involve significant numbers of children who commit atrocities, many of these children have been coerced, kidnapped, or traumatized into participating. As one study explains, the "story of child soldiers in many African conflicts…is the story of deliberate creation of perpetrators using the raw ingredients of the most vulnerable and malleable part of the population: disadvantaged children."[108] Local processes, such as the cleansing and reintegration ceremonies in Mozambique, which emphasize transformation more than punishment, may be particularly appropriate for former child combatants. In northern Uganda, reconciliation ceremonies "serve as a cultural strategy" for dealing with "abducted children both as victims and perpetrators of violence."[109]

In cases of mass violence, however, this does not necessarily apply only to children. The conflicts in Sierra Leone and Mozambique, among many others, involved the mobilization of combatants that depended heavily on coercion.[110] Furthermore, it is very often extremely difficult to distinguish the line between forced and voluntary recruitment.[111] And even if it is possible to clearly and firmly establish which acts constitute punishable crimes and which do not, in most cases it is just as difficult to identify precisely who committed each crime. As the Sierra Leone TRC report notes: "The mass based nature of these violations have the consequence that they remain anonymous. These situations make healing very difficult and make the reconciliation processes that take place at the community level even more important."[112] In Peru, explains Kimberly Theidon, those returning to villages were referred to with terms signifying varying degrees of guilt—"repentant, consciousness raised, rescued, tricked/duped"—in what seems a somewhat confusing way. "Ambiguity," she writes, however, "is what allowed this to work. In contrast with positive law, which is based on categories that are mutually exclusive, these categories are porous and fluid. There is a gray zone in communal jurisprudence that allowed for a greater flexibility in judging crimes and transgressors."[113]

A number of authors have made the case that local justice processes can be particularly useful for sorting out land and property disputes, which, while perhaps more minor than some crimes, can be an extremely important issue in need of resolution in postconflict societies.[114] It is also an issue that can be a major factor in the reintegration of ex-combatants and other returning groups. One report on nonstate justice in Burundi notes that the traditional legal system has historically played an important role in settling land disputes, and contends that it should take on an even greater postconflict significance with the return of refugees.[115] Lars Waldorf argues that in Rwanda, the lack of an appropriate forum to hear property disputes has led some people to make false accusations in the gacaca trials for land-related reasons:

> Local justice in transitional justice settings will be more effective and legitimate if it focuses on its ordinary subject matter—generally, property, restitution, and community reintegration. Property issues may seem trivial by contrast with the violence and suffering that has occurred, but they are an essential element of social reconstruction. Property (especially land) often plays an important role in today's brutal, intra-state conflicts, both as an underlying structural factor and as an inducement to violence, so resolving property disputes provides accountability for past violence while helping to prevent future conflict.[116]

## LIMITS OF LOCAL JUSTICE

It is important to note the limitations of local justice processes. For one, while they may in fact extend the reach of transitional justice significantly (in terms of perpetrators, victims, and community members), it would be a mistake to think that local justice processes can come even close to bringing justice in all possible cases. In Timor-Leste, for example, despite the participation of many more people than expected, "most potential deponents did not access the process."[117] Aside from the fact that the voluntary nature of many such processes allows many accused simply not to show up for a hearing (not everyone will agree that doing so is beneficial for their reintegration), even the most effective mechanisms of local justice will not bring justice to everyone. As with other forms of justice, although perhaps less so, local justice is subject to time and resource constraints.[118] The danger of unrealistic expectations should be considered.

At the same time, however, and conversely to the last point, the relative success of local processes might serve to discredit other transitional justice measures by creating a "justice gap." Again, for example, in Timor-Leste, as the CRP worked to hold perpetrators accountable for less serious crimes, while referring the more serious crimes to the formal legal system, it "remains to be seen whether the promise of the OGP [Office of the General Prosecutor] sanction for serious crimes, as inferred in the Regulation, will be brought into effect. A failure to do so will exacerbate concerns raised about a 'justice gap' where certain categories of people admitting to serious crimes might face no justice at all."[119] A situation in which people were sanctioned for confessing to minor crimes while those who confessed to much more serious ones were left untouched would certainly undermine some of the benefits of a transitional justice program as a coherent whole.

Finally, in Timor-Leste one of the criticisms of the CRP is that it was too perpetrator-focused. While many in local communities said that they valued the process, explains one report, "as a mechanism for achieving just outcomes for victims the CRP has been less consistent." "In its focus on the deponent reconciling with the 'community' the CRP has paid too little attention to the needs and rights of individual victims." The CRP did not, for example, require victim consent for the conclusion of a Community Reconciliation Agreement.[120] In all of the examples in this chapter, there would seem to be much room for more victim-centered, local transitional justice efforts, such as local, official, or unofficial truth commissions,[121] which may draw on existing practices in similar ways.

## CONCLUSION

This chapter has attempted to achieve three main objectives. First, it has tried to clarify the ways in which local justice processes in a postconflict and transitional justice context can serve as both justice and reintegration mechanisms. These processes share elements of the primary transitional justice approaches—prosecutions, truth-telling, reparations, and institutional reform—and they can facilitate reintegration through reconciliation and in other ways. Second, the chapter has raised some of the ways in which local justice processes are or might be linked with other transitional justice measures and DDR programs. Finally, the chapter has tried to present a balanced view of some of the main and contested issues surrounding the application of local justice in the aftermath of massive and serious human rights abuses. These issues include its practicality, local legitimacy, respect for international standards, subject matter, and limitations.

The chapter argues that local justice is not a substitute for other forms of justice or reintegration, but rather a complement with potential to contribute to and to be more firmly linked with other initiatives that share the goals of justice and reintegration. How this occurs in each case will depend on the context. As Connolly puts it, "the particular arrangement that is most appropriate in a given case will largely depend upon the history and culture of the state and local population, and not on a generalized balancing of pros and cons regarding the interaction between state and non-state systems."[122] It will also require time and resources. Local justice processes, even when complementing other initiatives, are flawed and limited. "Encouraging local justice means more than nodding permissibly in the direction of local justice initiatives," writes Drumbl. "It means committing resources, infrastructure, and human capital towards the institutions that will enforce such justice."[123] Similarly, Luc Huyse concludes that "the challenge of integrating traditional justice mechanisms into broader reconciliation and transitional justice strategies requires imagination, wide consultations, consensus building and capacity building, technical support, research and time."[124] In the interests of both justice and reintegration, it seems a challenge worth taking up. It is important, ultimately, that designers of transitional justice and DDR initiatives consider how local justice can be incorporated into a broader peacebuilding program, in which reintegration and justice are integral goals.

## NOTES

1   I would like to thank Paige Arthur, Pablo de Greiff, Ana Patel, and Lars Waldorf for comments on earlier versions of this chapter, as well as the participants in the project's May 2007 authors meeting for their feedback on a draft. The views expressed here do not necessarily reflect those of the ICTJ.

2   United Nations, Report of the Secretary-General, *The Rule of Law and Transitional Justice in Conflict and Post-Conflict Societies*, S/2004/616, August 23, 2004.

3   United Nations Security Council, *Statement by the President of the Security Council*, S/PRST/2004/34, October 6, 2004.

4   See Barbara Oomen, "Donor-Driven Justice and Its Discontents: The Case of Rwanda," *Development and Change* 36, no. 5 (2005): 887–910.

5   "[T]here is little information in the field of transitional justice on the role of local, traditional mechanisms and given the novel attempts to better incorporate such mechanisms into transitional justice strategies." Erin K. Baines, "The Haunting of Alice: Local Approaches to Justice and Reconciliation in Northern Uganda," *International Journal of Transitional Justice* 1 (2007): 97. "Despite the burgeoning literature on transitional justice, scant attention has been paid to local justice mechanisms." Lars Waldorf, "Mass Justice for Mass Atrocity: Rethinking Local Justice as Transitional Justice," *Temple Law Review* 79 (2006): 6. "The growing literature on transitional justice has tended to focus on the international and national levels...a politics of scale indicates a need for understanding 'transitional justice from below'; that is, for exploring how neighborhoods and communities also mobilize the ritual and symbolic elements of transitional justice." Kimberly Theidon, "Transitional Subjects: The Disarmament, Demobilization and Reintegration of Former Combatants in Colombia," *International Journal of Transitional Justice* 1 (2007): 67. The results of the largest research project to date on the topic were published in Luc Huyse and Mark Salter, eds., *Traditional Justice and Reconciliation after Violent Conflict: Learning from African Experiences* (Stockholm: International Institute for Democracy and Electoral Assistance [IDEA], 2008). Other comparative projects include "The Role of Non-State Justice Systems in Fostering the Rule of Law in Post-Conflict Societies," conducted by the United States Institute of Peace and the Fletcher School of Law and Diplomacy, in collaboration with the Centre for Humanitarian Dialogue; and Kieran McEvoy and Lorna McGregor, eds., *Transitional Justice from Below* (Oxford: Hart Publishing, 2008), the results of a project conducted by the Institute of Criminology and Criminal Justice at the Queen's University Belfast School of Law.

6   It focuses therefore on local processes in postconflict societies used to reintegrate ex-combatants and perpetrators of past human rights abuses. While there is some overlap, the chapter does not concentrate on the use of local processes as resolution mechanisms for current disputes or justice mechanisms for current crime, or as reconciliation

measures between communities. Nor does it discuss local initiatives that can be said to pursue justice primarily on behalf of victims, such as some unofficial truth projects (see Louis Bickford, "Unofficial Truth Projects," *Human Rights Quarterly* 29, no. 4 [2007]: 994–1035). This is not to say that the initiatives discussed here do not address the needs of victims or society, for I argue specifically that these processes usually contain a number of elements of the major approaches to transitional justice — prosecutions, truthtelling, reparations, and institutional reform — which seek justice for perpetrators, victims, and society in varying degrees. However, the perpetrator/ex-combatant is the focal point here.

7  Victor Igreja and Beatrice Dias-Lambranca point out how in Mozambique politicians have used the success of local processes "to justify their option for post-war amnesties, impunity and silence." The authors argue that "the fact that war survivors are engaged in everyday forms of attaining justice, reconciliation and healing should not be used as an excuse for state inaction vis-à-vis the violent past." Victor Igreja and Beatrice Dias-Lambranca, "Restorative Justice and the Role of Magamba Spirits in Post-War Gorongosa, Central Mozambique," in *Traditional Justice and Reconciliation after Violent Conflict*, 81-82. Similarly, the debate around transitional justice in northern Uganda is sometimes framed in terms a choice between *either* international justice *or* local justice, with mato oput presented as an alternative to the ICC. See James Ojera Latigo, "Northern Uganda: Tradition-Based Practices in the Acholi Region," in *Traditional Justice and Reconciliation after Violent Conflict*, 100, quoting the Ugandan minister of internal affairs as saying: "The traditional methods are both symbolic and real. They have worked. Instead of rushing for Western solutions, it is good we have revived them."

8  See, e.g., UK Department for International Development (DFID), "Non-state Justice and Security Systems," DFID Briefing, May 2004, 1–3; and Brynna Connolly, "Non-State Justice Systems and the State: Proposals for a Recognition Typology," *Connecticut Law Review* 38 (2005): 243–46.

9  Labels include "local," "traditional," "community," "indigenous," "informal," "nonstate," "popular," "restorative," and "cleansing," as well as "justice," "reintegration," "dispute resolution," "conflict resolution," "ritual," "ceremony," and "reconciliation." I focus here on local processes that draw on established or existing practices and focus on perpetrators. I use the term "local" instead of "community" because even within individual countries, the local processes being discussed often differ between communities. As one researcher notes about her work in Timor-Leste, "local systems vary from place to place. Terms such as 'community justice' do not give room for the various types of communities, individuals and social interactions which in this way are presumed to be homogenous." Aisling Swaine, "Traditional Justice and Gender Based Violence: Research Report," International Rescue Committee, August 2003, 11. See also Richard Wilson, *The Politics of Truth and Reconciliation in South Africa: Legitimizing the Post-Apartheid State*

(Cambridge: Cambridge University Press, 2001), 199: "we should not romanticize or reify the concept of community, since it is the product of conditions of the present, rather than something handed down from the mists of the traditional past. Who represents the community varies according to context, history and the position of the speaker. Communities are not homogeneous, and community justice is not a stable, given concept but is reworked in the cut and thrust of local politics." I do not use the terms "informal" or "nonstate" because local processes can be both quite formal and linked to or controlled by the state in varying degrees. Luc Huyse writes of a debate within the field of transitional justice about "two models at the extremes of a continuum. At one end is a strategy that is initiated, organized and controlled by (national or international) state institutions. Its procedures are formal and rational-legalistic.... At the other end of the continuum are policies that are community-initiated and community organized. They are predominantly informal and ritualistic-communal." He rightly points out, however, that "in real-world situations many transitional justice policies will combine, albeit to different degrees, ingredients of both extremes." Luc Huyse, "Introduction: Tradition-Based Approaches in Peacemaking, Transitional Justice and Reconciliation Policies," in *Traditional Justice and Reconciliation after Violent Conflict*, 5–6.

10    The gacaca trials in Rwanda, e.g., have been described as "ambitious, groundbreaking" (Amnesty International, "Rwanda: A Question of Justice," Amnesty International, December 2002, 2); a "radical break" from conventional transitional justice measures and an "unprecedented legal-social experiment" (Peter Uvin and Charles Mironko, "Western and Local Approaches to Justice in Rwanda," *Global Governance* 9 [2003]: 226, 228); and the "largest experiment in popular justice in history" (Peter Harrell, *Rwanda's Gamble: Gacaca and a New Model of Transitional Justice* [New York: Writers Club Press, 2003], 9. The Community-Based Reconciliation Process (CRP) in Timor-Leste has been described as "unique" and "innovative" (Piers Pigou, "The Community Reconciliation Process of the Commission for Reception, Truth and Reconciliation," Report for UNDP Timor-Leste, April 2004, 6, 31); and "a significant success" (Patrick Burgess, "A New Approach to Restorative Justice: East Timor's Community Reconciliation Processes," in *Transitional Justice in the Twenty-First Century*, ed. Naomi Roht-Arriaza and Javier Mariez-currena [New York: Cambridge University Press, 2006], 177). In Peru, Kimberly Theidon writes about "conciliatory practices" as a form of transitional justice at the village level being "very successful in terms of reincorporating arrepentidos [ex-Senderista guerrillas] and in breaking the cycles of revenge in these communities," while "national reconciliation" remains "several steps behind" (Kimberly Theidon, "Justice in Transition: The Micropolitics of Reconciliation in Postwar Peru," *Journal of Conflict Resolution* 50, no. 3 [June 2006]: 22, 24). Helena Cobban argues that in Mozambique "the combination of amnesties and community-based healing seems to have *worked*" (Helena Cobban, "The Legacies of Collective Violence: The Rwandan Genocide and the Limits of Law,"

*Boston Review: A Political and Literary Forum,* April/May 2002, 27). In a particularly sweeping statement, one commentator claims that "[t]raditional justice systems…which are restorative rather than retributive, have a better record than international criminal justice of ending savage cycles of retributive violence in deeply conflicted societies" (Ramesh Thakur, "East Timor: When Peace and Justice Collide," *International Herald Tribune,* August 31, 2005).

11   Huyse, "Introduction" and "Conclusion and Recommendations," in *Traditional Justice and Reconciliation after Violent Conflict,* 6–7, 188, 192.

12   Brynna Connolly observes that in general, whether it is in a postconflict situation or not, there is usually some degree of incorporation of informal justice systems into formal ones. She presents a typology of models of this incorporation, including complete abolition; incorporation with a formal role (such as gacaca); limited incorporation, in which the informal system exists independently but with state surveillance and accountability and avenues of appeal (such as the CRP); and, finally, coexistence. These models are not, she says, mutually exclusive. Furthermore, and importantly, the outcomes of these incorporation efforts can vary. They can fail, e.g., or they can succeed but undermine the benefits of the original informal processes, such as its flexibility and local legitimacy. If the process is "perceived as a government-imposed mutation of a customary dispute resolution process — or of what may not have even been traditional in the first place — then the justice project will be deprived of the public support that is its most vital asset." Connolly, "Non-State Justice Systems and the State," 245.

13   They do not, therefore, include private justice, which Jon Elster describes as justice "carried out by individuals against other individuals," and which "may also be seen as a substitute for, or preemption of, legal justice." Examples of private justice include extralegal killings in France and Italy after World War II, "deliberate and public humiliation" after the American War of Independence, "informal social ostracism" in Latin America, and even "vindictive rapes" in Europe in 1815 and at the end of World War II. Jon Elster, *Closing the Books: Transitional Justice in Historical Perspective* (Cambridge: Cambridge University Press, 2004), 97–98. It would be difficult to claim that these types of actions were based on local, established practices, and seem to be acts of revenge rather than justice; they certainly were not aimed at reintegrating people into communities. However, in many cases the extent to which a practice is established locally will be difficult to determine, blurring the line between local transitional justice and private justice.

14   Rosalind Shaw, "Rethinking Truth and Reconciliation Commissions: Lessons from Sierra Leone," United States Institute of Peace Special Report 130, February 2005, 12 (emphasis in original).

15   Waldorf, "Mass Justice for Mass Atrocity," 3, n. 12.

16   Huyse, "Introduction," 8.

17   Eugenia Zorbas, "Reconciliation in Post-Genocide Rwanda," *African Journal of Legal*

*Studies* 1, no.1 (2004): 36.

18   Uvin and Mironko, "Western and Local Approaches to Justice in Rwanda," 219.

19   Fausto Belo Ximenes, "The Unique Contribution of the Community-Based Reconciliation Process in East Timor" (paper prepared as part of the Transitional Justice Fellowship Program, cohosted by the International Center for Transitional Justice and the Institute for Justice and Reconciliation, May 2004), 4.

20   Laura Stovel, "When the Enemy Comes Home: Restoring Justice After Mass Atrocity" (paper prepared for Restorative Justice conference, Vancouver, June 1–4, 2003), 5.

21   J. Hudson and B. Galaway, "Restorative Justice and International Human Rights," in *Restorative Justice: International Perspectives*, ed. J. Hudson and B. Galaway (Monsey, NY: Criminal Justice Press, 1996), quoted in Mica Estrada-Hollenback, "The Attainment of Justice Through Restoration, Not Litigation," in *Reconciliation, Justice, and Coexistence*, ed. Mohammed Abu-Nimer (New York: Lexington Books, 2001), 74.

22   See, e.g., Wilson, *The Politics of Truth and Reconciliation in South Africa*, 200, discussing local justice in one township in South Africa: "By emphasizing the continued importance of retributive justice within their definition of community, residents position themselves in opposition to reconciliatory human rights talk."

23   Theidon, "Justice in Transition," 13, n. 5.

24   Ximenes, "The Unique Contribution," 17.

25   Chris Dolan and Jessica Schafer, "The Reintegration of Ex-combatants in Mozambique: Manica and Zambezia Provinces," Final Report to USAID — Mozambique, June 1997, 38.

26   Baines, "The Haunting of Alice," 104. See also Latigo, "Northern Uganda," 108. There are interesting questions about the differences between local and international understandings of the elements of justice and reintegration, such as acknowledgment of wrongdoing. Rosalind Shaw argues that in Sierra Leone, e.g., "social forgetting has been a cornerstone of techniques of reintegration and healing." Shaw, "Rethinking Truth and Reconciliation Commissions," 9. According to Trudy Govier, however, "it is crucial to understand that indigenous rituals do involve acknowledgment. These are non-Western forms of acknowledgment. If the ritual is remembered, then the absence and reincorporation of the person into his or her community is remembered as well. The ritual is not a form of forgetting; to apply a 'forgive and forget' label to it seems simply to be incorrect." Trudy Govier, *Taking Wrongs Seriously: Acknowledgment, Reconciliation, and the Politics of Sustainable Peace* (Amherst, NY: Humanity Books, 2006), 170.

27   Ezekiel Pajibo, "Traditional Justice Mechanisms: The Liberian Case," companion piece to *Traditional Justice and Reconciliation After Violent Conflict*, 23.

28   Patrick Burgess, "A New Approach to Restorative Justice," 177.

29   Baines, "The Haunting of Alice," 103.

30   Latigo, "Northern Uganda," 107.

31   Connolly, "Non-State Justice Systems and the State," 241.

32    Craig Etcheson, "Faith Traditions and Reconciliation in Cambodia" (paper prepared for the conference "Settling Accounts? Truth, Justice, and Redress in Post-conflict Societies," Harvard University, November 1–3, 2004), 14. See also Lisa Schirch, *Ritual and Symbol in Peacebuilding* (Bloomfield, CT: Kumarian Press, 2005).

33    Igreja and Dias-Lambranca, "Restorative Justice and the Role of Magamba Spirits," 61, 68, 76.

34    See, e.g., Daniel Philpott, *Politics of Past Evil: Religion, Reconciliation, and the Dilemmas of Transitional Justice* (South Bend, IN: Notre Dame University Press, 2006).

35    Theidon, "Justice in Transition," 17.

36    "Reconciliation, minimally, is the condition under which citizens can trust one another *as citizens* again (or anew). That means that they are sufficiently committed to the norms and values that motivate their ruling institutions, sufficiently confident that those who operate those institutions do so also on the basis of those norms and values, and sufficiently secure about their fellow citizens' commitment to abide by these basic norms and values." Pablo de Greiff, "The Role of Apologies in National Reconciliation Processes: On Making Trustworthy Institutions Trusted," in *The Age of Apology: Facing Up to the Past*, ed. Mark Gibney et al. (Philadelphia: University of Pennsylvania Press, 2008), 126–27.

37    United Nations Department of Peacekeeping Operations (DPKO), *Integrated Disarmament, Demobilization and Reintegration Standards (IDDRS)* (New York: DPKO, 2006), sec. 2.10, 5.

38    Sarah Michael, "Reintegration Assistance for Ex-Combatants: Good Practices and Lessons for the MDRP," Multi-Country Demobilization and Reintegration Program Working Paper No. 1, September 2006, 19.

39    Mark A. Drumbl, "Law and Atrocity: Settling Accounts in Rwanda," *Ohio Northern University Law Review* 31 (2005): 56.

40    Latigo, "Northern Uganda," 108.

41    Dolan and Schafer, "The Reintegration of Ex-combatants," 41–42.

42    Shaw, "Rethinking Truth and Reconciliation Commissions," 14–18.

43    Baines, "The Haunting of Alice," 110.

44    Lars Waldorf, "Transitional Justice and DDR in Post-Genocide Rwanda," Country Study (New York: International Center for Transitional Justice, 2009); www.ictj.org/en/research/projects/ddr/country-cases/2382.html.

45    Sarah Meek and Mark Malan, eds., "Identifying Lessons from DDR Experiences in Africa: Workshop Report," Institute for Security Studies, Monograph No. 106, October 2004, 34.

46    Theidon, "Transitional Subjects," 67.

47    DPKO, *IDDRS*, "Social and Economic Reintegration," sec. 4.30, 33.

48    Jeremy Ginifer, "Prioritising Reintegration," in *Sierra Leone: Building the Road to Recovery*,

ed. Mark Malan et al. (Pretoria: Institute for Security Studies, 2003), 46.

49  Dolan and Schafer, "The Reintegration of Ex-combatants," 66. In addition, the High Commission for the Reinsertion of Ex-Combatants in the Republic of Congo, according to one World Bank paper, is studying local processes and considering strengthening them as part of the national reintegration program there. Michael, "Reintegration Assistance for Ex-Combatants," 19.

50  Johanna Herman, "Reintegration, Justice and Reconciliation in the Great Lakes Region: Lessons from the Multi-Country Demobilization and Reintegration Program" (paper prepared for the Annual Convention of the International Studies Association, San Francisco, March 26–29, 2008), 2–3.

51  Baines, "The Haunting of Alice," 113.

52  In her discussion of how communities in Mozambique used local practices to "take the war out of society," which included their efforts to reintegrate ex-combatants, at whose very hands they may have suffered during the war, Carolyn Nordstrom writes that the "coherence, the truly national extent of this system of resisting and resolving violence was a surprise to many in Mozambique…a very nuanced and widely shared set of practices and cultural responses were transmitted from person to person, from province to province around the country along with the war." Carolyn Nordstrom, *A Different Kind of War Story* (Philadelphia: University of Pennsylvania Press, 1997), 147.

53  See Wilson, *The Politics of Truth and Reconciliation in South Africa*, 212. He points out, however, that such local courts may, despite their rejection of the concept of reconciliation and the truth commission, nevertheless end up facilitating "the kinds of solutions extolled by the TRC," such as the creation of "an environment less conducive to revenge killings" by channeling retributive sentiments through an institution.

54  Burgess, "A New Approach to Restorative Justice," 190.

55  Ibid.

56  Waldorf, "Transitional Justice and DDR." See also Bert Ingelaere, "The Gacaca Courts in Rwanda," in *Traditional Justice and Reconciliation after Violent Conflict*, 54: "the Gacaca and the reconciliation process in Rwanda in general are an extremely state-driven, state-owned and top-down process with people abiding by the principles, mechanisms, and discourses laid out for them."

57  Waldorf, "Mass Justice for Mass Atrocity," 9.

58  Ibid., 85.

59  Truth and Reconciliation Commission Act, 2000, para. 7.2, www.usip.org/library/tc/doc/charters/tc_sierra_leone_02102000.html; and An Act to Establish the Truth and Reconciliation Commission (TRC) of Liberia, Enacted by the National Transitional Legislative Assembly on May 12, 2005, art. VII, sec. 26(q), www.ictj.org/static/Africa/Liberia/liberiatrcact.eng.pdf.

60  Tim Kelsall, "Truth, Lies, Ritual: Preliminary Reflections on the Truth and Reconciliation

Commission in Sierra Leone," *Human Rights Quarterly* 27, no. 2 (May 2005): 378, 385, 390.

61  Sierra Leone Truth and Reconciliation Commission, *Sierra Leone Truth and Reconciliation Commission Final Report*, chap. 9: "Reconciliation," secs. 21, 121–24, October 2004.

62  Pajibo, "Traditional Justice Mechanisms," 15.

63  Agreement on Accountability and Reconciliation Between the Government of the Republic of Uganda and the Lord's Resistance Army/Movement, June 29, 2007 (Juba, Sudan), www.usip.org/pubs/usipeace_briefings/2008/accountability_reconciliation. pdf; and Annexure to the Agreement on Accountability and Reconciliation Between the Government of the Republic of Uganda and the Lord's Resistance Army/Movement, February 19, 2008 (Juba, Sudan), www.usip.org/pubs/usipeace_briefings/2008/account-ability_reconciliation_annex.pdf.

64  Tracy Dexter and Philippe Ntahombaye, "The Role of Informal Justice Systems in Fostering the Rule of Law in Post-Conflict Situations: The Case of Burundi," Centre for Humanitarian Dialogue, July 2005, 37–38.

65  Assumpta Naniwe-Kaburahe, "The Institution of Bashingantahe in Burundi," in *Traditional Justice and Reconciliation after Violent Conflict*, 175; and at 165: "the *bashingantahe* should be associated with and even play a potentially central role in any national transitional justice mechanism established to facilitate a return to peace and harmony in Burundian social life."

66  DFID, "Non-State Justice and Security Systems," 1–2.

67  Eirin Mobekk, "Transitional Justice and Security Sector Reform: Enabling Sustainable Peace," Occasional Paper No. 13, Geneva Centre for the Democratic Control of Armed Forces (DCAF), Geneva, November 2006, 49, 54.

68  Connolly, "Non-State Justice Systems and the State," 240, 257.

69  Uvin and Mironko, "Western and Local Approaches to Justice in Rwanda," 223.

70  Ibid., 227.

71  Ingelaere, "The Gacaca Courts in Rwanda," 35, 52.

72  Pigou, "The Community Reconciliation Process," 28.

73  Ximenes, "The Unique Contribution," 8.

74  Connolly, "Non-State Justice Systems and the State," 294.

75  Ibid., 278.

76  Justice and Reconciliation Project, " 'The Cooling of Hearts': Community Truth-Telling in Acholi-Land," Special Report, July 2007, 16.

77  Chris Lundry, "The Success of Tradition: Lisan and the Reintegration of East Timorese Militia Members" (paper presented at the conference "Challenges and Paths to Justice," Marquette University Institute for Transitional Justice, October 6–8, 2004), 6.

78  Diane F. Orentlicher, " 'Settling Accounts' Revisited: Reconciling Global Norms with Local Justice," *International Journal of Transitional Justice* 1 (2007): 20–21.

79  Waldorf, "Mass Justice for Mass Atrocity," 64–68. He describes gacaca as "unpopular

popular justice." Ingelaere describes them as "unpopular participatory justice," but claims that "ordinary Rwandans" still prefer gacaca to the national courts and the ICTR as a means for dealing with genocide crimes. Ingelaere, "The Gacaca Courts in Rwanda," 49, 51, 55.

80  Burgess, "A New Approach to Restorative Justice," 183.

81  Joe A. D. Alie, "Reconciliation and Traditional Justice: Tradition-Based Practices of the Kpaa Mende in Sierra Leone," in *Traditional Justice and Reconciliation after Violent Conflict*, 140.

82  See Sierra Leone Truth and Reconciliation Commission, *Final Report*, sec. 25; and Alcinda Honwana, "Children of War: Understanding War and War Cleansing in Mozambique and Angola," in *Civilians in War*, ed. Simon Chesterman (Boulder: Lynne Rienner Publishers, 2001), 135.

83  Refugee Law Project, "Peace First, Justice Later: Traditional Justice in Northern Uganda," Refugee Law Project Working Paper No. 17, July 2005, 27. See also Baines, "The Haunting of Alice," 98: "[In Uganda] local systems have broken down over the course of the conflict, raising concerns about the neutrality and capacity of elders and cultural leaders to adapt local approaches to crimes committed during the conflict." The same points are made regarding Liberia in Pajibo, "Traditional Justice Mechanisms," 15–16.

84  Alcinda Honwana, "Sealing the Past, Facing the Future: Trauma Healing in Rural Mozambique," Conciliation Resources, 1998, www.c-r.org/our-work/accord/mozambique/past-future.php.

85  Waldorf, "Mass Justice for Mass Atrocity," 10.

86  Drumbl, "Law and Atrocity," 67.

87  Schirch, *Ritual and Symbol in Peacebuilding*, 10.

88  Amnesty International, "Rwanda: A Question of Justice," 26.

89  Kenneth Roth and Alison Des Forges, "Justice or Therapy?" *Boston Review*, Summer Issue, July 2002.

90  According to Amnesty International, "the legislation establishing the Gacaca Jurisdictions fails to guarantee minimum fair trial standards that are guaranteed in international treaties ratified by the Rwandan government." Amnesty International, "Rwanda: A Question of Justice," 2.

91  Sierra Leone Truth and Reconciliation Commission, Final Report, 7.

92  Wilson, *The Politics of Truth and Reconciliation in South Africa*, 201, 205.

93  Refugee Law Project, "Peace First, Justice Later," 35.

94  "Is the fact that gacaca deviates from globalized constructions of the rule of law," Drumbl asks, "indicative of the failure or dangerousness of the project? What is the more important goal: conforming to often abstract notions of the rule of law or, rather, developing institutions most likely to promote peace and justice in a manner compatible with local histories and values? Is the rule of law an end in itself? A contextual,

socio-legal approach to post-conflict Rwanda might posit the potential for gacaca to attain the goals of building justice, a shared sense of citizenship, reconciliation, and reconstruction." Drumbl, "Law and Atrocity," 58. Similarly, Ariel Meyerstein argues that "any analysis must be couched within the particularities of Rwandan notions of justice and the prevailing socioeconomic conditions and not primarily from the basis of international human rights law." Ariel Meyerstein, "Between Law and Culture: Rwanda's Gacaca and Postcolonial Legality," *Law and Social Inquiry* 32 (Spring 2007): 470.

95 Baines, "The Haunting of Alice," 107.

96 Swaine, "Traditional Justice and Gender Based Violence," 2–3, quoted in Dolan and Schafer, "The Reintegration of Ex-combatants," 23.

97 Amnesty International, "East Timor: Justice Past, Present and Future," Amnesty International, July 2001, 39–42, also quoted in Dolan and Schafer, "The Reintegration of Ex-combatants," 23.

98 Owen Alterman et al., *The Law People See: The Status of Dispute Resolution in the Provinces of Sierra Leone in 2002* (Freetown: National Forum for Human Rights, 2003), 31.

99 Igreja and Dias-Lambranca, "Restorative Justice and the Role of Magamba Spirits," 80.

100 Burgess, "A New Approach to Restorative Justice," 185.

101 Timothy Longman, "Justice at the Grassroots? Gacaca Trials in Rwanda," in *Transitional Justice in the Twenty-First Century*, 211. See also Ingelaere, who argues that although women "have taken up an important role in the Gacaca proceedings," the system "remains biased against women because of its inadequacy for fully addressing sexual crimes." Ingelaere, "The Gacaca Courts in Rwanda," 52.

102 Naniwe-Kaburahe, "The Institution of Bashingantahe," 167.

103 Aude-Sophie Rodella, "Justice, Peace and Reconciliation in Post-Conflict Societies: The Case of Sierra Leone" (master of arts in law and diplomacy thesis, The Fletcher School, Tufts University, May 2003, 120). See also Alie, "Reconciliation and Traditional Justice," 145: "these tools can only complement the efforts of formal criminal justice systems, since only the latter are capable of dealing with complex issues such as war crimes and crimes against humanity."

104 Honwana, "Sealing the Past."

105 Latigo, "Northern Uganda," 114.

106 Refugee Law Project, "Peace First, Justice Later," 30. See also Baines, "The Haunting of Alice," 105.

107 See Roger Duthie and Irma Specht, "DDR, Transitional Justice, and the Reintegration of Former Child Combatants," in this volume.

108 Stovel, "When the Enemy Comes Home," 27.

109 Angela Veale and Akri Stavrou, *Violence, Reconciliation and Identity: The Reintegration of the Lord's Resistance Army Child Abductees in Northern Uganda* (Pretoria: Institute for Security Studies), Monograph No. 92, November 2003, 47. See also DPKO, *IDDRS*, sec. 5.30,

"Children and DDR," 26: "Cultural, religious and traditional rituals can play an important role in the protection and reintegration of girls and boys into their communities, such as traditional healing, cleansing and forgiveness rituals; the development of solidarity mechanisms based on tradition; and the use of proverbs and sayings in sensitization and mediation activities.... Reconciliation ceremonies can offer forgiveness for acts committed, allow children to be 'cleansed' of the violence they have suffered, restore cultural links and demonstrate children's involvement in civilian life. Such ceremonies increase the commitment of communities to the children's reintegration process."

110 Irae Baptista Lundin, Martinho Chachiua, Antonio Gaspar, Habiba Guebuza and Guilherme Mbilana, " 'Reducing Costs Through an Expensive Exercise': The Impact of Demobilization in Mozambique," in *Demobilization in Sub-Saharan Africa: The Development and Security Impacts*, ed. Kees Kingma (New York: St. Martin's Press, 2000), 190–91.

111 Honwana, "Children of War," 132.

112 Sierra Leone Truth and Reconciliation Commission, *Final Report*, sec. 30.

113 Theidon, "Justice in Transition," 19.

114 Connolly, "Non-State Justice Systems and the State," 293.

115 Dexter and Ntahombaye, "The Role of Informal Justice Systems." See also Naniwe-Kaburahe, "The Institution of Bashingantahe," 149: "During the current large-scale repatriation of refugees and internally displaced persons, the institution of *bashingantahe* is widely sought after for the settlement of family conflicts and property conflicts resulting from the seizure of property by individuals, and in some cases by the state itself."

116 Waldorf, "Mass Justice for Mass Atrocity," 72, 86.

117 Pigou, "The Community Reconciliation Process," 95.

118 Burgess, "A New Approach to Restorative Justice," 194–97.

119 Pigou, "The Community Reconciliation Process," 38.

120 Judicial System Monitoring Programme (JSMP), "Unfulfilled Expectations: Community Views on CAVR's Community Reconciliation Process," JSMP, August 2004, 45–47.

121 See Bickford, "Unofficial Truth Projects."

122 Connolly, "Non-State Justice Systems and the State," 294. See also Burgess, "A New Approach to Restorative Justice," 202: "There is an imperative to seek and implement more creative programs tailored to the specific needs of each situation. These approaches need to recognize that the basis of national reconciliation will often be at the grassroots level."

123 Drumbl, "Law and Atrocity," 73. See also Baines, "The Haunting of Alice," 114: "Moving towards the application of *mato oput* will require active consultation, time and legitimacy building."

124 Luc Huyse, "Conclusions and Recommendations," 194.

# CHAPTER 8

# Transitional Justice, DDR, and Security Sector Reform[1]

*Ana Cutter Patel*

"...security, development and human rights are preconditions for sustainable peace."[2]

In recent years, the concept of postconflict peacebuilding has emerged as a major focus of international policy interest. This has led to a simultaneous increase in new institutional arrangements, funding, and research that seek to reduce the risk of countries to lapse or relapse into conflict. Security is a primary preoccupation of peacebuilding efforts, and disarmament, demobilization, and reintegration (DDR) programs for combatants are often a first step in the process.[3] DDR can contribute to ending or limiting violence by disarming large numbers of armed actors, disbanding illegal or dysfunctional military organizations, and reintegrating ex-combatants into civilian or legitimate security-related livelihoods. DDR alone, however, cannot build peace, nor can it prevent armed groups from reverting to conflict. It needs to be part of a larger system of peacebuilding interventions, which include security sector or security system reform (SSR), transitional justice (TJ), good governance, and broader socioeconomic development programs.[4]

The focus of this chapter is on initiatives of DDR, SSR, and TJ as they relate in peacebuilding contexts. Of the three, DDR is the most clearly defined conceptually and programmatically. DDR seeks to remove weapons from the hands of combatants, take the combatants out of military structures, and help them to integrate socially and economically into society.[5] In contrast, SSR and TJ are broad concepts that represent a wide range of possible activities. According to the United Nations (UN), transitional justice "comprises the full range of processes and measures associated with a society's attempts to come to terms with a legacy of large-scale past abuses, in order to ensure accountability, serve justice and achieve reconciliation."[6] The range of TJ measures in any one country or region may include, among others, the establishment of domestic or international tribunals, truth-seeking efforts, programs that provide reparations for victims, and institutional reform (including SSR). The concept of security sector or security system reform is still somewhat disputed. The 2007 *OECD DAC Handbook on Security System Reform: Supporting Security and Justice (DAC Handbook)*, describes the security system as a broad range of security and justice institutions, including the armed forces, ministries of defense, the judiciary, and nonstate armed actors and groups.[7] The 2008 Report of the Secretary-General "Securing Peace and Development: The Role of the United Nations in Supporting Security Sector Reform" defines the security sector as the same institutions and actors, but with a narrower view of the roles of the judicial sector.[8] Apart from this discrepancy, reform in the security sector or security system is described in similar terms, as activities that aim to provide effective and accountable security for the state and its people.[9]

That there is a relationship between these three concepts is rarely disputed. Research and policy documents linking DDR and SSR are abundant.[10] In terms of DDR and TJ, this book represents the first major publication exploring that relationship, although a number of important articles and reports have contributed to establishing a link between the two.[11] There have been fewer attempts to consider the relationship between the three kinds of initiatives, in terms of either what it is or what it could be. This chapter is intended as a contribution toward filling that gap: first, by exploring the relationship between DDR and TJ; second, by examining the links between DDR and SSR; and third, by considering the connections between TJ and SSR.[12] Since there is little practical experience with situations in which the three programs have actually been linked, the arguments have the character of a proposal, although they make use of the existing literature, including papers developed for the research initiative on DDR and TJ of the International Center for Transitional Justice (ICTJ).[13]

Throughout this chapter I attempt to advance the claim that the implementation of transitional justice measures for accountability, truth, reparations, and institutional reform can contribute to the aims of DDR and SSR. The claim is based first on the premise that DDR programs that are informed by international humanitarian law and international human rights law are more likely to achieve the long-term objective of reintegrating combatants into civilian or legitimate security livelihoods, and be better supported by local and international communities. Moreover, I argue that DDR programs play an immediate and critical role as early security initiatives in the postconflict period, and thus have important implications for SSR. Finally, I look at the relationship between SSR and TJ and consider the concept of a justice-sensitive approach. In the conclusion, I propose that a justice-sensitive approach to DDR and SSR, which prioritizes building integrity, strengthening the legitimacy of security sector institutions, empowering citizens, and that coheres with other policy interventions will increase the likelihood of both their effectiveness and accountability, as well as contribute to the broader aims of peacebuilding and conflict prevention. Effectiveness, of course, is a worthy goal of any policy intervention, and what it means to achieve it in different domains is more or less familiar to us. There is much less clarity about what "accountability" as a policy goal means: the security community tends to define accountability in terms of the existence of government and civilian oversight mechanisms, as well as the legal framework, for the legitimate use of force.[14] Here, I will use the term more in the sense it has in transitional justice discussions, involving "accountability for specific acts,"[15] and therefore as a measure for challenging impunity and taking responsibility for violations of international human rights law and international humanitarian law that occurred in the past.[16] The argument, therefore, is one that seeks to establish the relevance of "dealing with the past"—and thereby of transitional justice measures—for both DDR and SSR.

It is important at this point to draw a distinction between links that suggest a kind of external coherence and those that involve a direct programmatic integration.[17] As with any other intervention in a postconflict, peacebuilding context, it is important to understand how DDR programs cohere with other aspects of a peace consolidation process, be they political, humanitarian, security-related, or justice-related, so as to avoid one process impacting negatively on another. This kind of external coherence may include some level of consultation or cooperation—for example, on public information strategies—but does not involve any kind of integration of programs.

## DDR AND TRANSITIONAL JUSTICE

Since the mid-1980s, societies emerging from violent conflict or authoritarian rule have often chosen to confront the legacies of serious human rights abuses with transitional justice measures. At the same time, programs for DDR of combatants have become integral elements of efforts to increase security in conflict and postconflict situations. These two types of initiatives—one focused on justice and accountability for victims and the other on security and the reintegration of former combatants—often overlap in the postconflict, peacebuilding period. The coexistence of DDR and TJ has implications for the success of both.

The relationships between DDR and TJ are important to consider not just because they overlap in a practical sense, but because they share the same long-term aims for peace and reconciliation. According to the UN, the aims of transitional justice are to ensure accountability, serve justice, and achieve reconciliation.[18] The guarantee of the non-recurrence of mass atrocities and the prevention of human rights violations and international crimes is recognized as the "first imperative" of justice efforts.[19] The establishment or renewal of trust is also an important complementary objective of transitional justice. By way of comparison, the UN Integrated DDR Standards (*IDDRS*) defines DDR processes as a means of increasing security, reestablishing state control over the use of force, preventing renewed violence, encouraging trust and confidence, and reconciliation.[20] Trust-building, prevention of renewed violence, and reconciliation therefore emerge as essential objectives for *both* types of processes.

This section considers how the establishment of DDR contributes to transitional justice, as well as how the implementation of transitional justice measures can contribute to the aims of DDR. I do not intend to minimize the potential for tension between DDR and transitional justice, or to disregard the possibility that in some contexts transitional justice may undermine DDR (and vice versa): both of these are possible outcomes of their coexistence. The point of this section, however, is that given this coexistence and shared long-term goals, it is important to consider how DDR and transitional justice, with a moderate degree of cooperation and coordination, may ultimately reinforce each other in positive ways.[21]

## DDR AND TJ: COHERENCE AND CONTRIBUTIONS

DDR programs can be an effective step in ending or limiting violence by disarming large numbers of armed actors and disbanding illegal, dysfunctional, or bloated military entities. The cantonment of fighters and the collection of weapons can help to stop the violence and halt ongoing human rights violations. For civilian populations that have suffered years of violence, DDR is often the first public indication that the war may really be over. The failure to remove weapons from the hands of fighters, break chains of command in illegal or illegitimate armed groups, and reestablish legitimate state control over the use of force can reduce the security situation of a country and undermine the prospects for transitional justice. Transitional justice measures, particularly those implemented in the national context, require some level of stability, so that those who participate, as witnesses, perpetrators, or victims, can be assured basic protections.

While it is generally accepted that DDR may contribute to increasing security, different reviews of DDR programs in Liberia and Sierra Leone, which correspond with anecdotal evidence from other contexts,[22] report limitations, including systems that exclude women, favor commanders, and provide incentives for staying in chains of command.[23] There is also little evidence as to the effectiveness of DDR programs in reducing stigmatization or violence among ex-combatants in their (re)newed life as civilians.[24] Additionally, DDR programs that provide benefits to ex-combatants in contexts where similar opportunities are not available to others in the community may be seen as rewarding violent actors.[25] For example, DDR carried out in situations without recourse to, or coordination with, justice mechanisms can result in gross inequities between ex-combatants, victims, and other war-affected populations, including the communities where ex-combatants seek to reintegrate, and may foster resentment and impede integration. The establishment of transitional justice measures may contribute to the aims of DDR by providing a means by which to recognize and address the rights of victims, as upheld by international human rights and humanitarian law and practice. The point is that this not only satisfies legal and moral obligations, but that in redressing the victims' claims to justice, their willingness to reintegrate returning ex-combatants may be increased, at least because of the mitigation of the sense of comparative grievance that victims often experience when DDR programs to benefit ex-combatants are established, while their claims remain totally unaddressed.

## ADDRESSING THE RIGHTS OF VICTIMS

Transitional justice measures are meant to address the rights of victims as upheld by the normative framework for transitional justice provided by the *Charter of the United Nations*, the Universal Declaration on Human Rights, international human rights law, international humanitarian law, international criminal law, and international refugee law. For example, widely ratified human rights and humanitarian law treaties require states to ensure punishment of specific offenses.[26] These treaties also require that victims of specified violations have access to remedies. Furthermore, treaty bodies repeatedly find amnesties that foreclose criminal prosecutions of gross violations of human rights to violate states' obligations under these treaties. A general or blanket amnesty that impedes victims' recourse to effective civil remedy would also violate this obligation.

Transitional justice offers a range of measures for upholding these rights by addressing the situations where systematic or widespread violations have occurred. These measures may be a part of the political package that is agreed to by the parties to a conflict in a cease-fire or peace agreement. A study by the Centre for Humanitarian Dialogue (HD Centre) of peace agreements from 1980 to 2006 finds that the seventy-seven peace agreements signed during that period contain 130 discrete justice mechanisms, plus thirty instances of amnesty.[27] Police and military reform with specific reference to international human rights standards, generally associated with SSR, comprise the largest category of justice mechanisms. There are forty-five references to other justice mechanisms, including human rights commissions, vetting, compensation (reparations), truth commissions, trials, and the incorporation of traditional justice.[28] The study finds that while amnesties were present in thirty of the seventy-seven peace agreements, very few general or unconditional amnesties have been included in peace accords from 2000 to 2006.[29] It is interesting to note that in several agreements since 2006—for example, in Kenya, Nepal, and the ongoing negotiation in Uganda—the discussions on justice have not been *whether* justice measures will be included but *what kind* of justice measures to include. While perhaps not yet statistically significant, these situations demonstrate a growing acceptance of transitional justice measures, an acknowledgment of international human rights and humanitarian law, and a simultaneous decline in general amnesties as a part of peace agreements.

### TJ CONTRIBUTION TO DDR

There may be inherent tensions between DDR and transitional justice. For example, in the case of prosecutions, DDR requires the cooperation of ex-combatants, while prosecutors seek to hold the war criminals among them accountable for their actions during the conflict. Yet transitional justice measures may also contribute to the realization of DDR aims by introducing an element of accountability and by providing some balance or equity between what is offered to ex-combatants and what is available to victims, in postconflict, peacebuilding contexts. The four main elements of a transitional justice policy—prosecution, truth-seeking, reparation for victims, and institutional reform—relate to DDR in a variety of ways. Experience suggests that accountability and redress for mass atrocities requires a comprehensive approach that includes elements of all of these approaches.

Prosecutions, in domestic courts, regional courts, or via hybrid or international courts, aim to fulfill the responsibility of national governments to investigate, prosecute, and bring to justice the perpetrators of specific offenses. Prosecutions can reduce the culture of impunity that often surrounds ex-combatants and therefore contribute to the consolidation of the rule of law. DDR processes also stand to gain if the distinction between ex-combatants and perpetrators of human rights violations can be firmly established. Obviously, not all ex-combatants are human rights violators. This is a distinction to which criminal prosecutions can make a contribution: prosecutions may serve to individualize the guilt of specific perpetrators and therefore lessen the public perception that all ex-combatants are guilty of serious crimes under international law.

Prosecution efforts may also remove spoilers and potential spoilers from threatening the DDR process. Most important, prosecutions may actually facilitate trust in the reintegration process and enhance the prospects for trust-building between ex-combatants and other citizens by providing communities with some assurance that those whom they are asked to admit back into their midst do not include the perpetrators of serious crimes under international law.[30] In Sierra Leone, the prosecution mandate of the Special Court for Sierra Leone was limited to top-level offenders. In this context, a strategy that focused on those with the most responsibility for crimes can be said to have served the aims of both accountability and DDR. The outreach strategy of the Special Court was specifically focused on providing communities with information on the mandate and objectives of the Special Court, and on allaying the fears of ex-combatants that the Special Court would indict them after their completion of DDR. These outreach initiatives responded to concerns that public misconceptions about the Special Court would inhibit ex-combatant participation in the DDR program.[31]

There has been a growing recognition that both individual victims and society as a whole have the right to know the truth about past violations, and that national governments have responsibility in giving effect to this right. Appropriate measures to ensure this right may include such processes as truth commissions that complement the role of the judiciary. Truth commissions have primarily focused on victims, but they can provide an opportunity for ex-combatants to tell their side of the story and/or to apologize. In some cases, truth-seeking efforts, with a sufficient public information and outreach capacity, may help break down rigid representations of victims and perpetrators by allowing perpetrators to tell their own stories of victimization, and by exploring and identifying the structural roots of violent conflict.

Often, ex-combatants (who in some cases have experienced extreme victimization) are reluctant to participate or to identify themselves as victims. In South Africa, for example, ex-combatant participation in that country's TRC was limited primarily to the amnesty hearings—relatively few made statements as victims of abuse or were given a chance to testify at victim hearings. As a result, ex-combatants in South Africa expressed a sense that "they had been left out of the process."[32] Such marginalization of ex-combatants from accountability and truth-seeking processes may hinder successful reintegration.

Truth-seeking initiatives may also contribute directly to reintegration and reconciliation processes. The Commission for Reception, Truth and Reconciliation (CAVR) in East Timor was the first truth and reconciliation commission to systematically take on the function of reintegrating perpetrators, among them many ex-combatants, by facilitating dialogue at the community level.[33]

Victims of gross violations of human rights and serious violations of international humanitarian law are also entitled to a remedy, including reparations.[34] Reparations programs, based on legislative or administrative measures, are meant to redress systemic and widespread violations of international law in the wake of conflict or authoritarian rule. In such situations large numbers of victims call for reparations, but their claims cannot be redressed through individual cases in courts of law. A reparations program may distribute a variety of benefits, ranging from the material to the symbolic—including cash payments, access to heath or educational benefits, official apologies, and monuments—in order to cover a larger portion of the universe of victims.[35]

Reparations programs for victims of human rights crimes can contribute to the reintegration efforts of a DDR program by acknowledging the violations committed against victims, providing some means of redressing these violations, and, thus, reducing the sense of grievance victims and communities may feel in the aftermath of violent conflict. In most postconflict settings, while ex-combatants participating in DDR often receive aid in the form of cash, counseling, skills training, education opportunities, access to microcredit loans and/or land, among other forms of support, victims of human rights violations receive nothing. The absence of reparations in the context of a DDR program can add to the perception that ex-combatants are receiving special treatment.[36] In Sierra Leone, for example, radio phone-in programs received comments full of resentment, such as, "those who ruined us are being given the chance to become better persons financially, academically, and skills-wise."[37]

The design of reparations programs can have positive implications for the entire community, contribute to the rebuilding of trust, and include elements of social healing—for example, by facilitating symbolic measures that recognize victims' rights.[38] DDR and reparations programs target different constituencies (ex-combatants in one case, victims in the other), with different objectives (security versus recognition/repair), so combining the two pro-grams is problematic. But it has been suggested that some degree of external coherence, such as a public policy approach that recognizes that the rights and needs of both communities are valued, may benefit both programs.[39]

Institutional reform to prevent serious abuses from recurring constitutes an important element of transitional justice. Such reforms aim to prevent violent conflict and human rights crimes by eliminating or transforming the structural conditions that gave rise to them in the first place. While institu-tional reform frequently includes skills training, supplying resources, and increasing organizational efficiency, institutional reform that aims to prevent human rights abuses would also include efforts to increase the legitimacy of the institution through such activities as "vetting, structural reform to pro-vide accountability, build independence, ensure representation, and increase responsiveness, as well as verbal and symbolic measures that reaffirm a com-mitment to overcome the legacy of abuse and an endorsement of democratic values and norms."[40]

One important aspect of institutional reform efforts in countries in transi-tion is vetting processes to exclude persons who lack integrity from public insti-tutions. Vetting procedures can screen current and new members of the armed forces, many of whom may be ex-combatants, for their possible involvement in human rights violations or international crimes. Vetting assesses a person's integrity, or adherence to human rights and professional standards, to deter-mine their suitability for public employment, including employment in the security sector.[41] Public employees who are personally responsible for gross violations of human rights or serious crimes under international law reveal a basic lack of integrity and violate the trust of the citizens they are meant to serve.[42] The citizens, in particular victims of abuses, are unlikely to trust and rely on a public institution, like the army or police, which retains or hires indi-viduals with serious integrity deficits. Such distrust can fundamentally impair the institution's capacity to deliver its mandate, as citizens look to other means for increasing their security or getting revenge, such as hiring private security or engaging in acts of retaliation or revenge. "Vetting processes aim at exclud-ing from public service persons with serious integrity deficits in order to (re-establish) civic trust and (re-)legitimize public institutions."[43]

## DDR AND JUSTICE FOR WOMEN

The experience of women associated with armed forces and groups often goes beyond the usual notions of victim and perpetrator. While this may also be true of male combatants, women returning to life as civilians frequently face greater social barriers and exclusion than men because of this association. Women may not participate in either DDR or transitional justice measures for a variety of reasons, including their exclusion from the agendas of these processes, the criteria for eligibility (such as one fighter–one gun criteria), the refusal of armed forces and groups to release women, a fear of further stigmatization, or a lack of faith in public institutions to address their particular situations. Their lack of participation can undermine their reintegration, bar those among them who have also experienced human rights violations from their rights to justice or reparation, and reinforce gender biases.

Transitional justice measures may facilitate the reintegration of women associated with armed forces and groups. Prosecutions initiatives, for example, may contribute to the reintegration of women by prosecuting those involved in their forcible recruitment, and by recognizing and prosecuting crimes committed against all women, particularly rape and other sexually based crimes.

Many women combatants, like their male counterparts, do not participate in truth commissions because they perceive these processes to be for victims, and they do not identify themselves as victims. Yet their participation may help the community to better understand the many dimensions of women's involvement in conflict, and in turn increase the probability of their acceptance.

Women associated with armed forces and groups have frequently endured such violations as abduction, torture, and sexual violations, including rape and sexual abuse, and may be eligible for reparations. Reparations can provide official acknowledgment of these violations, access to health or education, and material benefits that may facilitate their integration. Yet these women are commonly reluctant to explain what happened to them, particularly when it involves sexual violations, and less often come forward to claim their due.

## DDR AND SSR

DDR and SSR are connected in terms of their focus on increased security, their interventions with security actors, and their implications for each other. Approaches to DDR and SSR have broadened over the past ten years to embrace concepts of human security. It is now increasingly understood that DDR, as one of the earliest security initiatives in a postconflict context, should be considered and designed within the broad aims of an SSR framework.[44]

## EXPANDING MANDATES DDR-SSR

Since the end of the Cold War, the decline in the prevalence of interstate war and the increase in intrastate conflict have led to a broadening of the notion of the term "security." Where previously "security" concerned itself with the security of a state's borders and the absence of international conflict, the focus has begun to turn to more internally based issues, such as "human security" and development.[45] In an intrastate or civil war, a threat to national security is of less concern than the threat to locals from their own security institutions.[46] Thus, "human security," or threats to the well-being of citizens and their communities, has begun to receive attention equal to that of state security.[47]

## SECURITY SECTOR OR SYSTEM REFORM

The broadening of the concept of security has led to a simultaneous expansion of what is meant by the terms "security sector" and "security sector, or system, reform" (SSR). Traditionally, the term "security sector" related only to those institutions concerned with protecting a country from external aggression (that is, the army, navy, and air force), and with internal instability (that is, the police). This expanded definition provided by the *DAC Handbook* includes four main actor categories: core security actors; management and oversight bodies; justice and rule of law bodies; and nonstatutory forces.[48] "Core security actors" refers to the traditional "security sector" — those tasked with the national security of the country — and includes the armed forces, police, paramilitaries, presidential guards, intelligence services, navy, coastguards, reserves, and local security units; the "management and oversight bodies" include the executive and the legislature, ministries, financial and auditing bodies, and civil society organizations;[49] "justice and rule of law bodies" include the judiciary, prisons, police, investigating and prosecuting authorities, human rights commissions and ombudsmen, and traditional and customary justice institutions; and "nonstatutory forces" refers to liberation armies, guerrilla groups, private security/military companies, and political party militias.[50] This broader definition was adopted in a number of other core documents, including the United Nation's integrated DDR standards.

SSR now aims to reflect this broader concept of "security" as well as the implied wider range of security actors. The definition for SSR developed by the *DAC Handbook* has become a somewhat standardized version, though it is not necessarily universally agreed upon. The *DAC Handbook* is premised on the notion that security is a core component of development, governance, and the protection of human rights. The overarching objective of SSR is therefore to "increase the ability of countries to meet the range of security and justice challenges they face, in a manner consistent with democratic norms, and sound principles of governance and the rule of law."[51] The *DAC Handbook* identifies four main aims of SSR: the improvement of basic security and justice delivery; the establishment of effective governance, oversight, and accountability systems; the development of local leadership and ownership of the reform process; and the sustainability of security and justice service delivery.[52] In order to achieve these goals, SSR programs often focus on developing good legal frameworks (including strengthening the rule of law), effective oversight bodies (including civil society and the judiciary), and policies and procedures aiming to enhance human rights and international legal norms.[53]

The objectives of DDR have evolved in a similar way. Through the late 1990s, DDR programs were considered a technical military exercise, with no implications for parallel efforts to achieve justice. DDR is now perceived as fundamentally linked to other peacebuilding initiatives, including justice. The *IDDRS*, published in 2006, states that "[t]he DDR of ex-combatants is a complex process, with political, military, security, humanitarian and socio-economic dimensions."[54] The targets of DDR programs have also been broadened, at least conceptually, from a particular focus on men with guns to a current list of target groups that include combatants (men and women), children associated with armed forces and groups, men and women working in noncombat roles, ex-combatants with disabilities and chronic illnesses, and dependants.[55] The *IDDRS* also emphasizes the need to attend to the communities that receive ex-combatants, as they are also stakeholders in the DDR process.

## DDR AND SSR CONTRIBUTIONS TO SECURITY

DDR programs play an immediate and critical role as an early security initiative in a postconflict period in terms of both the supply and the demand of security. DDR supplies security when it is effective in terms of the disarmament, demobilization, and reintegration of ex-combatants. An unsuccessful DDR process can lead to increased insecurity and instability, and increases the demand for a reformed security sector to provide safety. For example, a lack of realistic employment options available to ex-combatants in the reintegration process can negatively affect the security situation.[56] In another example, a DDR process that does not present real choices between reincorporation into the national security forces or civilian reintegration can also lead to problems in the security sector. The late payments of stipends and the lag between demobilization and reintegration programs have resulted in a greater number of fighters in the Democratic Republic of the Congo (DRC) choosing to reinsert into the armed forces rather than into civilian programs.[57] This situation may also be traced back to ineffective training of ex-combatants during demobilization, training in skills that are not in demand in the market, or the inability of the local economy to absorb those reintegrating, among other reasons.[58] Such a situation can lead to large numbers of ex-combatants turning to crime as an alternative means of sustaining themselves.[59] This can place additional pressure on the SSR process, as attempts to respond to rising crime adds to the burden on the police, courts, and judiciary.[60]

Alternatively, if the SSR process leads to a poor security environment, many ex-combatants will not be willing to engage in DDR at all.[61] This has largely been the case in Afghanistan, where the presence of former warlords in leadership positions in the security sector, their alleged bias in favor of their ethnic group, and continuing insecurity have meant that few armed groups have been willing to demobilize and give up their weapons.[62]

## DDR AS A FIRST STEP IN SSR

DDR often sets out the parameters of the new security sector. Decisions concerning the overall number of combatants to be demobilized, as well as those relating to who will be kept on or be eligible for reconstituted security forces, such as the army or the police, will have consequences for SSR. DDR can directly affect who exits and who stays in the formal security sector. This means that DDR can determine the size of the resulting security forces, as well as the quality, or integrity, of those who make up those forces. In this sense, DDR is often one of the initial security system reform initiatives in many postconflict settings. The DDR program in the DRC aims to demobilize all ex-combatants and then either insert them into the Armed Forces of the Democratic Republic of the Congo (FARDC) or reintegrate them into civilian life.[63] Today, many analysts find that the army that has resulted from this process lacks trained soldiers and includes elements who have maintained ethnic loyalties and loyalties to their original groups, as well as alleged perpetrators of human rights violations. A few DDR programs have mandates to screen ex-combatants who are alleged perpetrators of violations of human rights and humanitarian law from receiving benefits, or, at a minimum, from reentering the security sector, but there is little evidence that such screening has actually been implemented.[64]

Furthermore, the manner in which employment choices are presented to ex-combatants in DDR programs may provide incentives or disincentives for reintegration in the armed forces. Such choices can potentially affect the representation of women or minorities in the security sector if the incentives for re-recruitment ignore their needs or interests. DDR program have not, for example, been particularly successful in bringing female combatants into the process: in most contexts, the number of women combatants who actually enter the DDR process is far lower than the estimated number of women in the armed groups.[65] Moreover, female ex-combatants are generally provided incentives to reintegrate into civilian life, rather than to incorporate into the security sector.[66]

DDR programs often operate alongside, but without a connection to, SSR initiatives. This lack of coordination or cohesion can lead to the reappointment of human rights abusers into the legitimate security sector. In Liberia, ex-fighters with notorious records of human rights abuses managed to get jobs in the security sector, a handful of whom were removed after public outcry.[67] In Uganda, Taban Amin, the son of the former dictator, was named as an alleged perpetrator of human rights crimes. He was then provided with amnesty under the Ugandan Amnesty Act, which shields him from future prosecutions. He was consequently offered a position in the Ugandan security forces. Such cases undermine public faith in security sector institutions, and can also lead to distrust within the armed forces.

## TJ AND SSR

The relationship between transitional justice and SSR is best understood by considering the forward-looking aims of justice. TJ is usually understood in terms of its focus on the past, but accountability, truth, and reparation without guarantees of nonrepetition are of limited use. The guarantee of nonrepetition of past violations is important because it is future-oriented. It implies that the restoration of the preexisting situation is not adequate. Taking the possibility of a repetition of abuses seriously forces the question of what has to change in order to prevent such abuses from occurring in the future. Often the required change is structural and calls for a reconsideration of what security and insecurity means for everyone in a society.

Structural reform that intends to transform the institutions and processes that enable violence and human rights abuses is essential to transitional justice. Given that massive systematic human rights violations are primarily carried out by state security forces or nonstate armed groups, there is a particular interest in the relationship between accountability and security sector reform.

SSR and TJ both seek to reform abusive security structures and build effective security sectors that respect human rights. "Transitional justice without SSR to prevent reoccurrence can only be incomplete justice."[68] SSR also stands to benefit from transitional justice. Similar to DDR, the focus on SSR by donors and national governments has been to improve effectiveness, rather than to strengthen accountability. Reform of these institutions, however, cannot happen in a vacuum, as if history did not exist. For example, the UN Peacekeeping Mission in Liberia completed its objective of training police officers by June 2007. Despite this, the effectiveness of the police was hampered by the continued mistrust of the people, who well remembered the role of the police in the armed conflict.[69] Heiner Hänggi recognizes the need to address the legacies of past conflict, including through DDR and TJ, as a third objective of SSR in transitional and postconflict countries, beyond effectiveness and accountability.[70] A thorough understanding of the root causes of abuse is necessary for developing the strategies to prevent future violations.

TJ offers a range of modalities for addressing the past. Prosecutions of leaders of security forces or armed groups for war crimes, or violations of international human rights and humanitarian law, criminalizes this kind of behavior, demonstrates that no one is above the law, and may act as a deterrent and contribute to the prevention of future abuse. Additionally, such processes may lead to the imprisonment of high-ranking members of the security forces and thus eliminate them as possible obstacles of reform. Truth commissions and other truth-seeking endeavors can provide critical analysis about the roots of conflict, identifying individuals and institutions responsible for abuse. Truth commissions can also provide critical information about the patterns of violence and violations, so that security sector reform can target or prioritize efforts in particular areas. In the case of the Sierra Leone Truth and Reconciliation Commission, there were specific recommendations for security sector reform, including a major decrease in military spending and compulsory human rights training for the military and the police.[71] Reparations for victims may contribute to trust-building between victims and government, including security sector institutions. TJ also contributes to meeting the challenge of accountability in SSR. Vetting is considered a tool of security sector reform; vetting on human rights grounds to exclude war criminals from public service contributes to dismantling abusive structures.

From a justice perspective, SSR should aim to build the integrity of the security system, promote its legitimacy, as well as empower citizens, in order to transform an overall abusive system into one that both respects and promotes human rights.[72]

## CONCLUSION: DDR, SSR, AND JUSTICE-SENSITIVE APPROACHES

This chapter has attempted to identify contributions that transitional justice can make to the aims of DDR and SSR, as well as to establish the connections between DDR and SSR. Comprehensive approaches to transitional justice may contribute to an understanding of some of the root causes of conflict, provide a measure of accountability and redress for past violations of international human rights and humanitarian law, and inform the institutional reform necessary to prevent the reemergence of violence. A justice-sensitive approach to DDR and SSR that acknowledges the potential contributions of transitional justice processes may facilitate more successful transitions from conflict to sustainable peace.

A justice-sensitive approach emphasizes four aspects of reform: integrity, legitimacy, civic empowerment, and coherence. Integrity, the first aspect of reform, refers to the adherence of the security system to the rule of law. Too often DDR and SSR efforts focus on the technical aspects of their respective mandates, yet equal efforts should be spent on preventing the recurrence of abuse. Screening ex-combatants on human rights criteria, vetting current and potential employees in the security sector, and contributing to new security sector institutions based on accountability are integrity-building measures. Legitimacy, the second aspect of a justice-sensitive approach, is indicative of the level of trust citizens have in the security system. TJ measures can contribute to trust-building in various ways—for example, by prosecuting perpetrators of war crimes, investigating and reporting on the root causes of the conflict in truth-seeking efforts, recognizing the violations perpetrated against victims through reparations, and by informing institutional reform.

TJ has a particular concern for the victims and survivors of abuses. Doing justice to victims means not only building effective, legitimate security systems, but empowering them directly. Civic empowerment is thus the third area of concern for a justice-sensitive approach. DDR programs, for example, can empower citizens, particularly representatives of communities where ex-combatants choose to reintegrate, by including them in the DDR program design process, informing them regularly about the reintegration process, and considering programs that offer benefits and opportunities to all members of the community.

Coherence, the fourth area of a justice-sensitive approach, implies not only internal coherence between various DDR and SSR efforts to build capacity, integrity, legitimacy, and civic empowerment (in response to the needs of the specific transitional setting), but external coherence with transitional justice measures, such as criminal prosecutions, truth-seeking, and reparations of victims.[73]

A justice-sensitive approach to DDR and SSR at the very least observes a "do no harm"[74] strategy, one that does not foreclose the possibility of achieving accountability in the future, and likewise does not undermine the achievement of security.

## NOTES

1    Thanks to Karen de Villiers Graff, an ICTJ intern, for developing a comprehensive literature review, to Alexander Mayer-Rieckh for his conceptualization of justice-sensitive SSR, and to Roger Duthie for enhancing the way the ICTJ talks and writes about it. I am particularly grateful to Pablo de Greiff for his visionary leadership and constant support.

2    United Nations Secretary-General, "Securing Peace and Development: The Role of the United Nations in Supporting Security Sector Reform, Report of the Secretary-General," A/62/659-S/2008/39 (January 23, 2008), Summary.

3    United Nations High-Level Panel on Threats, Challenges and Change, *A More Secure World: Our Shared Responsibility* (New York: United Nations Publications, 2004), 62.

4    Organisation for Economic Co-operation and Development (OECD) Development Assistance Committee (DAC), "Guidance on Evaluating Conflict Prevention and Peace-building Activities" (OECD Publishing, 2008), 18.

5    United Nations Department of Peacekeeping Operations (DPKO), *Integrated Disarmament, Demobilization, and Reintegration Standards (IDDRS)* (New York: DPKO, 2006), sec. 1.20.

6    United Nations, "The Rule of Law and Transitional Justice in Conflict and Post-Conflict Societies: Report of the Secretary-General," S/2004/616 (August 3, 2004), 4.

7    OECD, *OECD DAC Handbook on Security System Reform: Supporting Security and Justice (DAC Handbook)* (OECD, 2007), 22.

8    Report of the Secretary-General, "Securing Peace and Development," para. 14.

9    Ibid., para.17; and *DAC Handbook*, 21.

10  See, e.g., Nicole Ball and Luc van de Goor, "Disarmament, Demobilization and Reinte-
    gration: Mapping Issues, Dilemmas, and Guiding Principles" (The Hague: Netherlands
    Institute of International Relations, August 2006); Alan Bryden and Heiner Hänggi,
    eds., *Reform and Reconstruction of the Security Sector* (Geneva: Centre for the Democratic
    Control of the Armed Forces [DCAF], 2004); and Stockholm Initiative on Disarmament
    Demobilisation Reintegration (SIDDR) (Stockholm: Ministry of Foreign Affairs, 2006).

11  See, e.g., SIDDR.

12  The concept of a justice-sensitive SSR is developed in Alexander Mayer-Rieckh and
    Pablo de Greiff, eds., *Justice as Prevention: Vetting Public Employees in Transitional Societies*
    (New York: Social Science Research Council, 2007); and Alexander Mayer-Rieckh and
    Roger Duthie, "Enhancing Justice and Development through Justice-Sensitive Security
    Sector Reform," in *Development and Justice*, ed. Pablo de Greiff and Roger Duthie (New
    York: Social Science Research Council, 2009).

13  A description of the project is available at www.ictj.org/en/research/projects/ddr/index.
    html.

14  Mayer-Rieckh and Duthie, "Enhancing Justice and Development," 14.

15  Ibid.

16  Ibid.

17  For the notion of "external coherence," see Pablo de Greiff, "Justice and Reparations,"
    in *The Handbook of Reparations*, ed. Pablo de Greiff (New York: Oxford University Press,
    2006); and Pablo de Greiff, "Establishing Links Between DDR and Reparations," in this
    volume.

18  United Nations, "The Rule of Law and Transitional Justice," 4.

19  Ibid.

20  DPKO, *IDDRS*, 2.10

21  This argument is based on the thesis presented in Pablo de Greiff, "DDR and Reparations:
    Establishing Links Between Peace and Justice Instruments," in *Building a Future on Peace
    and Justice: Studies on Transitional Justice, Peace and Development*, ed. Kai Ambos, Judith
    Large, and Marieke Wierda (Berlin: Springer, 2009); and Roger Duthie, "Transitional
    Justice and Social Reintegration," in Stockholm Initiative on Disarmament Demobilisa-
    tion Reintegration, *Background Studies* (Stockholm: Ministry of Foreign Affairs, 2005),
    chap. 4.

22  See Sasha Gear, "Wishing Us Away: Challenges Facing Ex-combatants in the 'New'
    South Africa," *Violence and Transition* series, vol. 8 (Johannesburg: Centre for the Study of
    Violence and Reconciliation, 2002).

23  Kathleen Jennings, "The Struggle to Satisfy: DDR Through the Eyes of Ex-Combatants
    in Liberia," *International Peacekeeping* 14, no. 2 (2007): 1–15; and Dyan Mazurana, Khris-
    topher Carlson, with Sanam Anderlini, "From Combat to Community: Women and
    Girls of Sierra Leone," Case Study, Women Waging Peace and The Policy Commission

(Cambridge, MA, and Washington, DC: The Hunt Alternative Fund, January 2004), 16.

24 Macartan Humphreys and Jeremy Weinstein, "Handling and Manhandling Civilians in Civil War," *American Political Science Review* 100, no. 3 (2006): 429–47.

25 See, e.g., OXFAM International, "Compendium Note on Disarmament, Demobilization and Reintegration (DDR)" (May 15, 2007), www.oxfam.org.uk/resources/policy/conflict_disasters/downloads/oi_hum_policy_disarmament.pdf.

26 The 1948 Convention on the Prevention and Punishment of the Crime of Genocide; the International Covenant on Civil and Political Rights; the 1984 Convention against Torture and Other Cruel, Inhuman or Degrading Treatment or Punishment; the International Convention for the Protection of All Persons from Enforced Disappearance; the Geneva Conventions of 1949; the 1977 Protocol Additional (I) to the Geneva Conventions of 12 August 1949; and the Protocol Additional (II).

27 Leslie Vinjamuri and Aaron P. Boesenecker, "Accountability and Peace Agreements: Mapping Trends from 1980 to 2006," Centre for Humanitarian Dialogue Report (September 2007), 9–10.

28 Ibid., 14

29 Ibid.

30 See de Greiff, "Establishing Links," in this volume.

31 See Mohamed Gibril Sesay and Mohamed Suma, "Transitional Justice and DDR in Sierra Leone," Country Cases (New York: International Center for Transitional Justice, April 2009), www.ictj.org/en/research/projects/ddr/country-cases/2383.html.

32 Gear, "Wishing Us Away," 26.

33 See Emily Harwell and Lars Waldorf, "Ex-Combatants and Truth Commissions," in this volume.

34 United Nations, *Basic Principles and Guidelines on the Right to a Remedy and Reparation for Victims of Gross Violations of International Human Rights Law and Serious Violations of International Humanitarian Law*, A/RES/60/147 (December 16, 2005).

35 Office of the High Commissioner for Human Rights (OHCHR), "Rule-of-Law Tools for Post-Conflict States: Reparations Programmes" (New York and Geneva: United Nations, 2008).

36 See de Greiff, "Establishing Links," in this volume.

37 Jeremy Ginifer, "Reintegration of Ex-Combatants," in *Sierra Leone: Building the Road to Recovery*, ed. Mark Malan, Sarah Meek, Thokozani Thusi, Jeremy Ginifer, and Patrick Coker, *Monograph 80* (March 2003), www.iss.co.za/Pubs/Monographs/No80/Content.html.

38 Lisa Magarrell, "Reparations in Theory and Practice," Occasional Paper Series (New York: International Center for Transitional Justice, September 2007).

39 See de Greiff, "Establishing Links," in this volume.

40 Alexander Mayer-Rieckh, "On Preventing Abuse: Vetting and Other Transitional

Reforms," in *Justice as Prevention*, 483.

41 OHCHR, "Rule-of-Law Tools for Post-Conflict States: Vetting—An Operational Framework" (New York and Geneva: United Nations, 2006).

42 Ibid.

43 Ibid., 4.

44 DPKO, *IDDRS*, module forthcoming.

45 Michael Brzoska, "Embedding DDR Programmes in Security Sector Reconstruction," in *Security Governance in Post-Conflict Peacebuilding*, ed. A. Bryden and Heiner Hänggi (Geneva: DCAF, 2005), chap. 5.

46 Global Facilitation Network for Security Sector Reform (GFN-SSR), *A Beginner's Guide to Security Sector Reform (SSR)* (Birmingham: University of Birmingham, 2007), www.ssrnetwork.net/publications/ssr_beginn.php.

47 DPKO, *IDDRS*, sec. 2.10.

48 *DAC Handbook*, 22–23.

49 Ibid.

50 Ibid.

51 Ibid., 21.

52 Ibid.

53 Ball and van de Goor, "Disarmament, Demobilisation and Reintegration."

54 DPKO, *IDDRS*, sec. 1.10.

55 Ibid., sec. 2.10, Summary.

56 Ibid., sec. 2.10, Summary and Eirin Mobekk *Transitional Justice and Security Sector Reform: Enabling Sustainable Peace*, Occasional Paper 13 (Geneva Centre for the Democratic Control of Armed Forces, 2006).

57 United Nations Security Council, "Twenty-Seventh Report of the Secretary-General on the United Nations Organization Mission to the Democratic Republic of the Congo," S/2009/106 (March 27, 2009).

58 DPKO, *IDDRS*, 4.30; and SIDDR.

59 Brzoska, "Embedding DDR Programmes in Security Sector Reconstruction"; and DPKO, *IDDRS*, 4.30, Introduction

60 Alan Bryden, "Linkage Between DDR and SSR—Understanding the DDR-SSR Nexus: Building Sustainable Peace in Africa" (Issue Paper for Second International Conference on DDR and Stability in Africa, June 12–14, 2007).

61 Mark Knight, "Expanding the DDR Model: Politics and Organisations," in *Journal of Security Sector Management* 6, no. 1 (2008)

62 Patricia Gossman, "TJ and DDR in Afghanistan," Country Cases (New York: International Center for Transitional Justice, April 2009), www.ictj.org/en/research/projects/ddr/country-cases/2376.html.

63 See, e.g., Amnesty International, "Democratic Republic of the Congo," 2007 Annual

Report, www.amnestyusa.org/annualreport.php?id=ar&yr=2007&c=COD.

64  See, e.g., United Nations Mission in Sudan, "Disarmament, Demobilization and Reintegration: Role of National Commissions & United Nations," www.unmis.org/english/ddr-NC-UNrole.htm.

65  See, e.g., Tsjeard Bouta, "Gender and Disarmament, Demobilization and Reintegration: Building Blocs for Dutch Policy" (The Hague: Netherlands Institute of International Relations "Clingendael," 2005).

66  See Luisa Dietrich Ortega, "Female Combatants and Truth Commissions," in this volume.

67  Thomas Jaye, "DDR and Transitional Justice in Liberia," Country Cases (New York: International Center for Transitional Justice, April 2009), www.ictj.org/en/research/projects/ddr/country-cases/2381.html.

68  Mayer-Rieckh and Duthie, "Enhancing Justice and Development."

69  Jaye, "DDR and Transitional Justice in Liberia."

70  Heiner Hänggi, "Conceptualizing Security Sector Reform and Reconstruction," in *Security Governance in Post-Conflict Peacebuilding*, chap. 1.

71  Sierra Leone Truth and Reconciliation Commission, *Sierra Leone Truth and Reconciliation Commission Final Report*, vol. 2, chap. 3, trcsierraleone.org/drwebsite/publish/v2c3.shtml?page=7.

72  Mayer-Rieckh, "On Preventing Abuse."

73  Alexander Mayer-Rieckh, "A Justice-Sensitive Approach to Security System Reform" (International Center for Transitional Justice background paper, September 2006).

74  This phrase was coined for use in the developmental context by Mary Anderson, *Do No Harm: How Aid Can Support Peace or War* (Boulder: Lynne Rienner, 1999).